Presents

THE
GRIDIRON'S
GREATEST
LINEBACKERS

JONATHAN RAND

FOREWORD BY MIKE SINGLETARY

Publisher: **Peter L. Bannon**

Director of Production: **Susan M. Moyer**

Art Director: **K. Jeffrey Higgerson**

Developmental Editor: **Kipp A. Wilfong**

Senior Graphic Designer: **Kenneth J. O'Brien**

Copy Editor: **Cynthia L. McNew**

Acquisitions Editor: **Bob Snodgrass**

Printed in the United States of America.

ISBN: 1-58261-625-6

Sports Publishing L.L.C.
www.sportspublishingllc.com

RIDDELL® is a trademark of RIDMARK, INC.
used by permission.

ACKNOWLEDGMENTS

When you're plowing back as far as six decades, you need a lot of help to bring pro football history alive. Fortunately for me, I received that help.

This book could not have been written without the generous cooperation of so many who've had outstanding careers in professional football, nor without the aid of outstanding research libraries.

First, I'd like to thank the linebackers themselves, those ranked among the top 25 and other outstanding players, who were so generous with their time and recollections. Their keen memories and senses of humor breathed fresh air into this work.

This project enabled me to stay in touch with some exceptional coaches and executives who've made sports writing so much fun for me over the years. They include coaches Pete Elliott, Marv Levy, Marty Schottenheimer and Don Shula, general manager Ernie Accorsi and former player personnel director Gil Brandt.

I appreciate the help of several former Kansas City Chiefs, most of whom I was able to sit down with—Bobby Bell, Willie Lanier, Jim Lynch, Ed Budde, Walt Corey and Len Dawson. Thanks also to Black and Blue Division veterans Ed O'Bradovich, Greg Landry and Veryl Switzer.

I also want to thank the sports writers who filled in some blanks for me. They include Bill Handleman, Jerry Izenberg, Alex Marvez, Gary Myers, Len Pasquarelli and Don Pierson.

I'm also indebted to some of the exceptional public relations staffs in the NFL, notably those headed by Kevin Byrne in Baltimore, Harvey Greene in Miami, Bill Johnson in San Diego, Bob Moore in Kansas City, Lee Remmel in Green Bay, Jim Saccomano in Denver and Aaron Salkin in Atlanta.

My research could not have gotten started without Chad Reese and his library staff at the Pro Football Hall of Fame. I'm also grateful to Kathy Lafferty and her colleagues at the Spencer Research Library at the University of Kansas.

This project could not have gotten off the ground without my editors at Sports Publishing L.L.C. I want to thank Bob Snodgrass for conceiving the theme and Kipp Wilfong for his editing and guidance. The sponsorship of Riddell, Inc., also is much appreciated.

This book definitely would not have been possible without the support and patience of my wife, Barbara Shelly, and our son, Steven. They made sure I'd have the time and space to complete this project. The constant encouragement of my older children, David and Danielle, also gave me a big lift.

Jonathan Rand

TABLE OF CONTENTS

Mike Singletary wasn't all that big or fast, but cut an imposing figure as the middle linebacker of the Bears' famous "46" defense. His smarts and toughness put him in 10 consecutive Pro Bowls and made him the leader of a defense that put on one of the most dominant Super Bowl performances ever in a 46-10 victory over the Patriots in January 1986.
AP/WWP

FOREWORD

Linebacker isn't just a position. It's a commitment and a state of mind. It's a search on the football field for what we seek in life—a healthy balance, though achieving that balance in professional football may not always be so good for your health.

Linebacker is the balance between the big guys in front of you—the defensive line—and the guys behind you—the defensive backs. He's always that balance, in terms of knowing when to be ferocious and knowing when to think. Knowing when to lead and knowing when to listen. Knowing when to use your strengths, but not allowing them to become a weakness by thinking you can do everything.

You need to be able to take on a 350-pound tackle and at the same time chase down guys who run a 4.4. That's balance. People say the linebacker position has really changed, that it's become a more athletic position. Well, it really hasn't changed. Linebacker is not just about how fast you can run or how high you can jump or how many times you can bench-press 225 pounds.

It's more about commitment, about how hard you're willing to work and push yourself and how many times you will get up after you've been knocked down. Will you quit? How hard will you study? Can you be depended on when it really, really counts? Linebacker will always be about vicious collisions, blood and broken bones and pride. It's about reaching down for a little more when there really isn't anything left. Basically, it's about paying the price to be called a linebacker.

During my 12 years playing middle linebacker for the Chicago Bears and my experience coaching linebackers for the Baltimore Ravens, this position has become very special to me. So excuse me if I seem proprietary.

I never wanted to be an offensive lineman. I never wanted to carry the ball, never wanted to catch the ball, never wanted to touch the ball. The guys who do that are the enemy. It seemed contradictory. In my mind, I couldn't adjust to the idea of hitting the guy with the ball and then carrying the ball. Some guys can do it. It works for them. It just didn't work for me. I'm a linebacker. That's all I am. That's all I ever wanted to be.

There are a lot of guys out there who call themselves linebackers, but the guys in this book are the guys who paid the price to be linebackers.

They paid it through leading by example. By understanding what's going on every play. Understanding what everybody's doing every play. By playing like a warrior even though you're 40 points behind or when it's third and one and if they score, you go home. It's about a lot of different things.

Mostly it's about the guy with the football never wanting to come your way again. You want them to think twice about coming into your area. A linebacker is about being ferocious, being an animal, delivering a blow, and at the same time it's about anticipating what the next play is going to be. You have to think like the other quarterback, you have to think like the coach on the other side. You have to be savvy. And you have to have heart.

You want the defense to take on the personality of its leader, and that should be the middle linebacker. He's the signal caller, and he takes the heart and soul of the defense and pins it on himself. He won't give excuses and will not accept any.

Every linebacker has to know: I'm not playing at this level just for me; I'm playing at this level for everybody. If I do my job first, it creates something special. It creates the spirit and confidence of the defense. You can't explain it. The only way to explain it is…you'll know if it's not there.

Linebackers become great when they learn how to trust that their teammates will do their jobs. A linebacker is also about respect—respecting those you play with and against, week in and week out. Respecting your opponent enough to prepare to the best of your abilities and to wake up every day knowing you have to prepare for your opponents even harder than they are preparing for you. You have to keep asking yourself, "What's my edge? How do I get that edge?"

Linebacker ultimately is about being thankful for those who surround you, the other 10 guys on the field. You have to respect their strengths and weaknesses and respect them for what they do to make your job easier. Every linebacker, if he's honest with himself, will be grateful for the other 10 guys with him.

To be able to play the linebacker position, I looked to others before me—Dick Butkus, Willie Lanier, Tommy Nobis, Mike Curtis, Ray Nitschke, Lee Roy Jordan, Jack Lambert, any of those guys. When I was coming up, I said to myself: "I have something to look up to. At the same time, I want to set a new standard and be better than any of them." I said that out of respect.

We continue to pass the torch to one another. We continue to seek out guys to take it to another level and nurture our love for the position and our love for the game. True greatness is like fine wine. It really is defined over time, year in and year out. Whether the team is good, bad or great, the linebacker is always leading…always thinking…always blitzing…always believing that "Somehow, some way, we're going to win this game."

To future linebackers, I need you to look at this book and look at the guys who dedicated themselves to greatness. If you think you're ready to fill these shoes and take it to the next level, the steps get bigger every time.

Are you willing to get into this vicious circle of love? If you're willing to be nasty, ferocious and take the next step, we welcome you with open arms. If you're not willing, the circle is closed. The challenge is on, and the challenge is yours.

People will want to know who I think is the best.

All of them were the best.

It depends on what day you saw them. If you were fortunate enough to see any of these guys on a given day, doing what they did best—whether it was blitzing, tackling, making an interception or taking over a game—you would have said, "He's the best. No one else can do that. It's just not going to get any better than that."

And you know what? If you asked any of them, some might be shy about it, but as a final answer they would tell you, "I'm the best." And if they said anything less, they wouldn't be in the circle.

—Mike Singletary

INTRODUCTION

The image of an NFL linebacker is a hammer pounding a nail. But not everything about the position is that blunt.

"First, you have to have something loose up here," said Kansas City Chiefs linebacker Bobby Bell while he was playing his way into the Pro Football Hall of Fame. "A linebacker is an in-between man. You've got to be able to spot the run or go deep and help out the secondary. You've got about a tenth of a second to read a play and decide whether you're going to come up for the run or go back for a pass. You've got to be two guys in one. Big enough to play and tackle like a lineman and fast enough to go after all that speed."

There has to be a lot more in a linebacker's toolbox than just a hammer. And the position is as full of contradictions as it is of head-knocking.

Linebackers play with a fury. But they can't afford to lose their heads. They rely on instinct. But they'd better do their homework. They're known as the sport's ultimate tough guys. But often they're only as tough as their defensive lines.

If linebacking was as simple as hammering a nail, the best at the position would be a cinch to identify. Instead, great linebackers are constantly misevaluated in the draft. From Joe Schmidt to Ted Hendricks to Mike Singletary to Ray Lewis, NFL teams have overlooked Hall of Fame-type linebackers. They were too skinny, too small or too slow…or so the thinking went.

"Aside from the size and strength and all that, I look for consistency, which includes intelligence and a feel for the game," said Len Dawson, a Hall of Fame quarterback and longtime NFL analyst on radio and television.

"Some guys are physically great specimens but don't have a clue what's going on. There are others, like Nick Buoniconti, who didn't have the physical attributes but are smart and know something about the game and the position they're playing."

When NFL coaches discuss prerequisites for great linebackers, instinct always comes first. Only animals are supposed to have instincts, but let's face it—the best linebackers have a lot of animal in them.

"There's a great deal of instinct involved," said Hall of Fame coach Marv Levy.

"You have to be tough, but they have to understand what they're doing. Once they're in motion, things happen pretty darn quick. Do I go into the guy? Duck under him? Go over the top? You don't have time to think that through every time. Almost all those reactions are instinctive."

Hardly anybody paid attention to linebackers in the NFL's early decades. Teams had no more than two, anyway. Then Chicago Bears middle guard Bill George became a middle linebacker in 1954, and a position was born. Joe Schmidt put middle linebackers on the map, and Sam Huff, with his famous CBS documentary, glamorized them.

The speed and collisions in *The Violent World of Sam Huff* were the very characteristics that helped propel pro football to the top of America's sports mountain. The spectacle of Huff, Dick Butkus, Jack Lambert or Lewis closing in for the kill has always been a crowd pleaser. Such stars as Bell, Jack Ham and Lawrence Taylor showed that outside linebackers could be impact players, too.

"They all have that streak in 'em—kill or be killed," said Walt Corey, a former Kansas City Chiefs linebacker who was defensive coordinator for the Buffalo Bills' four Super Bowl defenses. "But in order to play great defense, you have to have a great defensive line."

Sure enough, most great linebackers played behind strong defensive fronts that kept blockers at bay so linebackers could make the plays. The ones short on help, like Butkus and Tommy Nobis, suffered knee injuries that shortened their careers or diminished their range.

Of the 25 stars in this book, 14 have been traditional middle linebackers, usually the highest-profile linebackers because they're always in the middle of the action. But middle linebackers also are defensive quarterbacks. Today, this involves calling for adjustments before the snap, but linebackers like the Cowboys' Lee Roy Jordan actually called defensive plays from scratch.

"Coaches got a little smarter and started signaling in the calls," Corey said. "But some adjustments still have to be made. The free safety will help him out. The game has changed so much."

Speed, as much as size or strength, has become a linebacker's best friend, though a few gifted players possess an awesome combination of both.

"You don't realize how fast some of these guys today are," Corey said. "If [offensive linemen] stood toe to toe and punched it out, you had a chance. It's not that way any more."

The prototype linebacker over the past 40 years has switched from Ray Nitschke or Butkus to the Ravens' Lewis or the Bears' Brian Urlacher, a 254-pounder quick enough to have played at safety in college.

"They say Butkus is the guy who changed the way the game is played," Dawson said. "The physical part of it, yeah, but he didn't have to worry about pass coverage. If anybody came into his territory, it was legal to unload on him.

"I think of the linebackers in Pittsburgh—Lambert, Ham and [Andy] Russell—that was a fast group. They got involved in coverage."

But the intangibles for great linebackers stay constant from one era to the next.

"It's all about a passion for the game," Lewis told *NFL Insider's* Ray Didinger. "You look at the great middle linebackers—and I've studied them—they're different in certain ways. Butkus was big and physical. Nitschke and Lambert were just plain nasty. Willie Lanier could run from sideline to sideline. Singletary, you see those eyes—so intense—locking in on the offense like a chess player.

"But what's the one thing they all have in common? A passion for the game, a passion for playing that position. That's where it starts. You can study and lift weights and all that other stuff, but if you don't have that passion, you'll never be a great middle linebacker."

—Jonathan Rand

ABOUT THE RANKINGS

I was taking a cab to the Metrodome for a Vikings-Packers game, and the 60ish driver began rattling off the names of his childhood NFL heroes and asked if I thought they would still be stars if they faced today's bigger men. I suggested that if his old-timers were born generations later, they'd be bigger, stronger and faster because of better diets, medical care and training methods. They'd have better facilities and bigger coaching staffs, too.

I figured I'd convinced the cabbie he was trying to compare apples and oranges, but he must not have heard a word. "So, you think Sid Luckman coulda played today?" he asked.

Sports fans love such speculation. Could Babe Ruth, with his carefree conditioning, be a dominant slugger today? Could Wilt Chamberlain have scored 100 points in today's NBA? Could Dick Butkus have covered today's receivers out of the backfield?

I don't see any sense in trying to pull athletes out of the context of their times. If Butkus had no peer at stopping the run when offenses ran the ball like crazy, that's good enough for me. We don't downgrade George Washington as a president just because he never had to confront a nuclear crisis.

These rankings are compiled from my three decades of covering pro football and dozens of interviews with NFL players, coaches and executives. The main criteria are a linebacker's individual performance and statistics, contributions to team success and historical importance. Individual statistics, surprisingly, are not especially helpful.

"Linebackers are difficult to evaluate because there is a lack of statistics," said Matt Millen, a linebacker with three NFL teams before he became the Detroit Lions' general manager.

Counting tackles might seem the best way to evaluate linebackers, but they aren't even an official NFL statistic. They're compiled by individual teams, but the league and its official statistician, the Elias Sports Bureau, have never discussed guidelines for what constitutes an unassisted or assisted tackle. Though tackles are now revised by coaches reviewing game films, they once were recorded solely by statistics crews on game day, and their accuracy can be suspect.

The Atlanta Falcons' media guide, for instance, credits Tommy Nobis with 296 tackles over 14 games in 1966. I know experts back then routinely said, "Nobis makes all the tackles," but they probably didn't mean he actually made *all* the tackles.

Besides, as former Buffalo Bills defensive coordinator Walt Corey, said "The middle linebacker should lead the team in tackles, if everybody's doing their job up front the way they should."

Because football is the ultimate team game, no other major professional sport makes it so difficult to separate the success of an individual from that of his team.

Were Nobis a Packer and Ray Nitschke a Falcon, might their legacies be reversed?

In evaluating greatness in the NFL, especially for defensive players, there's unquestionably a bias toward stars on championship teams. That's why the Hall of Fame is dominated by them. Quarterbacks, running backs and wide receivers at least have the benefit of extensive statistics, which enables such backs as O.J. Simpson and Barry Sanders to get their due despite their lack of championship rings.

Even on a championship team, the impact of an offensive playmaker is most easily evaluated. Could the 49ers have won four Super Bowls without quarterback Joe Montana? No way. Could the Steelers could have won four Super Bowls without middle linebacker Jack Lambert, their defensive quarterback? That's a tougher question.

Of the 25 linebackers here, all but four have played in a Super Bowl or NFL championship game, and most played behind superb defensive lines. It's probably not coincidental that Butkus and Nobis, the only top 25 players who never played in the postseason and often weren't well shielded from blockers, suffered serious knee injuries that shortened or diminished their careers.

Linebackers from the two-way era, with two notable exceptions, are excluded here if they were best known for their offensive prowess. Clyde "Bulldog" Turner and Chuck Bednarik went into the Hall of Fame as centers, but Turner led the NFL with eight interceptions in 1942 and Bednarik made his most famous plays as a linebacker.

With all due respect to your personal favorites who are missing, here's my ranking of pro football's 25 greatest linebackers heading into the 2003 season.

THE TOP 25

1. DICK BUTKUS

"He should be at the top of the list," thundered Hall of Fame coach Don Shula, an NFL player or coach for 43 years. Some might argue with him, but not many.

Butkus was a mean, devastating tackler with a knack for being in the right place at the right time. His size, 6'3" and 245, lust for contact and ability to force turnovers set Butkus apart. He set the bar for run-stuffing middle linebackers and played during the position's golden age.

But unlike most other top-flight linebackers, Butkus never played on a championship team, or even a playoff team, and lacked a strong supporting cast. A knee injury in 1970 filled the last three years of his nine-year career with excruciating pain and diminished range. That Butkus could build such a legacy in an injury-shortened career speaks to his extraordinary talent.

"The Miss America contest has a lot of beautiful girls, but only one is Miss America," said Hall of Fame coach Marv Levy, loath to single out one linebacker as the best. "Butkus is the Miss America of linebackers, I guess."

2. LAWRENCE TAYLOR

He didn't actually invent the position of rush linebacker; he just played it as nobody had before. Taylor, 6'3" and 237, was a devastating pass rusher, with 142 career sacks, and a hard and reckless hitter. He was the player every opponent had to keep an eye on during every play and was the signature player of the Bill Parcells era in New York that produced two Super Bowl victories for the Giants.

3. RAY NITSCHKE

He was the heart of a defense that helped win three NFL championships and two Super Bowls and led the NFL in fewest points allowed three times. With his gap-toothed ferocity and blood-splattered uniform, Nitschke was the epitome of the blood-in-the-mud linebacker. A panel of sports writers in 1969 named him "the best linebacker in the NFL's 50 years." He belongs near the top yet.

4. JOE SCHMIDT

He gave the middle linebacker position its first splash of glamour and enhanced its reputation as a thinking man's position. Though just 6', 222, he used his quickness to frustrate blockers, was an exceptional tackler and seldom made a mistake. He helped win two NFL championships and led defenses that boasted every bit as much talent as Lombardi's Packers.

5. JACK HAM

According to seven-time Pro Bowl linebacker Andy Russell, "If there was only one linebacker on the Steelers, Jack Lambert and I would've been on the bench." Ham was arguably the best all-around outside linebacker ever. An exceptional athlete, he was strong enough to stop the run and quick enough to cover receivers. He made big plays in big games and played in three of the Steelers' four Super Bowl victories.

6. BOBBY BELL

Those who disagree that Ham was the best all-around outside linebacker ever probably would pick Bell. He was such an outstanding athlete, he probably could've played any position. Bell returned six interceptions for touchdowns and remains a standard used by scouts when they spot a prospect with superior skills and play-making ability. "He reminds me of Bobby Bell," they'll say. But nobody else really does.

7. JACK LAMBERT

No middle linebacker before him played both the run and pass at such a high level. He was the last piece of the "Steel Curtain" defense, and his aggressiveness, quickness and play calling helped cement the best defensive dynasty of all time. The "Dracula" image embellished his reputation but belied his superior speed and smarts.

8. RAY LEWIS

Many already would put him in the top three, but it's dicey to rank anybody that high before he's played nine or 10 years. Lewis hits like a Butkus clone but also has astonishing range to chase down ball carriers and knock down passes, as he did while earning MVP honors in the Ravens' Super Bowl victory in January 2001. For such a hard hitter, he remained remarkably healthy until he suffered a shoulder injury that ended his 2002 season and required arduous rehabilitation.

9. WILLIE LANIER

The only middle linebacker generally considered better during Lanier's prime was Butkus, and that wasn't unanimous. Lanier didn't just debunk the myth that a black couldn't play middle linebacker in pro football—he demolished it, just as he figuratively did many a ball carrier. He also was nimble in pass coverage and led a defense that held Minnesota to just one touchdown in the January 1970 Super Bowl.

10. DAVE WILCOX

He's living proof of how a Hall of Fame-caliber player can slip through the cracks of history if he's on a losing team in a mid-sized media market. When Ham and Russell wanted to watch film of a technically superior outside linebacker, they studied Wilcox. He took on Hall of Fame tight ends, and his strength and soundness made him difficult to block. Wilcox finally got to Canton 26 years after he retired.

11. TED HENDRICKS

Because of his lanky physique, personnel experts didn't always know what to make of him and coaches didn't always know where to play him. But Hendricks was a turnover-forcing machine and peerless at blocking kicks. He helped win four Super Bowls, including three with the Raiders, who couldn't win the big one until Hendricks became an integral part of their defense. He played 215 consecutive games.

12. MIKE SINGLETARY

As his old defensive coordinator Buddy Ryan said, the only difference between Lewis and Singletary is that Lewis is bigger. Singletary was a hitter in the Butkus mold and an intense and stabilizing influence in the middle of a defense laden with as many eccentrics as stars. You can imagine some great defenses still having been great with another middle linebacker, but the Bears' 46 defense is not one of them.

13. CHUCK BEDNARIK

He was the last of the 60-minute men, and when you consider Bednarik's tenacity, endurance and war heroism, he's got to be as tough a man as you'll find on this list. He helped the Eagles win two NFL championships, and his vicious but clean game-saving tackle of Frank Gifford in 1960 is the most famous hit in pro football history. Despite dishing out and absorbing tremendous punishment, Bednarik missed only three games in his 14 seasons.

14. SAM HUFF

Nobody glamorized the middle linebacker position as much as Huff did in his famous CBS documentary. That may have been a mixed blessing for him, because some experts suggest he was overrated and merely in the right place at the right time—in New York just as pro football's popularity was exploding. He was an ideal fit for coordinator Tom Landry's 4-3 defense, and considering that Huff played in six championship games and had epic battles with Jim Brown and Jim Taylor, how overrated could he have been?

15. BILL GEORGE

He's credited with becoming the first true middle linebacker when he backed up from his middle guard position in 1954. He was strong enough to plug the middle against the run and was an excellent blitzer and signal caller. He was a star on the defense that intercepted Giants quarterback Y.A. Tittle five times in the 1963 championship game and was Mr. Linebacker in Chicago before Butkus came along.

16. TOMMY NOBIS

He's the best of the old-time linebackers not in the Hall of Fame and better than some who are. Nobis was tough, quick and instinctive, and early in his career he routinely was mentioned in the same sentence as Butkus and Nitschke. Weak supporting casts and knee injuries diminished his play and, even worse, his legacy.

17. DAVE ROBINSON

He was probably the first to play the Lawrence Taylor position, though there wasn't nearly as much of a need to rush the passer back then. Robinson's size, strength, speed and reach made him tough against the run and pass. He made big plays in big games and starred on three championship teams, including the first two Super Bowl winners.

18. CLYDE TURNER

Like Bednarik, his greatest fame rests at center, but he also led the NFL with eight interceptions in 1942 and had four interceptions in five NFL championship games. Turner was so fast and strong that he even successfully filled in at running back. It gets dicey trying to compare him with modern linebackers, but we'll trust the late George Halas when he described Butkus as the best linebacker he'd coached since Turner.

19. MIKE CURTIS

He was the raging bull of linebackers and versatile enough to move from the outside to the middle for the Colts. He was mean, quick and dogged and played a key role for two Super Bowl defenses. TV analyst and former Raiders coach John Madden in 1986 rated Curtis, Butkus, Lanier and Nitschke as the best middle linebackers he'd ever seen.

20. LEE ROY JORDAN

Some defensive teammates were greater players, but nobody exercised more leadership for the Cowboys as they grew from "Next Year's Champions" to "America's Team." Jordan was a powerful locker room presence and loved to hit, whether on Sundays or in practice. He weighed barely 200 when a season ended and would be a Hall of Famer if he'd been 25 pounds heavier.

21. RANDY GRADISHAR

He usually knew where the ball was going, got there quickly and almost always made the tackle. Gradishar was an every-down inside linebacker and leader of the "Orange Crush" defense, which led the Broncos to their first Super Bowl. He'd be better remembered if the Orange Crush had a longer shelf life, and Gradishar's supporters insist he's vastly underrated.

22. NICK BUONICONTI

Though undersized, he recklessly threw his body around and was leader of the "No Name Defense," which helped the Dolphins achieve the first perfect season in the modern NFL. He was among the top interceptors ever among linebackers and played in three Super Bowls. The No Names formed an all-time great defense despite lacking an obvious Hall of Fame player, though voters gave Buoniconti the benefit of the doubt.

23. HARRY CARSON

He stood out on the Giants' defense even when the franchise hit bottom. Once Parcells, then Taylor, arrived in New York, Carson capitalized on his talent and became a locker room leader for a Super Bowl champion. Like Gradishar, his identity suffered a tad at inside linebacker in a 3-4 defense, where the inside spots lack the visibility of a middle linebacker in a 4-3.

24. GEORGE CONNOR

At 6'3" and 240, he was first of the Butkus-sized linebackers. He showed his superior aggressiveness and mobility when he was moved from tackle to linebacker to stop a sweep the Eagles had been using to beat everybody else. Connor played offensive and defensive tackle early in his NFL career and in 1946 at Notre Dame became the first winner of the Outland Trophy, which honors college football's top lineman.

25. JUNIOR SEAU

He was the pride of the Chargers' franchise for 13 seasons and led them to their first Super Bowl in January 1995. Despite suffering from a pinched nerve in his neck that sometimes made his left arm numb, Seau was credited with 16 tackles, including 12 unassisted, as the Chargers upset the Steelers 17-13 in the AFC championship game. Also a strong pass rusher, he was the NFL's best linebacker who played throughout the '90s.

DICK BUTKUS

Dick Butkus begins talking in a low voice, humbly and almost uncomfortably, as if he's embarrassed that anyone would ask him to reminisce about his historic career. But then his passion starts to build.

Butkus recalls how determined he was to play pro football even when he was in grade school, how he loved to punish ball carriers until they'd cough up the ball and how he'd sooner swallow pain than give an opponent the satisfaction of knowing he'd made Butkus ache. Then there's a sneer on his face and gravel in his voice, and you know you're talking to the middle linebacker who rocked ball carriers as nobody had before.

"Talking to him is kind of like talking to Jack Nicklaus," said Mike Singletary, who picked up Butkus's torch as a Hall of Fame middle linebacker for the Bears. "He can be very cerebral and calm and all of a sudden there's a dark side to him. Whether it's the smirk, the eyes, the tone…that crazy streak, you know it's there and you know he's definitely a linebacker."

Butkus was not, of course, just any linebacker. Despite playing only nine seasons, without a strong supporting cast and never on a playoff team, Butkus is still remembered, three decades after his retirement, as without peer at his position.

"To this day, people regard him as the best of all time," said Ed O'Bradovich, a defensive end who played with Butkus for seven years. "The way Dick would hit people…if they had the amount of cameras from all the different angles they have today and the way they make these sound bites, they might have to bar the guy.

"Tackling wasn't good enough. Just to hit people wasn't good enough. He loved to crush people. That takes a sense of timing. You cannot teach that. When he made that tackle, he exploded into 'em. He not only put the fear in the running backs, but in the offensive linemen, too."

Green Bay Packers running back MacArthur Lane once said: "If I had a choice, I'd sooner go one on one with a grizzly bear. I pray that I can get up every time Butkus hits me."

Butkus was in high school when he began to develop the devastating tackling style that would become his signature. While playing fullback at Chicago Vocational High School, he realized the best way to tackle was the way he hated getting tackled.

"It wasn't hitting me low with the perfect tackle around the waist," Butkus said. "What bothered me was when somebody hit me high and wrapped their arms around my arms and I had nothing to break my fall. And when I'm getting hit like that, boy, it really took concentration to hold on to the ball and also brace for hitting the ground.

"I thought, all right, that's what I'm going to start doing. I'm going to put my head in someone's sternum and it won't be picture perfect, but I'll tell you what—they won't come back. I'll put 'em on their backs and somewhere along the line, they'll cough up the ball and that's the whole thing. The idea of hitting somebody hard is not for your ego, it's to make them forget about the ball. Big deal if you're making picture tackles but they're making first downs. The idea is getting the ball."

Butkus was playing golf in the Bayer Celebrity Pro-Am, a Champions Tour event in Parkville, Mo., in May, 2003, and during a break demonstrated his fumble-forcing technique. He slipped a massive forearm under his interviewer's arm and made a yanking motion to show how he'd knock the ball loose. Butkus had 25 fumble recoveries, an NFL record when he retired, and 22 interceptions.

"He personally took the ball away from our offense in two games one season," recalled Don Shula, then coaching the Baltimore Colts. "On one play, we handed off to Tony Lorick, and the next thing I know, Butkus had the ball going the other way."

Butkus's total of forced fumbles wasn't recorded, but it's safe to assume it would have dwarfed his total of recoveries.

1

Dick Butkus, shown here during the 1970 preseason, was at the height of his powers after the five most dominating seasons anybody had seen from a middle linebacker. During 1970, though, he suffered a knee injury that never healed properly and shortened a still-legendary career.
AP/WWP

"A lot of 'em I didn't get because I pulled too hard and the ball fell a little farther than where I could get it," he said, chuckling.

Bears tacklers were taught that the first one in should make the tackle and the second one in should try to strip the ball.

"Dick would make the tackle and take the ball at the same time," O'Bradovich said, laughing. "He'd eliminate the middle man and do it himself."

Miami Dolphins quarterback Bob Griese was understandably anxious the first time he faced Butkus. He lined up behind right guard Larry Little, who jumped when he felt Griese's hands.

"When Dick is on the other side of the line, glaring at you with those boiling eyes, it makes you wish you could trade places with the equipment boy," Bears running back Brian Piccolo told Cooper Rollow of the *Chicago Tribune*.

Though Detroit Lions quarterback Greg Landry doesn't recall Butkus being especially intimidating, he said Butkus never failed to be a distraction.

"The thing he would do is jump in the line and growl at you," Landry recalled.

"I remember one time Ed Flanagan, our center, hollered at Dick to stop because he couldn't hear the signals. I almost started laughing."

Despite his growling, Butkus insists he wasn't quite the animal some people portrayed him as being.

"I got burned in college by a writer and my first few years [in the NFL] I never talked that much, so they didn't know I ate with a knife and fork," he said.

"They thought the way I played was the way this guy is—he's not together. Those stories, like me biting somebody's finger, that's all bull. It was so hot in August, playing in Miami, and Abe Gibron always made us play the full [exhibition] game. So I told the defensive tackle, 'Let's get in a fight and get out of this.' He started the fight and I got thrown out and they said I bit somebody's finger. I said, 'Who'd I bite? If I bit somebody, there'd be blood on my shirt.' Forty years later, now it's probably somebody's arm."

Landry tells one classic Butkus tale, though, which he said he witnessed. Lions rookie running back Altie Taylor, after a victory over the Bears in October 1969, made the mistake of saying Butkus was overrated. Teammates reminded Taylor they'd have to face Butkus again at Wrigley Field in the final game of the season.

"We called a play to Altie Taylor, an end sweep towards the old third base line, maybe 30 yards from the brick wall," Landry recalled. "Altie ran out of bounds and started slowing down and here comes 51 at him. Next thing he knows, 51 is still coming at him. Next thing, you see a football in the air and Altie Taylor jumping over the wall.

"He came back to the huddle all glassy eyed and said, 'That guy's crazy!' Dick chased him right out of the ballpark. There were things at Wrigley Field that Dick could get away with."

Butkus and the Bears at first seemed a match made in heaven because he was never far from Chicago. Butkus went out of his district to play for Chicago Vocational coach Bernie O'Brien, then went to Illinois and led the 1963 team to a Rose Bowl win.

Ed Budde, a Michigan State guard who became a Pro Bowl fixture for the Kansas City Chiefs, could've warned NFL blockers about Butkus.

"[Coach] Duffy Daugherty was talking to the whole team," Budde recalled, "and said, 'Illinois has this linebacker, Butkus, who thinks he's tough. You know what we're gonna do? We're gonna go right at him.'"

Budde was quite dubious of this strategy and said, "He must've made 80 percent of the tackles that day."

Illinois coach Pete Elliott, who was Butkus's presenter at his Hall of Fame induction, recalls Butkus's all-around determination.

"I don't think he ever missed a class, never failed a course, never missed a practice, was never late for a bus or any team function, and what an example for the rest of the team," Elliott recalled.

There was at least one time, though, when teammates didn't follow Butkus's example. Elliott canceled a practice prior to a Saturday spring scrimmage because of inclement weather, and all his players cheered. Except one. Butkus sat by his locker with his head down.

"He felt he needed to practice so he could play well in the scrimmage," Elliott said. "It's an amazing thing, very indicative of him."

Butkus had decided early that nobody was going to outwork him and said, "I had total tunnel vision. I was a furniture mover and did all these hard things because weightlifting wasn't in vogue. In high school, I was always thinking, somewhere in this country there's a guy working harder than I am. When I got to college, I thought the same thing. And I felt that way in the pros. I couldn't get enough, I couldn't play enough."

"**Tackling** wasn't good enough. Just to **hit** people wasn't good enough. He loved to **crush** people."

—Ed O'Bradovich

Perhaps somebody out there was working harder than Butkus. But if there was anybody more talented, his college coach sure didn't know about him.

"I never saw or heard of a better football player," said Elliott, who also was head coach at Nebraska, California and Miami and was an assistant to St. Louis Cardinals coach Bud Wilkinson in 1978.

"He had the greatest instincts I've ever been around. He was fast, but not extremely fast. He just anticipated where the guy was going to throw the ball. And he was as good a tackler as there ever was.

"He had a fire within him to be the best. I saw him get mad, but I did not see him go into a frenzy. He always wanted to hit, he wanted to make good tackles. But I never saw him do anything unsportsmanlike or dirty. I never saw him slug people, or anything like that. Some of the tackles he made…a back would be running at full speed, Butkus hits him and he starts going backwards."

Butkus didn't slow down in the NFL. He was the third overall pick of the 1965 draft behind fullbacks Tucker Frederickson and Ken Willard, drafted by the New York Giants and San Francisco 49ers, respectively. It didn't take long for Bears middle linebacker Bill George, an eventual Hall of Famer, to appreciate Butkus's talent.

"The minute that guy walked into camp, I started packing my gear," said George, who left a year later. "There was no way he wasn't going to be great."

Butkus wasn't NFL Rookie of the Year because teammate Gale Sayers sewed up the award by scoring six touchdowns in a late-season game. Butkus did, however, make his first of eight consecutive Pro Bowls.

Like all great linebackers, Butkus had a keen nose for the ball.

"It's being prepared and watching movies," he said. "People always go back to what they do best, even the best of them. [John] Unitas had tips, if you looked long and hard enough. If you can figure it out, you're a step ahead."

Landry can vouch for Butkus's ability to read keys.

"The challenge he created, a lot of times as I was calling the cadence, he'd leave his position and guess the play," Landry recalled. "Maybe he detected a lineman or a back giving something away, but that was one of the strengths he had. It was too late in the cadence to call an audible and he'd jump right in the hole."

If Butkus guessed wrong, he'd jump somewhere else. And there was method to his madness.

"I know," Butkus said, "a lot of guys would say, 'Butkus is running all over the place.' Yeah, but I took care of my responsibility. Am I supposed to stay there and not make the tackle? I took the attitude, 'I got no help. I've got to make the tackle.' If somebody else made it, I got ticked off that it wasn't me. I don't put my trust in anybody else but me."

Butkus had good reason for that attitude. The Bears finished 9-5 his rookie season, but during his career never again won more than seven games and never made the playoffs. Butkus played most of his career with ordinary defenses and weak offenses.

"Maybe that says something about what I did," Butkus said. "I would just go position by position with our team versus Nitschke's, Lambert's or Lanier's. Who's in front of you? If I've got three Hall of Famers in front of me, it should be easy for me, right? If maybe you have one, it's a little different."

A stronger supporting cast, especially up front, would've kept more blockers off Butkus and perhaps extended his career. He suffered a right knee injury in 1970, which never healed properly despite surgery and left him in pain the rest of his career.

"You could see he was dragging his leg," Landry said. "But he was always there and gave 100 percent. I'd like to have seen him in the locker room after a game. I don't know if he'd be able to lift off his pads, because he looked like he gave everything in those three hours."

But after he had to leave the field because of unbearable pain in the fifth game of the 1973 season, Butkus had little left to give. He retired after that season and in '74 sued the Bears for mishandling his injury. He received a $600,000 settlement.

"They always claim that my threshold of pain was great, but it ran in my family," Butkus said. "One of my brothers, Don, was a welder and he was soldering in his garage in his bare feet and hot solder was dropping on his feet. He didn't even flinch. It smelled like burnt chicken feathers and he didn't interrupt what he was soldering.

"It just makes me want to throw up nowadays when a guy gets hurt, his face is buried in the grass and the trainer is talking to his earhole. The guy gets up and takes his helmet off and runs off the field. I'm not saying how tough we were, but why would I give you the benefit of having you put me out?

"That's what I had to go through my last three years. Guys were taking shots, clipping me, trying to tackle my foot and twist it even more. For what? To make their name that they put me out? I never gave 'em the satisfaction, even if I had to crawl. Today, it's like they have the ambulance ready.

"A friend of my brother played in high school and broke his leg and ran off the field just so the other guy didn't know. That's the way I learned. Many times I caught a knee or got kicked in the chest and got the air knocked out of me. I wasn't going to let them know. It's all a psych game. I'm not going to give you any advantage.

"If you made a good block on me, I'll kick you when I'm getting up. That shaking hands bull…I would've been great with [Vikings coach] Bud Grant because he wouldn't have had to warn me about shaking hands after a game. How the hell can you do that—this good sportsmanship thing—when it's so superficial? You mean to tell me you're not going to try to get me? C'mon."

Before his knee injury, Butkus was nimble enough to return 12 kickoffs and once gained 28 yards on a fake punt attempt. He twice caught passes for extra points after the snap for the conversion kick went awry. He once said the favorite play of his career was a leaping catch for the extra point that beat the Washington Redskins, 16-15, in 1971.

"It'd take me all day to run 100 yards, but 30 yards sideways or on an obstacle course, I was pretty quick," Butkus said.

Many, including San Diego Chargers coach Marty Schottenheimer, question whether Butkus would've been quick enough to be dominant in today's NFL.

"Butkus today perhaps wouldn't perform as well," Schottenheimer said. "He was 245 and as big as some of the linemen he was playing against. He's a good friend and all of that, but clearly it's a different game."

When Schottenheimer told him that, Butkus replied: "I think I could find a spot."

Three decades after Butkus's retirement, his name remained synonymous with the position he played. He credits his acting career for keeping his name alive.

"I think the staying power is because of the exposure," Butkus said. "If I hadn't done the commercial work and some of the other TV stuff, the name probably would've died like a lot of others. When you get these ex-players as announcers and people see their faces every weekend, that's recognition—'Oh yeah, he's the best.'

"They've got this college award named after me [for the nation's top linebacker] and believe me, I had nothing to do with it and it's kind of embarrassing. People say, 'You should be honored, you should be glad people are asking you for your autograph.' It's nice that I can do things like that—if they're sincere about it, that's fine.

"But if you know me, it doesn't really matter. If nobody asked me [for an autograph] from today on, I'll go on living because I know what I did. How many guys can say they did what they set out to do since they were eight or 10 years old? I did it, so I don't have to get verification by being remembered 30 years after I'm done playing."

Maybe not. Yet Butkus remains the most unforgettable linebacker of them all.

Dick Butkus had a nose for the ball and was quick to close on anybody carrying it. St. Louis Cardinals running back Willie Crenshaw finds a hole here in an early-season game in 1969, but Butkus is about to stop him after a five-yard gain.
AP/WWP

LAWRENCE TAYLOR

Football players talk about "turning off the switch"—trying to rejoin the civilized world after spending three hours locked in a hard-hitting, brutal and sometimes nasty contest. Most players flip the switch without a great deal of difficulty.

But few NFL players have had more trouble turning off the switch than did Lawrence Taylor. The recklessness that made him one of the very best linebackers in pro football history also caused him a heap of trouble.

"Sunday is a different world," Taylor once said. "It's like a fantasy world which I'd rather live in. Then I go back to the rest of the world and that's when the trouble starts."

Most of Taylor's troubles involved substance abuse, though some of his remarks could make people cringe, too. He sounded downright cold-blooded during an interview before the Super Bowl against the Denver Broncos in January 1987.

"I can be a SOB," Taylor said five days before kickoff. "Nasty, lousy, mean people are the guys who get the farthest. That's just the nature of the game. I love the contact. It makes the game real enjoyable. I can go two or three games without a kill shot—that's when the snot comes from [the quarterback's] nose and he starts quivering on the ground. You want to run the film again and again."

Taylor may have been laying it on a bit thick, because the previous season he was distressed when he inadvertently broke the leg of Washington Redskins quarterback Joe Theismann in a Monday night game. Theismann's lower leg was bent grotesquely, and Taylor urgently called for help. He didn't want to talk about, much less relish, that tackle.

Taylor was named the NFL's Most Valuable Player in 1986 and became the first defensive player to win that award since Alan Page of the Minnesota Vikings in 1971. Taylor was a difference maker for two Super Bowl champions, and it's not often a defender becomes the signature player for a championship team.

John Madden, TV analyst and former Oakland Raiders coach, described Taylor as "the single most intimidating defensive player in the league, a guy you can't run away from or block out, a guy who can change your whole approach to a game."

Madden also said that Taylor "defensively has had as big an impact as any player I've ever seen. He changed the way defense is played."

Taylor, who totaled 142 sacks and made 10 Pro Bowls, brought a fresh approach to outside linebacker. Pouncing from the weak side, his combination of speed, strength and aggressiveness enabled him to play his position as few ever had.

"L.T. was a defensive end; he just stood up," said New York Giants general manager Ernie Accorsi. "It was a 3-4 and he was the fourth defensive lineman. His greatness was rushing the passer. If you played against him and he was in coverage, you breathed a sigh of relief."

Giants coach Bill Parcells and defensive coordinator Bill Belichick were not about to allow any opponent a sigh of relief. So Taylor rushed the passer and clobbered ball carriers, forcing 33 fumbles and recovering 10. He also made nine interceptions.

"There comes a time in a game when you know a key play is coming up," Taylor said on ESPN.com. "You can just feel it in the air. There are guys who shun those moments. It's like in basketball. There are guys who want to shoot the last shot and others who want to pass off. I want that shot."

As if Taylor wasn't sufficiently motivated, Parcells would invent the insult that the Redskins didn't think he was still in his prime. Six of Taylor's 20.5 sacks in 1986 came in two games against the Redskins.

2

NEW YORK GIANTS
Years: 1981-93
Height: 6'3" Weight: 237
Number: 56
Hall of Fame: 1999
Born: February 4, 1959

When Lawrence Taylor was on the sideline, that's exactly where opponents wanted him. Taylor was the New York Giants' signature player and an imposing presence as he led two Super Bowl-winning defenses during his Hall of Fame career, from 1981-93.

Taylor could absorb pain just as impressively as he inflicted it. Many remember him best for playing despite a muscle tear in his right shoulder in a Monday night game at New Orleans in 1988. The Saints, 9-3, had a golden opportunity to wreck the playoff chances of the Giants, who stood 7-5 and were missing quarterback Phil Simms and Pro Bowl linebackers Harry Carson and Carl Banks. Taylor, wearing a harness to keep his shoulder in place, totaled seven tackles, three sacks and two forced fumbles in a 13-12 Giants victory.

"I wanted to cry because I felt like somebody had torn my shoulder off," Taylor said after enhancing his reputation for playing hard even with excruciating pain. Once after

Lawrence Taylor didn't always need to throw a quarterback to the ground to ruin his view. It's hard to imagine Vikings quarterback Jim McMahon can see what's going on downfield as Taylor, who totaled 142 sacks, swoops in to help win a January 1994 playoff game, his last appearance in Giants Stadium.
AP/WWP

Taylor suffered a concussion, a trainer hid his helmet to prevent him from returning to the game. Taylor missed only one game, because of a broken bone in his foot in 1989.

Unfortunately for Taylor, his recklessness brought him as much attention off the field as on the field. He checked into drug rehabilitation after the 1985 season, and though he bounced back with his best season ever, more trouble seemed inevitable when Taylor claimed he'd cured his addiction by playing golf.

He failed an NFL drug test during the 1987 preseason and was suspended for 30 days after failing another test the next summer. His drug problems escalated after he retired. He entered drug rehabilitation twice in 1995 and was arrested on drug charges in 1996, '97 and '98.

Taylor's conviction for the 1998 arrest eventually resulted in an $1,100 fine and six-month revocation of his New Jersey driver's license. He wasn't imprisoned, despite the drug arrests, a conviction for income tax evasion and a 1997 arrest for failing to make child support payments.

But the 1998 drug arrest, in Florida, intensified controversy around the 1999 Hall of Fame balloting, held annually before the Super Bowl. Taylor was eligible for the first time and was an obvious selection based on his career. Though Hall of Fame guidelines stipulate that a candidate should be judged solely on performance, Taylor's off-the-field behavior also invited discussion among electors when they met in Miami.

Electors strongly indicated in news stories that they would elect Taylor. Yet he denigrated the electors as a bunch of hypocrites who were criticizing him for his drug problems while they supposedly got drunk and chased little girls on Miami Beach.

Electors, perhaps deaf and numb to Taylor's tirades and antics over the years, voted him in.

For those wanting to give Taylor the benefit of the doubt, his son, Lawrence Jr., offered a touching presentation speech in July at Canton. He said, in part: "When I reached my teens, and I read about all his accomplishments on the field and his mishaps off the field, that helped me know, love and respect my father even more. I admire my father because he is never one to not admit when he's done something wrong. And even though it's never reported, he does so many things right. I love my father. I would do anything for him, just as he would do anything for me or my sisters. If I could pick anybody to be my father, I'd pick Lawrence Taylor every time."

Taylor suggested he'd learned a hard lesson when during his induction speech he said: "I think what I want to leave the people is that life, like anything else, can knock you down. You know, anybody can quit. A Hall of Famer never quits. A Hall of Famer realizes that the crime is not being knocked down. The crime is not getting up again."

Taylor and seven teammates from their Super Bowl days returned in January 2001, at coach Jim Fassel's invitation, to Giants Stadium the day before a 41-0 victory over the Minnesota Vikings in the NFC championship game.

"You've got what you want right here," Taylor said as he addressed Fassel's players. "You can't ask for anything better than this: playing this game, you're 60 minutes away [from the Super Bowl], here at Giants Stadium.

"Most of us played our whole career as a Giant, and to be a Giant is very special and very dear to us, and we care about what happens to you guys. We're really proud of you. You've worked hard and you've done the little things to get the job done, but it's not over yet. There's still one more game to go before you get the prize. I know how special it was, how exciting it was. This is what it's all about."

RAY NITSCHKE

S undays were good days for the Packers playing offense. They didn't have to confront middle linebacker Ray Nitschke, whose vicious hitting never took a day off.

Nitschke, mainstay of five championship defenses, was as tough on his teammates as he was on opponents. Coach Vince Lombardi's pet drill was the "nutcracker," better known today as the "Oklahoma" drill. An offensive lineman, in a confined space, leads a running back against a defensive player, who tries to shed the block and make the tackle.

David Maraniss, in his Lombardi biography, *When Pride Still Mattered*, recounts tight end Gary Knafelc's dread in facing Nitschke, "a second-year linebacker out of Illinois, who seemed to be salivating for his chance to slap and whack and pound the hell out of him."

Lombardi, trying to rebuild a chronic loser when he arrived at Green Bay in 1959, also loved to run his trademark sweep against his defense.

"This was too much like the nutcracker drill for Nitschke," Maraniss wrote. "He loved it. Blood spurting out from his knuckles, smeared on his pants, some of it his, some Knafelc's."

The drill was run repeatedly and didn't end until Knafelc, who by this time feared Nitschke more than Lombardi, said: "Coach, by this time even Ray knows it's a sweep."

Nitschke, who died in 1998 from a heart attack, explained that going all out, every day, on every play, was the only way he knew how to perform.

"Intensity was the only way I felt I could survive," he said. "I practiced diligently. I came to play every day. I never went out on a football field without being ready to play.

"It's a survival type of thing. You've got to like contact. If you're not willing to hit people, you don't belong on the field. You want them to have respect for you when they run a play at you. You want them to be a little shy and a little shyer the next time. You want them to remember you're there."

Packers quarterback Bart Starr, for one, was grateful he didn't have to look over the line at Nitschke, whose ferocity was underscored by his missing upper front teeth.

"Ray played with such a recklessness and fierceness that he developed a reputation fast that here was a guy you avoided, if at all possible," Starr said.

"But he never did things in the sense that he would overrun tackles in a wild rage. He just loved to hit people."

Nitschke also made some of his biggest plays in some of the biggest games of the Lombardi era. On defense, only he, linemen Henry Jordan and Willie Davis and safety Willie Wood were with Lombardi for all six championship games over eight years. They lost only one.

Nitschke came up with two fumble recoveries and a pass deflection in the Packers' 16-7 victory over the New York Giants in the 1962 NFL championship game and was named Most Valuable Player. He made one of four Packer interceptions in a 37-0 rout of the Giants in the 1961 NFL championship game, played before a record-breaking 55 million TV viewers.

Nitschke was credited with nine unassisted tackles in a 33-14 win over the Oakland Raiders in Super Bowl II in January, 1968. His vicious hits on running back Hewritt Dixon on the first two plays set the tone for the Packers.

"Hewritt was quivering like a tuning fork, Ray hit him with such ferocity," recalled Lee Remmel, who became Packers executive director of public relations after covering the team for the Green Bay *Post-Gazette*. "That seemed to neutralize him for the rest of the day.

"He was the epitome of controlled violence on the football field. He was probably the most intense football player I've ever seen, and I've been watching pro football since 1946. He only had one speed, and that was all out. I don't think there's any doubt he was one of the best in the history of the game."

3

GREEN BAY PACKERS
Years: 1958-72
Height: 6'3" Weight: 235
Number: 66
Nickname: Wildman
Hall of Fame: 1978
Born: December 29, 1936
Died: March 8, 1998

Ray Nitschke was caught here in an unfamiliar spot. When the Packers' defense was on the sideline, the Hall of Fame middle linebacker usually could be found kneeling near coach Vince Lombardi. When the Green Bay defense was on the field, Nitschke usually could be found putting devastating licks on any opponent carrying the ball.
VERNON J. BIEVER PHOTO

Nitschke, showing the rough edges of his childhood, could bring thunder off the field, too. He was three when his father was killed and 13 when his mother died, and an older brother raised him. Nitschke grew up poor and tough in the Chicago area and came to the Packers as a free spirit and hard drinker.

Before one game in Los Angeles, Nitschke walked into a hotel bar where Lombardi and friends were drinking. Nitschke already was breaking a team rule by entering the bar, then compounded his indiscretion by sending Lombardi a drink. Wood told the *Post-Gazette* that Lombardi wanted to cut Nitschke because of that episode but was talked out of it by a players' committee.

Nitschke married Jacqueline Forschette of Green Bay in 1961 and stopped drinking a few years later. Now, his reputation as a wild man was confined to the field.

"I was real rowdy, real obnoxious, especially when I was drinking," Nitschke said. "I was mad all the time and took it out on everybody off the field. I was a hard guy to get along with.

"I grew up belting the other kids in the neighborhood. My brother was wonderful to me, but I never really had any discipline, not anyone to tell me when to go to bed. I felt I was somebody who didn't have anything, and I took it out on everybody else."

Nitschke's opponents must've breathed a sigh of relief during the 1961 season when he, running back Paul Hornung and wide receiver Boyd Dowler were called up to active duty as part of President John Kennedy's military response to the Soviets' construction of the Berlin Wall.

Lombardi, with his team off to a 4-1 start, tried, to no avail, to pull strings and get Nitschke and Hornung deferred. The coach had to settle for having all three play on weekend passes, and they also were able to practice for the title game against the Giants.

Because the Packers had so many other stars and the Chicago Bears' Dick Butkus burst on the scene in 1965, Nitschke was named to only one Pro Bowl, in 1964. But in 1978 he became the first defensive player of the Lombardi era elected to the Pro Football Hall of Fame.

"It's a **survival** type of thing. You've got to like **contact**. If you're not willing to **hit** people, you don't belong **on the field**."

—Ray Nitschke

"To play for the Packers was a privilege," Nitschke said. "The 1967 Ice Bowl victory over Dallas was the greatest satisfaction I've ever received in football. To see my coaches and teammates in tears in the locker room after the game, it's a time I'll always remember."

The Packers' 21-17 victory over the Cowboys was one of the NFL's classic games, largely because it was played with the temperature 13 degrees below zero and the wind chill minus 46. Nitschke, despite frostbitten toes, refused to sit near the sideline blowers and kept to his superstitious habit of kneeling near Lombardi.

"But he **never** did things in the sense that he would overrun tackles in a **wild rage**. He just loved to **hit people**."

—Bart Starr

Hall of Fame officials were touched by Nitschke's devotion to the shrine, and he returned faithfully for the annual induction ceremonies and members' luncheon. He seemed to take his membership as seriously as any game he'd played.

"He was a fire eater," recalled Pete Elliott, the Hall of Fame's former executive director. "He'd chew 'em out if they didn't get back for Hall of Fame weekend. Invariably Ray Nitschke would get up at the luncheon and make a fiery talk: 'This is the greatest fraternity, you've got to come back.' And they looked forward to it. They'd all ask, 'When is Nitschke going to talk?'"

Nitschke always spoke gruffly, yet even in his playing days presented a dramatically different portrait out of uniform. When he'd put in his bridgework and put on horn-rimmed glasses and a turtleneck sweater, he was barely recognizable as the middle linebacker of the Packers.

Even after his MVP performance in the 1962 championship game, he initially stumped the celebrity panel of the TV show *What's My Line*. It must've been hard to believe this bald, gentle-looking man knocked people down for a living.

"Off the field, you hardly would have identified Ray as being a middle linebacker," Starr said. "He was meek and mild and easygoing, very respectful of others. When they met him, people couldn't believe that here was the wildman linebacker they had been watching all these years. He was a classic example of Dr. Jekyll and Mr. Hyde."

Nitschke lost his teeth as a junior at Illinois while covering a kickoff. He was hit in the mouth with a helmet and his two front teeth were knocked out while two others were broken into stumps. Nitschke put cotton in his mouth and played the rest of the game.

"You've got to have the proper temperament," he said years later, "to take lots of bruises and physical abuse and come back the next week."

Nitschke, though proud of his play and temperament, was sensitive to his image as a brute. He wanted people to understand that once a game was over, he wasn't interested in knocking heads.

"People see you as a gladiator," he said after his retirement. "They don't see you in the community, so they're quick to judge you. People would tell me all the time, 'You're not the same guy I see on the field.' I wasn't. I'm not today. I have a lot of compassion for people."

Nitschke, relegated mainly to special teams, retired during training camp of 1973. He was elected to the Hall of Fame five years later, in his first year of eligibility.

"My spirit is still there," Nitschke announced upon retiring. "But the numbers game got to me. There's no room on the roster for a third middle linebacker, so I'm retiring."

Two decades later, the man still was unforgettable. Even as the Packers were climbing back to the top in 1996, defensive end Sean Jones wondered if they were performing up to Nitschke's standards.

"What people don't understand outside Green Bay is that we have to exorcise those ghosts: Willie Wood, Willie Davis, Bart Starr, Ray Nitschke," Jones said. "I think Ray Nitschke thinks we stink."

Nitschke died while visiting family and friends in Florida, and when Hall of Famers hold their annual luncheon now, a beloved member is missing. Not in spirit, however. The event is now officially named the Ray Nitschke Luncheon.

Ray Nitschke must've been delighted to see Bears quarterback Rudy Bukich, and not Hall of Fame running back Gale Sayers, running with the ball. Nitschke fights off Sayers's block and takes dead aim at Bukich, who scrambles while trying to spot an open receiver. VERNON J. BIEVER PHOTO

JOE SCHMIDT

T he way Don Shula tells it, Joe Schmidt stopped the Green Bay Packers from celebrating Thanksgiving in Detroit. The Packers visited the Lions every Thanksgiving from 1951-63 and in '62 took a 10-0 record into Detroit against a team with defensive stars Dick "Night Train" Lane, Dick LeBeau, Wayne Walker, Yale Lary, Roger Brown, Alex Karras, and Schmidt, their captain and middle linebacker.

The Lions sacked Bart Starr 11 times and gave the Packers their only loss, 26-14, in a championship season.

"We completely dominated them, and Joe was unbelievable," recalled Shula, a Hall of Fame coach who was then the Lions' defensive coordinator. "After that game [and a 13-13 tie in 1963] Lombardi refused to come and play us every year. It was just a game where the fans wanted the defense to be on the field the whole game."

The Lions' defense that year always seemed to be on the field the whole game. The Lions' only losses were 9-7 at Green Bay, 17-14 at New York and 3-0 at Chicago. An offensive juggernaut they were not.

"We were good enough on defense to win it all," Schmidt recalled. "Unfortunately, a couple of circumstances didn't happen. Just like life."

Schmidt played in three NFL championship games, all against the Cleveland Browns, and the Lions won titles in 1953 and '57. They lost the '54 title game 56-10, then a year later made a move that changed Schmidt's legacy and the way defense was played in the NFL.

Schmidt, the strong-side linebacker in a 5-2 alignment, moved to the middle in a 4-3, which was just catching on. Bill George of the Chicago Bears in 1954 was credited with becoming the first true middle linebacker; then Schmidt became the position's signature player. He made 10 straight Pro Bowls and totaled 24 interceptions.

"Schmidt's mobility took some of the load off the defensive backs on pass defense," Lions coach Buddy Parker once recalled. "In fact, his style of play brought about the zone defenses, revolving defenses and the modern defensive look of pro football."

Though coaches realized the 5-2 alignment left a hole in the middle, that posed no problem as long as the strong-side linebacker jammed the tight end.

"Then they started pulling the tight end off the line of scrimmage and using a slot situation," Schmidt recalled. "I'd just pound the tight end—then you were allowed to do that. As a result, they pulled him off the line to give him more freedom so he could escape and get in the pattern more.

"What happened then is they started pulling me back once in a while and we'd go to a 4-3. It evolved from necessity."

Though not especially big, Schmidt was smart, tough, quick and had played middle linebacker in high school and at the University of Pittsburgh. Lombardi described him as "a cat, and not the purring kind."

According to *The Detroit News,* Shula determined that in 1961 Schmidt made just seven mistakes in judgment or execution in 890 defensive plays.

"That was the kind of intelligence he had and he was a field general on defense, similar to what [Miami quarterback] Bob Griese was on offense," Shula recalled. "It was a quiet leadership. He wasn't a rah-rah guy. He led by example. Everybody just looked up to him."

Even opponents. Sam Huff, the New York Giants' middle linebacker during their glory years of the 1950s and '60s, recalls being keenly aware of Schmidt's presence when the Lions visited Yankee Stadium in 1962.

"I watched him all the time, probably a lot more than he watched me," Huff recalled. "We had never met and I looked across the field and said to myself, 'This is my turf, you're playing in Yankee

4

DETROIT LIONS
Years: 1953-65
Height: 6' Weight: 222
Number: 56
Hall of Fame: 1973
Born: January 18, 1932

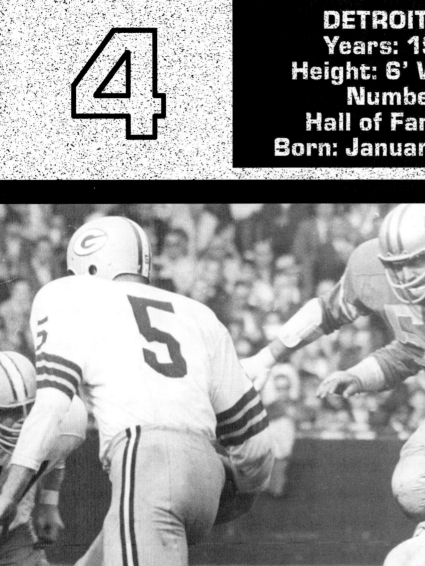

This leap by Joe Schmidt (56) over Green Bay fullback Jim Taylor should explain why Packers coach Vince Lombardi likened Schmidt to a cat. Schmidt zeroes in on halfback Paul Hornung (5).

VERNON J. BIEVER PHOTO

Stadium and this will be my day.' I admired him for what he had done for the game. I had to prove to Joe Schmidt who I was and that I could do his job."

Huff, through his famous TV documentary, enhanced the tough-guy image George and Schmidt helped create. Schmidt, however, sounds sheepish about the middle linebacker mystique.

"The middle linebacker gets more credit than he should be given," he said. "Everything is funneled to you. If you like to tackle and go to the ball, it's the easiest position on the field

"I used to say, 'The guys in front of me lather and I shave.' That's how simple it is. Maybe because I did it so long, I never looked at it as something difficult."

Schmidt was grateful the facemask came along in the NFL about the same time as the middle linebacker. When Schmidt joined the Lions, players wore only a chinstrap on their helmets. He had suffered a concussion in college and didn't want to wind up looking like an old-time NHL goalie.

"I'd bump into Gump Worsley once in a while at the Lindell AC, and he didn't have a tooth in his head," Schmidt said, referring to the famous Detroit bar. "Those guys were nuts.

"Some people considered a facemask a sign of cowardice. When I wore one, my defensive coach, Buster Ramsey, said, 'You can't see.' I told him, 'I can see perfectly.'"

Ramsey wasn't always wrong, though. He's credited with convincing the Lions to draft Schmidt, who suffered severe injuries every season at Pitt, including torn knee cartilage and a concussion as a senior. The Lions didn't draft him until the seventh round in 1953, and general manager Nick Kerbawy barely acknowledged Schmidt when he, along with second-round draft choice Gene Gedman, first visited the Lions' offices. Kerbawy told Schmidt where he could catch a bus to the Lions' training facility, then asked Gedman, a running back from Indiana, if he'd like to play golf.

Schmidt didn't receive such a hot reception from Lions' veterans, either. His arrival allowed the club to trade Dick Flanagan, a popular returning starter, and the veterans froze out Schmidt until midseason. By 1956, however, he was their player representative, and he voted for the formation of the NFL Players Association.

Schmidt could appreciate the need for a union, because during his career he earned more from a Detroit auto parts supply business, which he still owned at age 71, than he earned as a Lion. Player representatives in his day were mostly stars, because marginal players who became union leaders tended to have short careers.

"So generally they elected guys who were pretty well established," Schmidt recalled. "There were a lot of problems in the beginning to the point the union was almost disbanded. I don't think players today realize the heartaches and problems these guys went through—the possibility of losing their jobs—to get the union established.

"I had a heck of a time collecting dues. A couple of guys would say, 'I'll get you next year.' I'd say, 'No, I have to have it this year.' Guys never thought it would get to where it's developed today."

Schmidt eventually got his taste of management. Just one year after serving as Lions linebackers coach under Harry Gilmer, Schmidt was named Lions head coach in 1967. He compiled a 43-35-7 record, unmatched by any of the eight full-time head coaches who succeeded him prior to Steve Mariucci's hiring in 2003. But Schmidt, explaining that coaching no longer was fun, resigned after the 1972 season.

"I was frustrated by some things I wasn't able to have control over to my satisfaction," he recalled. "As a result, it was time for me to get out of there. When I look back, I didn't have the experience to be a head coach. I had a good staff, I knew football. The thing I had to do was create an environment conducive to young guys working and having a good time. That promotes winning.

"We lost to Dallas 5-0 [in the 1970 playoffs], which was sort of ridiculous. If we'd gotten by them, we'd have played the 49ers and we'd beaten them previously. Then we would've played Baltimore in the Super Bowl. Like everything in life…a couple of turns here and there. We had a good run and a good record."

Schmidt was known as a players' coach and during his year as an assistant received a good primer in handling hard cases. The Lions picked up Joe Don Looney, a talented but eccentric running back, and when Looney skipped a practice, Schmidt found him in a dormitory room. When Schmidt told Looney he'd be fined if he didn't come to practice, Looney asked Schmidt how long he'd been going to practice every day.

"Fourteen years," Schmidt replied.

Looney suggested, "Joe, you ought to take a day off once in a while."

Moviegoers might best remember Schmidt as the Lions' head coach from the movie *Paper Lion*, the adaptation of George Plimpton's book about his tryout at quarterback during a Lions training camp. Considering Schmidt's quiet dignity, he understandably had a dim view about being in a movie.

"Once the newness wore off, we all thought we were movie stars," he joked. "I thought, 'This is going to make jackasses out of everybody.' I thought we'd all be laughingstocks. But it turned out to be a pretty good movie in everybody's eyes."

Paper Lion was so good, in fact, it may have done for sports cinema what Schmidt had done for middle linebackers.

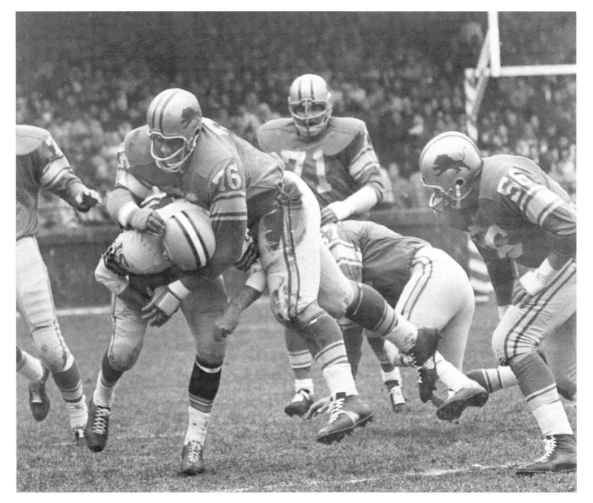

Middle linebacker Joe Schmidt (56) always said his defensive linemen made his job easy and here's why. He's joined here by Alex Karras (71) and Roger Brown, who's taking down Packers quarterback Bart Starr. The Lions sacked Starr 11 times in a 1962 game that dealt the Packers their only loss that season.
VERNON J. BIEVER PHOTO

JACK HAM

 ew York Giants general manager Ernie Accorsi was a publicist at Penn State in the late 1960s when Jack Ham was helping make that school Linebacker U. Ham was a year behind two-time All-American Dennis Onkotz, and both worked with linebackers coach Dan Radakovich.

"Ham asked Radakovich, 'Coach, will I ever be an interceptor like Onkotz?' " Accorsi recalled. "He said, 'Not as long as you cover backs the way you do. They'll never throw you the darn ball. You're going to have to learn how to let them get open.' "

Ham's 32 career interceptions tie him for most among Hall of Fame linebackers. But his pass defense was just the highlight of a remarkable repertoire, and many consider Ham the best all-around outside linebacker in pro football history.

"Jack was the last true linebacker who did it all," Accorsi said. "He was great against the run, great at dropping. He was a great blitzer, though they didn't blitz that much because with that front four, they didn't have to.

"He had a nose and a knack. For a pure outside linebacker, he was the best. Ham was just unbelievable."

The Steelers were able to draft Ham in 1971, as well as Jack Lambert three years later, in the second round. Both were considered too light for first-round picks.

"When I was at Baltimore," Accorsi recalled, "we had a coach in our draft room and when they picked Ham, he said, 'What do they need, a strong safety?' I won't tell you his name, but I was going to send him an invitation to the induction ceremony."

Though getting Ham in the second round was a coup for the Steelers, it was insulting for Ham. Even worse, he'd been drafted by a perennial loser. Little did he know he would become a key player for arguably the best defensive dynasty in NFL history.

"The Giants and San Diego both told me they were going to take me number one and I'm naïve enough to believe the banter the day before the draft," Ham said from his drug-testing company in suburban Pittsburgh.

"So the combination of being drafted in the second round and by Pittsburgh… I've lived in this area my whole life and thought I'd have the opportunity to live somewhere else for six months. I remember being at the College All-Star Game, all the guys were saying, 'Too bad you got drafted by Pittsburgh, it's such a lousy team.'

"Then all of a sudden, we got some pretty good drafts."

The Steeler draft in 1974 included four future Hall of Famers: wide receivers John Stallworth and Lynn Swann, center Mike Webster and Lambert. The Steelers were strong enough in 1972 to give the undefeated Miami Dolphins a scare in the AFC championship game, eight days after the "Immaculate Reception" stunned the Oakland Raiders.

But the Raiders had little trouble knocking off the Steelers in a wild-card playoff game at Oakland in '73, and a return trip to Oakland for the '74 AFC title game marked a historic gut check for the Steelers.

With the score 10-10 in the third quarter, Ham made his second interception. Raider quarterback Ken Stabler was getting blitzed and threw to the sideline for running back Charlie Smith, but Ham got to the ball first. His return inside the Oakland 10 set up a Terry Bradshaw pass to Swann that put the Steelers ahead to stay. That win was the takeoff point for a run of four Super Bowl victories in six years.

"We had a pretty good football team before that," Ham recalled. "But that put us over the top and we became a great football team."

Ham consistently stepped up in big games. He made 18 unassisted tackles in three postseason games in 1978. In that season's AFC championship game, a 34-5 win over the Houston Oilers, he had two fumble recoveries and an interception. He made 21 fumble recoveries in his career.

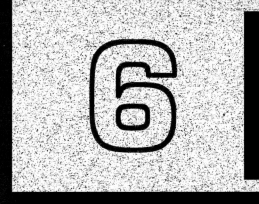

KANSAS CITY CHIEFS
Years: 1963-74
Height: 6'4" Weight: 225
Number: 78
Hall of Fame: 1983
Born: June 17, 1940

Even three decades after Bobby Bell's retirement, NFL personnel experts routinely cite him as the measuring stick by which all other fast, strong and versatile outside linebackers are measured. Bell's all-around athletic skills rarely have been matched.
KANSAS COLLECTION, U. OF KANSAS

Though Bell could've played several positions, outside linebacker suited him best. With such linemen as Jerry Mays, Curley Culp and Buchanan tying up blockers, Bell was especially hard to stop.

"That gave me a free rush," he recalled. "Kind of like what Lawrence Taylor was doing, I was doing that back in the '60s. When I blitzed, they didn't have a chance."

Bell could be punishing, too. He once picked up 250-pound Houston Oiler guard Sonny Bishop and threw him into the quarterback for a seven-yard loss.

"I wanted them to know I was there, not just that play but all day, every game, every year," Bell said. "I didn't want them to say, 'Bobby was great last week, but he didn't show up this week.' If you're going to make the Hall of Fame, you've got to be consistent.

"If you pound on a door long enough, it's going to come down and you'll find the weak spot. If you pound on a guy all day long, that's the name of the game. If [my opponent] leaves the game that day and doesn't say that Bobby Bell was the toughest guy he ever played against, in my mind I didn't do my job. It was my way of getting everybody's attention. I wanted to let 'em know up front the old man was here to stay."

Bell stayed on the field as much as he could. He played on nearly all special teams and snapped for punts and place kicks. Stram, at Bell's Hall of Fame induction in 1983, said, "He is the only player I have seen who could play any position on a team and that team could still win."

Bell said remaining on the field as much as possible enhanced his concentration.

"Very seldom would I go to the bench," he recalled. "I always sat on my helmet and watched the field. If the offense went three and out, I'd snap for the punt and run out and play defense. When you're in the game 85 percent of the time, you're warm and your attention span never comes down."

Bell played in two Super Bowl games and the first three postmerger Pro Bowls, but is best remembered by many for a goal-line stand in a 13-6 victory over the New York Jets in a 1969 divisional playoff game. That win paved the Chiefs' way to a Super Bowl victory over the Minnesota Vikings.

The Jets trailed 6-3 but had first down on the one, and after two plays went nowhere, they called for quarterback Joe Namath to fake a handoff to fullback Matt Snell, roll out and pass to Snell. The Chiefs called for a blitz, which should have played right into Namath's hands, except Bell didn't bite. He stepped between Namath and Snell and waited for the quarterback to commit. Namath hesitated and was sacked.

"He had no business being there," Namath said. "If he reacts normally, it's a sure touchdown."

The Chiefs then beat the Raiders for the AFL championship and a berth in the Super Bowl, where the Chiefs followed the Jets' example of stunning a heavily favored NFL opponent. Bell maintains a soft spot for the AFL, partly because it expanded opportunities for black players and enabled teammate Willie Lanier to become pro football's first black middle linebacker.

Deep south colleges were still at least a decade away from recruiting black athletes when Bell was a high school star in Shelby, N.C. Though North Carolina coach Jim Tatum could not recruit Bell, he wanted to keep him away from Notre Dame or Michigan State, both upcoming North Carolina opponents. Bell's high school couldn't afford game films, and Tatum convinced Minnesota coach Murray Warmath to recruit Bell, sight unseen.

"He told Warmath if I didn't make the team, he'd pay for his scholarship," Bell said.

Bell and quarterback Sandy Stephens were among five black Gophers, and Bell said all felt they had something to prove. Minnesota was voted national champion in 1960 and the next season played in a second straight Rose Bowl game.

"It was like living in a glass house, because now my people all over the country were watching us," Bell said. "We were pioneers. You could call it pressure. We were out there to play football, get an education and do well so the people behind us would have a chance."

Bell would experience yet another dramatic chapter in U.S. history less than a decade later. He joined several other NFL stars in 1968 on a three-week tour of hospital bases in Vietnam, where the U.S. was fighting Communist forces, and Thailand, where many U.S. airmen were based. Five hours after the players arrived in Saigon, the Vietnamese capital, fighting broke out and Viet Cong soldiers tried to storm the players' hotel. Bell roomed with Buffalo quarterback Jack Kemp, and a mortar shell exploded under their window.

"They killed the MPs at the hotel; I crawled on my knees up and down the hotel steps," Bell recalled. "They were shooting in the windows. They finally got us out of there 10 days later. I don't talk about it much. It was a nasty affair."

There isn't much else Bell won't talk about. He talks to strangers in restaurants and elevators. He'll phone people he's met in passing to wish them a happy birthday or anniversary. In every town he visits for a speech or trade show appearance, he'll phone any Hall of Famer who lives nearby.

Bell especially enjoys restaurants because he formerly owned a small chain of barbecue places in the Kansas City area. After spending nearly three hours in Applebee's, he kiddingly tells the waitress it's his birthday. She brings him cake to go and Bell grins mischievously.

Some diners obviously recognize Bell, but most don't. If he didn't impress some of his peers as looking like a pro football player when he was young, strapping and fresh out of college, it's understandable if some don't recognize Bell now.

"No one ever asked me if I won a beauty contest after I knocked 'em on their tail," he once said. "Not even Buck Buchanan."

The Chiefs, fresh off their Super Bowl victory in January, went to Baltimore on Sept. 28, 1970 for the second Monday Night Football game ever played. Bobby Bell uses his speed and power to sack Colts quarterback John Unitas in a 44-24 Kansas City victory.
TOPEKA CAPITAL-JOURNAL

JACK LAMBERT

I t's no knock on Jack Lambert to say the myth is bigger than the man. Lambert was, after all, on the light side for a middle linebacker.

And the Lambert myth is so entertaining, so full of what both the bloodthirsty and romantics think pro football is all about, that only a killjoy would dare debunk it. And like many myths, those about Lambert contain some truth. So in the interests of truth—or should we say half truth?—the myth is a good place to start.

Lambert, who helped make the "Steel Curtain" defense arguably the best of all time, is widely portrayed as a gap-toothed wildman who intimidated opponents into submission. Quarterback John Elway in 1983 made his first NFL start at Pittsburgh and noticed that Lambert wasn't exactly the kind of player he'd faced while at Stanford.

"He had no teeth and he was slobbering," Elway recalled. "I was thinking, 'Get me out of here, I should've become an accountant.'"

Lambert would be the first to admit that for a quarterback, the Steel Curtain was not a welcome sight.

"He also saw Joe Greene and a bunch of other guys," Lambert said from his Worthington, Pennsylvania home. "I don't think a lot of people felt comfortable looking at our defense. [Bengals quarterback] Ken Anderson would come in our locker room after games and said, 'You guys are awesome.'

"I don't think anybody said anything. I think we all knew it."

Lambert also would be the first to admit he was aggressive.

"I played the way I had to play," he recalled. "I weighed about 218 pounds. If I hadn't played aggressively, they would've carried me off the field on a stretcher."

Opponents and teammates polished Lambert's image more than he did.

"I don't care for the man," Dallas Cowboys linebacker Thomas "Hollywood" Henderson once said. "He makes more money than I do, and he don't have no teeth. He's Dracula."

Chimed in Steeler defensive back J.T. Thomas: "He's so mean he hates himself."

Lambert's image for nastiness was ratcheted up by three penalized hits on Cleveland Browns quarterback Brian Sipe and his famous knockdown of Cowboys safety Cliff Harris.

Lambert was first penalized for a late hit on Sipe in 1978 and was mobbed by angry Browns. The Steelers' next game was on a Monday night against the Houston Oilers, and with quarterbacks Terry Bradshaw and Dan Pastorini within earshot, Lambert was interviewed about the Sipe incident. "Quarterbacks should wear dresses," Lambert suggested.

Lambert was twice ejected from games for hitting Sipe as he was throwing, but said he considered Sipe fair game because he was rolling out.

"I was all for protecting the quarterback as long as he's in the pocket," Lambert said. "Once he's running with the ball, he deserves to be treated like any other player. I got penalized in Cleveland [in 1981] for hitting him too hard. I never really understood that."

In the January 1976 Super Bowl, Harris raised Lambert's ire by tapping Steeler kicker Roy Gerela on the helmet and taunting him for missing a field goal attempt. Lambert threw Harris to the ground but wasn't penalized.

"It wasn't something I thought about—it was a split-second thing, but I couldn't permit anyone to intimidate our team," Lambert said then. "Luckily, I didn't throw any punches or I probably would have been thrown out of the game."

That knockdown could not have surprised anybody who'd scouted Lambert at Kent State. That included Wayne Rudy, also the Kansas City Chiefs' trainer.

7

PITTSBURGH STEELERS
Years: 1974-84
Height: 6'4" Weight: 218
Number: 58
Nickname: Dracula
Hall of Fame: 1990
Born: July 8, 1952

A powerful linebacking trio was a hallmark of the "Steel Curtain" defenses that helped the Pittsburgh Steelers win four Super Bowls in six years. When Pro Bowl right outside linebacker Andy Russell retired after the 1976 season, eventual Hall of Famers Jack Ham and Jack Lambert (58) were joined by Loren Toews (51), who closes in on Kansas City Chiefs quarterback Mike Nott.

"Wayne said, 'This is the toughest guy I've ever seen,'" recalled Walt Corey, then a Chiefs assistant. "I said, 'He's so skinny. When you look at him on film, you say he'll never make it in the pros.'

"He was fortunate he went to Pittsburgh, with that great line. He got to mirror you mentally and he saw things happen a lot before they did happen, and became a heck of a force for Pittsburgh."

A news release from the Pro Football Hall of Fame went so far as to suggest the Steelers lacked a great defense until Lambert came along because they'd allowed 33 points in a 1973 playoff loss to the Raiders. Considering the Steelers already had three Pro Bowl linebackers and their famous front four, it seemed farfetched to suggest that Lambert put the steel in the curtain by replacing Henry Davis.

Not even teammate Andy Russell, who calls Lambert "the best middle linebacker I ever saw," would go that far. Lambert, a second-round pick in 1974, was an obvious boon to the Steeler defense. But safety Donnie Shell made the team as an undrafted free agent that year, and the Steelers became more balanced by also drafting wide receivers Lynn Swann and John Stallworth and center Mike Webster.

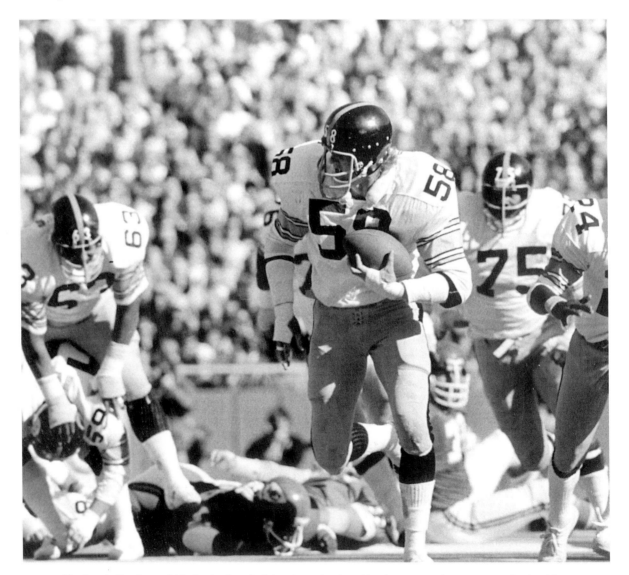

Pittsburgh Steelers middle linebacker Jack Lambert developed such a reputation as an unrelenting hitter that his extraordinary coverage skills often were overlooked. But once Lambert got his hands on the ball, he wasn't much fun to deal with, either. Here he's returning one of the 28 interceptions he made on his way to the Hall of Fame.
KANSAS COLLECTION, U. of KANSAS

"Those 33 points to the Raiders…that was a very good team, and if they were on and got things going, they could hurt us," Russell recalled. "They were very impressive. I don't think it had anything to do with Henry Davis.

"Jack Lambert was the icing on the cake, the last piece of the puzzle and a great player with a lot of other great players."

Where some saw a maniac, Russell saw savvy. Russell was a seven-time Pro Bowl player, has written two books about his Steeler days, and, playing opposite Jack Ham, was a master technician on the Steel Curtain's weak side.

"They'd say what made him a great player was his aggressiveness—he was so tough," Russell recalled. "Fans loved that stuff, but what it was—the guy was so smart, he never made a mistake. He was brilliant on the football field, almost contrary to his image.

"Technique-wise, he was superb. That's how he survived. He was a tall string bean, but he had great speed, great anticipation and a great knowledge of the game. All those things are why this image as a rock 'em-sock 'em guy who'd duke it out with you is really not what made him a great player.

"Opponents weren't intimidated. You don't intimidate these offensive linemen in the NFL. You beat them with speed and anticipation and things of that nature."

Steeler fans loved Lambert's style, because it was a perfect fit for a city that embraces toughness and hard, honest work. And Lambert loved Pittsburgh's rabid football following and small-city feel.

"If I played in New York City, I don't know what I would've done—I would've lost my mind," he said.

"I would tell rookies in Pittsburgh, 'They want to see somebody playing hard every week. If you keep your nose clean and stay out of trouble, these people will take care of you for the rest of your life.' "

Lambert, however, didn't want anybody taking care of him once he retired. He moved to rural western Pennsylvania and became a deputy game warden for nine years. Since then he's devoted himself to managing, umpiring and groundskeeping for a youth baseball league in which his four children have played. Friends and neighbors pay little mind to Lambert's glory days.

"I've been here for so long, they all really couldn't care less," he said. "If they did, I'd move."

Lambert made nine straight Pro Bowls and totaled 28 interceptions, and his fourth-quarter interception in the January 1980 Super Bowl killed the Los Angeles Rams' last chance to prevent the Steelers from winning their fourth Super Bowl in six years. Lambert often was freed up to use his 4.7 speed to cover receivers because his front four, led by Greene, didn't need much help.

"The Dick Butkuses and guys like that made devastating hits, but we played pass defenses that they couldn't have even attempted," Russell said. "You're restricted by what defenses you can play if the guy's not mobile. If you allow for the complexities Lambert allowed us to play, that makes a huge difference. That's why I would put Lambert as the best middle linebacker ever.

"He could run with the tight ends and could cover the first back out of the backfield on the weak side, man for man. He was so quick, he could do that. He'd make the tackles—they might not have been devastating, because he wasn't 250. Who could hit the hardest? That's irrelevant."

As for Lambert's missing teeth, they were casualties of a collision during a high basketball practice in Mantua, Ohio. That's just 30 miles of north of Canton, so Lambert was right at home for his Hall of Fame induction speech in 1990.

"If I could start my life all over again, I would be a professional football player," he said, "and you damn well better believe I would be a Pittsburgh Steeler."

RAY LEWIS

No other linebacker in NFL history established himself as as much of a star on the field and as notorious off the field as Ray Lewis did in just one year.

Between the end of the Super Bowl in January 2000 and the end of the Super Bowl a year later, Lewis took a tumultuous ride. It started with his arrest on two counts of murder and ended with him voted Most Valuable Player of a 34-7 Super Bowl victory over the New York Giants. He became only the second player ever to win both Super Bowl MVP and NFL Defensive Player of the Year honors in the same season.

Lewis, considered too small to play middle linebacker by many NFL teams, was the 26th player drafted in 1996. Ravens rivals were burned for their oversight when Lewis, even as a rookie, blasted ball carriers, harassed quarterbacks and knocked down passes. Starting in 1997, he earned five straight Pro Bowl berths and climaxed his 2000 season with one of the best postseason performances ever for a defensive player.

In the Super Bowl, Lewis was all over the field as he made five tackles, three unassisted, and defensed four passes. During a 24-10 victory at Tennessee in a divisional playoff game, Lewis made 12 tackles and stole the ball from running back Eddie George for an interception that Lewis returned 50 yards for a touchdown.

Lewis was the heart and soul of a unit that in the 2000 season allowed just one touchdown in four postseason games and set 16-game regular-season records by allowing just 165 points and 970 yards rushing. The Ravens had four regular-season shutouts, and the Giants' lone Super Bowl score came on a kickoff return by Rod Dixon.

"That hurt," Lewis said after the game. "There'd never been a shutout in the Super Bowl, and that's what we were working for. But our defense knows that they didn't score on us."

Before kickoff, Lewis told tight end Shannon Sharpe and running back Jamal Lewis that the defense needed only a 10-point lead. The Ravens led 10-0 at halftime, and Ray Lewis told Sharpe, "You did what you were supposed to do. Game over."

The Giants clearly were in for a long day when Tiki Barber ran a sweep in the first quarter that might've been a big gainer, except Lewis ran across the field and chased him down. With his running game shut down, Kerry Collins was forced to throw and was intercepted four times.

That victory, in Tampa, Florida, capped a week in which Lewis became the first player ever at a Super Bowl to field questions about street killings. During the annual Tuesday media session, Lewis was asked to address the events after a post-Super Bowl party outside an Atlanta night spot a year earlier. Richard Lollar and Jacinth Baker were stabbed to death in an early-morning brawl allegedly involving Lewis and his companions.

Lewis initially was uncooperative with police and was charged with two counts of murder under a law that allows a murder charge against anyone involved in a fatal fight. Two men in Lewis's group, Reginald Oakley and Joseph Sweeting, were accused of the stabbings.

The trial began in May, 2000, and the prosecution's case quickly fell apart because of unreliable testimony. Lewis had spent 15 nights in prison in January and eventually agreed to a misdemeanor plea of obstructing justice. Lewis also agreed to testify against Oakley and Sweeting, but his testimony wasn't damaging to either and both were acquitted. Lewis also was fined $250,000 by NFL commissioner Paul Tagliabue. Though Lewis at the Super Bowl was available for questions about the murder trial, he didn't answer them. "I'm not here to please y'all," he said defiantly. "The person you want it from isn't going to talk about it. I'm not here to justify, that chapter is closed."

But that chapter may never be closed. Because the killings went unpunished and unexplained, a divide endured between Lewis's supporters and critics. Was he a falsely accused man who showed

8

Middle linebacker Ray Lewis was attempting a short-lived comeback from an early-season shoulder injury when the Ravens visited Miami in Nov., 2002. Lewis plugs a hole as tackle Maake Kemoeatu stops Ricky Williams during the Dolphins' 26-7 victory. Lewis soon after underwent season-ending surgery.
MARC SEROTA/REUTERS LANDOV

great inner strength by rebounding with a spectacular season, or a wayward celebrity whose lack of initial cooperation sabotaged a murder investigation?

"After I fought for my life in Atlanta, everyone said, 'Ray Lewis will never be the same player he was,'" Lewis said. "Well, they were absolutely correct. I'm not the same player. I'm better.

"If someone said to you: 'Ray is going to go through pure hell and by the end of the year he's going to be Defensive Player of the Year,' you would go, 'How?' If you read it in a book, you wouldn't believe it."

Lewis became just the sixth defensive player in the first 35 Super Bowls to win the MVP Award. Harvey Martin, a Dallas Cowboys end, in 1977 was the only previous player to win both major defensive awards in one season.

It takes an optimistic back to run up the gut of the Baltimore Ravens' defense, because Ray Lewis, a perennial Pro Bowler, seldom yields much ground. The Denver Broncos' Olandis Gary shouldn't have been surprised to find Lewis waiting for him with open arms.
MOLLY RILEY/REUTERS/LANDOV

"I played with John Elway, and as much as John was the heart and soul of that team, Ray is the heart and soul of this team," said Sharpe, who played for two Super Bowl champions hip teams in Denver.

Before the Ravens' Super Bowl win, Marcus Allen, now a Hall of Fame running back, joined other NFL experts in recognizing how much Lewis, just 25, had achieved so soon.

"I think he's redefining the middle linebacker position," Allen said. "He's been able to cover ground, he's able to cover multiple offensive weapons, and he's strong at the point of attack. He's aggressive, but never out of control, and he's fundamentally sound.

"He's always in the right place at the right time. He's a very, very intelligent player. He hurts people, too. He leaves an impression."

> "He's always in the right **place** at the right **time**. He's a very, very **intelligent** player. He **hurts** people, too. He leaves an **impression**."
>
> —Marcus Allen

Lewis, like most great linebackers, had a strong supporting cast to help him win a championship. But unlike the stars of yesteryear, he saw his cast diminished by free agency and the salary cap. In 2002, the Ravens had to gut their roster, and seven starters from their Super Bowl defense were gone.

Lewis started out, however, as if 2002 might be his best season yet. He totaled 69 tackles, two interceptions and a fumble recovery before he suffered a partially dislocated shoulder late in the third quarter at Cleveland in week four. Lewis tried to come back after missing five games, but season-ending surgery was unavoidable.

"I wanted to put this team on my back and get them back to the playoffs, but this is the best thing for me to do right now," Lewis said in late November. "This is so frustrating and it's so hard not playing, especially the home games."

The Ravens finished 7-9, and Lewis faced an arduous rehabilitation for 2003. The Ravens added a defensive wrinkle by hiring linebackers coach Mike Singletary, leader of the Bears' defense that saw its fewest-points record broken by the Ravens.

"He [Lewis] wants to be on a level all by himself; he wants to be the best," Singletary said before the 2003 season. "I think his heart can take him where he wants to go. The sky's the limit, and I'm excited about what he brings.

"I'm excited to help him get the little things. To me, he's definitely a glass that's somewhat empty. He wants it empty. He's asking questions. To me, that's a hunger, a willingness to be great. That's important."

WILLIE LANIER

T he Chiefs hit the jackpot in the second round of the 1967 draft, the first common draft after the AFL-NFL merger. With two second-round picks, the Chiefs drafted middle linebackers Jim Lynch from Notre Dame and Willie Lanier from Morgan State.

Lanier could not have known then that he, Lynch and left linebacker Bobby Bell would form one of the best linebacking trios in pro football history and become enduring friends. What concerned Lanier back then was whether he'd get a square chance to play middle linebacker. Blacks who played that position in college typically were moved outside, much as black college quarterbacks wound up as receivers or defensive backs.

"Quarterback, center, middle linebacker, free safety…anybody in the middle of the offense and defense…players who had to make judgments and think…blacks did not exist and didn't have opportunities," Lanier recalled.

"I was very keenly aware of it at the time. I wasn't sure if I would have the opportunity to play the position, regardless of what team drafted me. The Chiefs initially tried me at outside linebacker, and I thought, 'Oh, that's to be expected.'"

That was understandable, though. Lynch had been drafted ahead of Lanier and came from Notre Dame, a cradle of successful pro players. But he didn't see special significance in which linebacking spot either of them played.

"Here's how dumb I was," Lynch recalled. "It never dawned on me there hadn't been a black middle linebacker in pro football. It had to be in Willie's mind. I was oblivious to it, and he wasn't carrying any chip on his shoulder, whatsoever.

"It was never a 'me-or-him' competition. It was an attitude of, 'See if you can play.'"

Lanier stayed in the middle, Lynch moved outside, and they roomed together for most of their careers.

Lanier is convinced the American Football League, co-founded in 1960 by Lamar Hunt, then owner of the Dallas Texans, accelerated progress for blacks in pro football. Hunt moved his team to Kansas City in 1963, and his Chiefs gained a big edge in the AFL by scouting previously overlooked black colleges.

"I told Lamar that without him forming the AFL and the league's interest in small colleges, a lot of opportunities would've gone unfulfilled," Lanier said. "Jobs wouldn't have been there—not only for players from the black colleges, but the total number of players who were black."

Lanier became a starter four games into his rookie season but endured an injury that would affect the way he played football and viewed life. In the seventh game, a 52-9 win over the Denver Broncos, he dove over a blocker to make a tackle and hit his head against the runner's knee. Lanier remained on the field for a few plays but went over to the wrong huddle and collapsed.

"I had a severe hematoma [potentially fatal bleeding], which was worse than a concussion," Lanier said. "Having had that, being unconscious for an hour and a half and going to the Mayo Clinic, mine was a clear understanding others didn't have. My own mortality was very clear to me in the first year."

Lanier missed four games because of that injury, yet missed only one more game the rest of his career. Though he was still known as a devastating tackler, he was determined to tackle with less recklessness and better technique. He resumed playing with extra padding on his helmet, but that became more of a trademark than a safety feature. Lanier said he never found evidence that the padding gave him extra protection.

Lanier also realized he needed to start planning for life after football and briefly retired after the 1974 season to start a business career. But if he was trying be more careful about his tackling, opponents didn't seem to notice.

9

KANSAS CITY CHIEFS
Years: 1967-77
Height: 6'3" Weight: 245
Number: 63
Nickname: Contact, Honey Bear
Hall of Fame: 1986
Born: August 21, 1945

Willie Lanier's reputation as a ferocious hitter made it easy to overlook his impressive quickness and pass coverage skills. Here he returns one of the 27 interceptions he made during an 11-year career with the Kansas City Chiefs that landed him in the Hall of Fame.

Hewritt Dixon, an Oakland Raiders running back, once described a Lanier tackle like this: "Part of me landed one place and the rest of me someplace else. I pulled myself together and went on, just like a mountain had never fallen on me."

Quarterback Craig Morton, while playing for the Dallas Cowboys, said, "[Dick] Butkus is a friend of mine and a helluva linebacker, but Lanier has to be the best."

Lanier strove to be known as more than a bruiser, though. He was a sideline-to-sideline tackler and read coverages well enough to make 27 interceptions, which he returned for 440 yards and two touchdowns. He recovered 15 fumbles, too.

"I realized very clearly that part of being physical is not that you need a good mind," he said. "[Defending] the passing game is where you're supposed to think—understand conceptually, be the general, be in position to make things happen."

Lanier, a securities executive in Richmond, Virginia for more than two decades, isn't interested in telling old football stories. He recalls them reluctantly and says he can't imagine anyone is still interested in hearing them.

"The Super Bowl stands out, the longest game stands out," he said, referring to a 23-7 victory over the Minnesota Vikings in Jan., 1970 and a 27-24 playoff loss to the Miami Dolphins in double overtime in 1971.

"I played 149 games, missed five games, thought I was highly productive and walked away healthy."

Longtime Chiefs fans recall Lanier for much more than that. According to one popular account, Lanier, with tears streaming down his face, told his defensive teammates that they could not let the New York Jets get into the end zone despite a first down at the Kansas City one as the Chiefs were clinging to a 6-3 lead in the 1969 playoffs. The Chiefs held them to a field goal in a 13-6 win.

While the Vikings were trying to come back in the fourth quarter of Super Bowl IV, Lanier intercepted a pass at the Chiefs' 34-yard line.

During grudge matches between the Chiefs and Oakland Raiders, collisions between Lanier and 230-pound fullback Marv Hubbard were a featured attraction.

"Nice-looking fellow, real innocent-looking, isn't he?" Lanier once asked. "Well, nobody comes at you harder than he does. He's an old-fashioned fullback."

Hubbard didn't disagree. "I get this nasty little thrill out of sticking my helmet into somebody's stomach," he said. "It's as much fun as scoring touchdowns."

Each player usually got in his share of licks. In a 16-14 Chiefs victory in 1971 that clinched the division title, Hubbard ran for 77 hard-earned yards, and Lanier made 10 unassisted tackles. In a 16-3 Chiefs victory at home early in 1973, Lanier helped hold Hubbard to 28 yards rushing and returned an interception 17 yards for a touchdown. Hubbard bounced back later that year with 31 carries for 115 yards, including a 31-yard touchdown run that got the Raiders rolling in a 37-7 win.

AFL linebackers had a hard time getting recognized on an equal footing with their NFL counterparts until the Jets and Chiefs won back-to-back Super Bowl games. Butkus was the standard by which other linebackers were measured, but Lanier didn't see why he should play second fiddle to anybody. Starting in the 1968 season, he made eight straight AFL All-Star Games or Pro Bowls.

"I was really hungry on proving I was better than Butkus," Lanier once said. "But after the fifth year, when I was selected All-Pro, it proved to people what I felt all along. Now the desires have become more teamward. That's why I haven't made a statement like that about being better than Butkus in a year and a half."

Chiefs Pro Bowl guard Ed Budde faced most of the toughest linebackers of his era and didn't consider Lanier second fiddle to anybody, either.

"There was no façade about anybody," Budde said, "because in my mind every day I played against the best linebacker who ever played, and that was Willie Lanier."

Lanier made his final Pro Bowl in the 1975 season, his first under coach Paul Wiggin, who inherited a declining team from Hank Stram. When Lanier's contract ended, in 1977, Wiggin had been fired and the Chiefs finished 2-12, their most dismal season ever. Lynch and Lanier, two of the last holdovers from the Chiefs' Super Bowl champions, went out together.

"Like anyone else, when you go into something, you want to reach the top," Lanier said upon retiring. "It's been that way for me in football. You want recognition and the respect of the people you play with. But I didn't want to play on and on until they trade you or you have to retire. Why not go out when you're on top?"

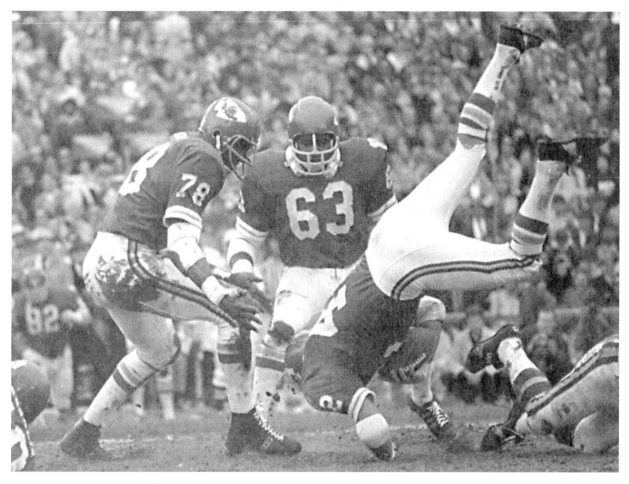

Linebackers Bobby Bell and Willie Lanier were at the heart of a Kansas City defense that smothered the Vikings in Super Bowl IV. Bell (78) and Lanier, who made a fourth-quarter interception in the Chiefs' 23-7 win, watch safety Johnny Robinson recover a second-quarter fumble by Minnesota wide receiver John Henderson.
KANSAS COLLECTION, U. of KANSAS

DAVE WILCOX

I t's hard to say exactly why Dave Wilcox fell off the radar screen of public recognition from the end of his exceptional career until his induction into the Pro Football Hall of Fame 26 years later.

Maybe it was because he played in San Francisco when that city was a black hole for national media coverage. Maybe it was because he played mostly for ordinary teams and never experienced a playoff victory. Maybe it was because after he retired, Wilcox moved back to Oregon and kept a low profile.

Then again, maybe it was because Wilcox couldn't stop reminding people that he was on the field when Chicago Bears rookie running back Gale Sayers scored six touchdowns against the 49ers in a 61-20 rout at Wrigley Field on December 12, 1965.

"He was the quickest and fastest person," Wilcox said from his home in Eugene, where he played at the University of Oregon.

"I never did meet Barry Sanders, and they talk about how quick he was. But Gale Sayers was playing in mud and quagmires, and if he could have played on that same [artificial] stuff…holy cow!"

It's hard to imagine that Wilcox was to blame for Sayers having one of the biggest scoring days in pro football history. Wilcox, then a second-year player, was best known for his ability to shed blocks, get to the right spot and knock people down.

"What I do best is not let people block me," he once said. "I just hate to be blocked."

Joe Schmidt, a Hall of Fame linebacker for the Detroit Lions and their coach during Wilcox's career, said, "The lead block had to really come out hard to take him out because he was so strong."

Strength wasn't the only asset that made Wilcox so effective on the strong side. He prided himself on acquiring sound fundamentals, especially from Mike Giddings, the 49ers' linebackers coach from 1968-73.

"He knew the difference between winning and losing a game was taking a wrong step somewhere," Wilcox said. "I really enjoyed doing those fundamental things. Those were great athletes we played against.

"The tight ends were Ron Kramer [in Green Bay], John Mackey [in Baltimore], Mike Ditka [in Chicago] and those guys. You had to figure out a way to get an edge somewhere. And that goes back to fundamentals. I loved the game, it was like a chess match to me.

"I wanted to know everything I could—keeping your balance and leverage at certain angles. I don't know that other coaches taught their guys to do those things. I knew what my responsibility was and had to be in place to get that done.

"It's pretty hard to chase somebody down when you're laying on the ground. The way they get you down is to knock your feet out from under you."

Wilcox's peers took notice of his attention to detail. Pittsburgh Steelers Hall of Fame linebacker Jack Ham recalls that he and teammate Andy Russell would watch any game tape of Wilcox they could find.

"The 49ers were terrible most of his career, but we watched his technique and I always admired the way he played," Ham said. "If he played with the Steelers, he would've been in the Hall of Fame the first time he was eligible."

Wilcox didn't like missing a game any more than he liked missing an assignment. In his 11 seasons, he was sidelined for only one game, when cartilage that was torn in a 1970 exhibition game in Miami eventually became so painful he had to sit out. Another time, he kept playing despite a broken toe.

10

Dave Wilcox's 11-year career with the 49ers included seven Pro Bowl berths, but was largely forgotten until Hall of Fame electors reconsidered his credentials and voted him in with the class of 2000. Wilcox was among his era's most versatile outside linebackers.

"Overall, I didn't have many problems," he recalled. "I guess I'm lucky that way. And I knew what I was doing. If you keep them away from your feet, they're not going to hurt your ankles. If you're out of position, that's when you get hurt."

Though Dave Wilcox was best known for his toughness, technique and ability to shed a block, he was a savvy pass defender, too. Here in a 1969 game he moves into position to make one of his 14 career interceptions.
AP/WWP

The 49ers of the 1960s were best known for such stars as quarterback John Brodie, halfbacks R.C. Owens and John David Crow and wide receiver Gene Washington. But it wasn't until their defense improved that the 49ers won Western Conference titles in 1970, '71 and 72. Those also marked three of Wilcox's seven Pro Bowl seasons.

"He may have been the best man at his position that I have ever seen in pro football," said Paul Wiggin, a 49ers defensive assistant from 1968-74 and later head coach of the Kansas City Chiefs.

Wilcox finally made the Hall of Fame as the Seniors Committee nominee, but for him, honors were just gravy. Football enabled him and two brothers to get college educations, an enormous opportunity for a family that could relate far better to the writings of John Steinbeck than Grantland Rice.

"My parents moved to Oregon from Oklahoma in 1935, the Dust Bowl and all that," Wilcox said. "We had a truck, we didn't have a car. No way were we going to be able to go to college, so football helped us get out of that.

"I didn't want to milk cows for the rest of my life. Football's not everything in our lives, but it's been a great career. People said, 'What would you change?' I said, 'Nothing.'

"Some guys at my age seem very bitter. It would be wonderful if we could all make millions of dollars, but we can't go back 30 years and bring [our salaries] up to date. I've had more fun watching my kids."

Wilcox's son, Josh, was a tight end with the New Orleans Saints from 1998-99. Another son, Justin, became linebackers coach at California, though Wilcox said he couldn't help him much.

"My son is talking about all this [technical] stuff and I'm wondering, 'What is he talking about?'" Wilcox said, laughing. "I tell him, 'Defense is pretty simple. Just tell your guys not to let the guy with the ball get over the goal line.'"

Wilcox sometimes could make it look that easy.

"The lead **block** had to really come out **hard** to take him out because he was so **strong**."

—Joe Schmidt

When John Madden coached the Oakland Raiders, he described his star linebacker like this: "Ted's elevator doesn't go all the way to the top."

Then again, Ted's elevator had a long way to go. Hendricks stood six feet seven and was built more like a scrawny basketball player than an outside linebacker. Though Hendricks was an All-America defensive end at the University of Miami, 32 players, including 11 defenders, were picked before the Colts took him in the second round of the 1969 draft.

"He was skinny," explained New York Giants general manager Ernie Accorsi, who joined the Colts in 1970 as their public relations director.

The Colts used Hendricks's lack of heft as a negotiating ploy. He visited the Golden Beach, Florida home of owner Carroll Rosenbloom, and his son, Steve, a team executive, insisted on weighing Hendricks.

Hendricks weighed just 218 and spent his NFL career ignoring advice to bulk up. He never did get heavier than 235 but evidently carried all the bulk he needed. Over 15 years, Hendricks played 215 consecutive games, made 26 interceptions and 16 fumble recoveries, blocked 25 kicks and scored four safeties. He also earned four Super Bowl rings, the last three with the Raiders.

Hendricks already was named to four Pro Bowls before the Raiders in 1975 signed him away from the Packers, who'd obtained him from the Colts in 1974. Under free agency rules of those days, the Packers received two first-round draft choices as compensation. The Raiders weren't shortchanged, though, because Hendricks made an impact for them on and off the field.

He once broke the monotony of training camp at Santa Rosa, California by riding a horse on to the practice field while wearing his uniform and using a traffic cone as a lance. He doesn't recall any of the Raiders being especially shocked.

"I guess Madden had seen everything with our group and everybody else had seen everything," Hendricks recalled, laughing. "I borrowed the horse from a friend of mine's daughter who was going out to ride in Santa Rosa. I just asked her to bring it over to the practice field. We were anxious for the season to start and get going."

Hendricks could not have found a more appreciative audience.

"Most Raiders loved to party, but Ted Hendricks was a party all by himself," wrote quarterback Ken Stabler in his autobiography, *Snake*.

Stabler recalled that one Halloween, Hendricks came to practice with a pumpkin squashed on his head as a helmet. During a Monday night game, he put on a fake nose when a camera zoomed in on the Raider bench.

"He got the reputation of being an eccentric, but once a game started he went like gangbusters," said Madden, who coached Hendricks from 1975-78. "Great players make great plays, and I can't think of any defensive player who made more big plays for us."

Raiders assistant Myrel Moore joined the list of Hendricks's frustrated strength coaches. He had a weight machine for his linebackers, but Hendricks responded by hanging empty cans, which he marked "500 lbs," on each side of a bar. When Moore had his linebackers push a heavy medicine ball to help them fend off low blocks, Hendricks stole the ball, put it in his trunk and left it in a local bar.

Despite his stork-like legs, Hendricks didn't let blockers get at them. Walt Corey, former Buffalo Bills defensive coordinator, preceded Hendricks at Miami under defensive assistant Walt Kichefski.

"Kichefski stressed using your hands and not getting knocked off your feet," Corey recalled. "As long as Hendricks's legs were, you could never get to his darn feet. And he must've had two sets of eyes."

11

BALTIMORE COLTS, GREEN BAY PACKERS and OAKLAND and LOS ANGELES RAIDERS
Years: 1969-83
Height: 6'7" Weight: 235
Number: 83
Nickname: The Mad Stork
Hall of Fame: 1990
Born: November 1, 1947

Ted Hendricks holds the ball after coming up with one of his 42 career turnovers. He played for three Super Bowl championship teams during his nine years with the Raiders, and Howie Long, left, said he considered Hendricks and Pittsburgh's Jack Ham two of the best outside linebackers he ever saw.

Blockers who tried to cut his legs sometimes were kicked in the helmet as Hendricks leaped over them. He once knocked out fullback Marv Hubbard, his roommate, in practice and acquired the nickname, "Kick 'em in the head Ted." He liked that a lot better than his more popular nickname, "The Mad Stork."

Though Lawrence Taylor is credited with inventing the rush linebacker position in the 1980s, Hendricks played a similar role for the Raiders. They used Hendricks sparingly in 1975 but came to utilize his talents for rushing the passer, smothering the run and covering receivers.

"They experimented with that standup rushing linebacker, and Tony Cline was doing that before he got hurt—that's who I replaced in the [1975] championship game," Hendricks recalled. "We didn't do it as extensively as Taylor did it—he was a continual pass rusher, and I don't know if he ever dropped back to a passing situation."

Hendricks started in '76 and won his first of three Super Bowl rings as a Raider. Though previously branded as a team that couldn't win the big one, the Raiders won three Super Bowls in eight seasons by a combined score of 97-33. They routed the Minnesota Vikings, Philadelphia Eagles and Washington Redskins.

"I remember that those games were over with before the third quarter, but each one was different," Hendricks said. "[Minnesota's] Fran Tarkenton would always roll out to our

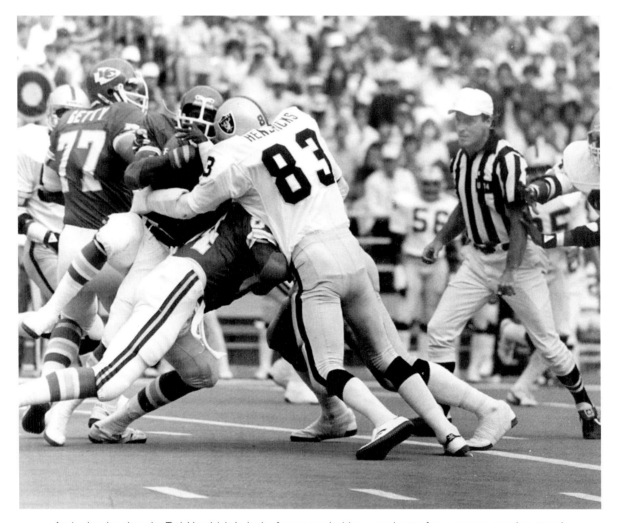

Anybody who thought Ted Hendricks's lanky frame made him a pushover for a strong running attack was sadly mistaken. When he wasn't harassing quarterbacks or blocking kicks, Hendricks (83) used his strength and long arms to smother ball carriers. He provided a big lift to a Raiders defense that didn't allow more than 14 points in any of three Super Bowl victories over eight years.
KANSAS COLLECTION, U. of KANSAS

defensive left, and I wound up chasing him all day. In the Philadelphia game, I only had three plays run to my side, but I blocked a kick before halftime. That gave us a boost in our spirits and deflated them going in to the locker room."

Hendricks's first Super Bowl, in stark contrast, was a white-knuckler. The Colts and Dallas Cowboys, in January 1971, combined for 11 turnovers in a sloppy offensive show before the Colts pulled out a 16-13 victory on Jim O'Brien's 32-yard field goal.

"That was an exhausting game," Hendricks recalled. "It seemed like each down was a decisive play. I was all tensed up the entire game."

Between his first two Super Bowls as a Raider, Hendricks was removed in passing situations. He became a three-down player again when Charlie Sumner took over the defense in 1980, and Hendricks made the Pro Bowl in each of the last four years of his career. Typically, an offense had no clue where he was coming from.

"I'd always have fun with the offensive linemen," Hendricks recalled. "I would walk around and assume different spots where they'd think I'd be rushing from. My defensive linemen knew where I was coming from. We had a lot of games going on."

Hendricks's final game was a 38-9 Super Bowl win over the Redskins. When Ted's elevator made its last stop, he got off at the top.

"He got the **reputation** of being an eccentric, but once a game started he went like gangbusters. **Great players** make great plays, and I can't think of any **defensive** player who made more big plays for us."

—John Madden

MIKE SINGLETARY

Mike Singletary insists that too much was read into his eyes. His penetrating, wide-eyed stare was Singletary's signature as a middle linebacker, and many read into his unsquinting eyes a coldness, malevolence or both. The way he saw it, he merely was being observant.

"My eyes were as open as they were for only one reason—to see the entire field," Singletary explained. "I'd get back just far enough—three and a half yards—and it was like looking at a movie, and I didn't want to miss any of the parts."

Singletary didn't miss many scenes. He broke a Bears record by making 10 straight Pro Bowls and a club defensive record by making 172 starts. He also led one of the strongest defenses in pro football history.

"Mike is the modern-day Ray Nitschke," said George Seifert while he was coaching the San Francisco 49ers. "He has set the standard for what coaches and scouts look for in inside linebackers."

The 1986 Bears allowed just 187 points, fewest in a 16-game regular season until the Baltimore Ravens, who hired Singletary as linebackers coach in 2003, allowed 165 points in 2000. The '85 Bears weren't too shabby on defense, either. They allowed just 198 points in the regular season, shut out both playoff opponents and yielded seven yards rushing while totaling seven sacks in a 46-10 Super Bowl victory over the New England Patriots.

That unit, playing coordinator Buddy Ryan's 46 defense to perfection, will be long remembered, no matter how often its record is broken.

"It was just everybody talking the same language," Singletary recalled. "It's not very often you're striving for greatness and everybody can truly see it. For once, I was fortunate to be with a group of guys who could see it. Everybody was talking about the Super Bowl, and being part of something like that is unlike anything else you will experience in sports."

The Bears began talking, or, more accurately, rapping about the Super Bowl during the regular season. They performed the "Super Bowl Shuffle," a rap video, and ignored the time-honored rule to never look beyond the next game. But those Bears were talented and bold enough to speak their minds, and Singletary joined in on the video.

"Unfortunately," he said, laughing. "It was kind of stupid, but it was a great motivator and it brought us together."

While Singletary's hard-knocking play and role as captain made him a symbol of the Bears' defensive dominance, his deeply religious, serious and stable nature made him a curious fit amid a unit of wildmen.

Tackle Steve McMichael was nicknamed "Mongo" and "Ming the Merciless." Nose tackle William Perry was nicknamed "The Refrigerator," for an appetite that would cause him to eat his way out of the NFL. Singletary once confided to Don Pierson of the *Chicago Tribune* that when outside linebacker Otis Wilson said before a game that he wanted to go out and kill somebody, Singletary suspected he really meant it.

"Somebody's got to have some sense, somebody's got to be stable," Singletary said. "God had given me a great opportunity to balance out a situation. Whatever it was, keep the peace. Keeping the peace is the only way you can progress. Chaos sends you backwards, and it didn't take much to send us into chaos."

The night before the Super Bowl, the Bears' defense was scheduled to meet on its own for a final review of the game plan. Some players began screaming they'd seen enough of the game plan, destroyed the portable blackboard that was to be used for drawing plays and declared themselves ready. They were ready, indeed.

12

CHICAGO BEARS
Years: 1981-92
Height: 6' Weight: 230
Number: 50
Nickname: Samurai
Hall of Fame: 1998
Born: October 9, 1958

Mike Singletary gave the impression that his laser-beam stare alone could freeze a ball carrier. Singletary, in reality, still had to make the tackle and gets the angle he needs here on the Giants' George Adams. Singletary always took a good look at his target.

"I'm not sure you want to take these characters home, but you definitely want to take them to war," Singletary said. "You know you're going to win.

"Buddy always told me, 'Son, you're the captain out there, you're the leader. If somebody gets out of line, you have to take care of it.' I took that personally, I represented him on the field."

Ryan told Singletary a bunch of other things that he also took personally. Ryan told Singletary, a second-round draft choice in 1981, that he lacked what it takes to succeed in the NFL. Then throughout Singletary's rookie season he referred to him only as "Number 50." For a player who hit so hard at Baylor that he cracked 16 of his helmets in four years, such disrespect was shocking.

"Buddy was the best thing that ever happened to me," Singletary said. "I was such a stubborn guy. I was already mad because I didn't go in the first round, then I get there and he tells me I'm too short, too slow, too fat and too dumb. I say, 'What's going on here? It's a conspiracy.'

"He saved me from myself because I came to Chicago and already thought I was God's gift to linebackers. I came to camp late and my first day, Dan Hampton was asking Alan Page something, and I told them, 'Shut up, get in the huddle and let's go.'

"Buddy says, 'Son, do you know who you're hollering at?' I said, 'I don't care, it's my huddle and you keep your mouth closed.' That was the beginning of a long year and a half. He realized this kid was full of himself, and I guess I was. He humbled me and put me in a position where I could learn. Guys respected me then, but I earned it."

These rain-soaked fans in Kansas City could not have realized that in this 1981 game they were getting a glimpse of the Chicago Bears' championship future. Rookie Mike Singletary (50) enjoyed his coming-out party, making 10 tackles and recovering a fumble in a victory over the Chiefs. He would emerge as the leader of coordinator Buddy Ryan's "46" defense, named for safety Doug Plank, who joins Singletary here.
KANSAS COLLECTION, U. of KANSAS

Even while relegated to Ryan's doghouse, Singletary became a starter in the seventh game of the 1981 season. A few weeks later, he had his coming-out party, with 10 tackles and a fumble recovery in a 16-13 upset victory in overtime at Kansas City.

Still, Ryan removed Singletary in passing situations because he didn't consider him a complete linebacker. By 1983, Singletary was playing every down and was named defensive captain. Two years later, the Bears reached their zenith.

Of the Patriots' 10 points in the Super Bowl, three came after a recovery of Walter Payton's fumble on the first possession. The Patriots' lone touchdown came early in the fourth quarter with the Bears ahead 44-3.

"I felt bad for the Patriots," Singletary recalled.

Before the NFC championship game, a 24-0 victory over the Los Angeles Rams, Singletary delivered a pep talk that left his defensive teammates screaming and throwing furniture. Singletary showed how pumped up he was when he dropped Eric Dickerson for a loss on a third-and-one play late in the first quarter.

"Mike hit Dickerson so hard, I don't think he knew where he was," Bears linebacker Wilber Marshall said.

Singletary was named NFL Defensive Player of the Year in 1985 and '88 and while winding up his career decided he'd like to coach. But Singletary, whose family would grow to seven children and who asked his wife, Kim, to present him at his Hall of Fame induction, was worried that coaching would detract from his family life.

"I began to go around the league and ask different coaches I respected, 'How did they balance coaching and family?'" Singletary recalled. "Every one said, 'My wife did a great job raising the kids,' and I made the decision, as much as I loved football, that wasn't going to work.

"I kept in touch with football, have some buddies coaching and they're asking me questions—what drill should they do? And I'd been out of the game 10 years. It was a hobby for me. I still sat down and wrote out plays, never knowing if I'd get back in the game."

Singletary's coaching appetite was whetted in the fall of 2002, when Baylor fired Kevin Steele and interviewed Singletary before hiring Guy Morriss.

"Going through that process, I realized this is what I should be doing," Singletary said. "This is who I am. I don't have to practice this. It's very natural for me."

The Ravens, whom Singletary joined in January 2003, seemed the right fit for him.

"I wanted to go to a team that cares about winning, where I can learn and they won't be intimidated by me being there and I wanted to go to a team that's family-friendly," Singletary said.

"I don't want to be in the office [all night]. In football, no one's inventing anything new. Don't let me outsmart myself."

The Ravens also gave Singletary the chance to serve on the same defensive staff with Buddy Ryan's son, Rex, and to coach Ray Lewis, the NFL's best middle linebacker. Singletary already knew how he wanted to approach this job.

"How much does a person want to learn?" he asked. "You can't pour water into a glass already full. That's one thing—how open and receptive is that student? How creative and willing is the teacher?

"Some of my best professors were the ones that reached beyond conventional ways of doing things and had me understand their desire to get it across. To me, the sky's the limit. I believe I'm a better teacher than a coach."

Singletary, clearly, was starting a new career with his eyes open.

CHUCK BEDNARIK

C huck Bednarik can look up from the telephone in his Coopersburg, Pennsylvania home and study the photograph that defines his career.

Bednarik, the Eagles' center and linebacker, is pumping his right fist in celebration after forcing the fumble that wrapped up a pivotal 17-10 victory over the New York Giants midway in the 1960 season. Frank Gifford, on the receiving end of a Charlie Conerly pass and the most famous tackle in pro football history, is on his back, unconscious. Gifford, one of the most popular Giants ever, suffered a severe concussion and would not play again until 1962.

Bednarik, unaware of how badly Gifford was hurt, went into a victory dance once he saw teammate Chuck Weber recover the fumble. The Yankee Stadium crowd, assuming Bednarik was gloating over Gifford's injury, became incensed. Bednarik has always insisted he was celebrating the win, not the injury, and has felt no need to apologize for a clean, if vicious, hit.

"I have that picture right here, and you know what?" Bednarik asked. "I sell about a thousand of those a year. People request it. I send it autographed. I'm standing over him, he's out like a light and I saw the recovery. With a clenched fist and my eyes closed—and it happened to be where he was laying—I said, 'This…game is over.'

"It's a shot that people dream about. If you go down the field, doing a down and in, and you're coming across, you have to look at that quarterback throwing the ball and at the same time I'm coming straight across. It's a head-on collision and I happened to get that forearm out and hit him high on the chest. That's when he flipped, his head's bent, the ball came out of his hands and he's unconscious for a minute or two."

Bednarik and Gifford have since bumped into each other in more peaceful circumstances, such as Hall of Fame functions.

"He said to me, 'I made you famous, didn't I?'" Bednarik said, laughing.

"If you do anything, do it in New York. It happened to be in New York and it was Frank Gifford."

Bednarik was famous in his own right. He was pro football's last true two-way player and was inducted into the Hall of Fame as a center, though at linebacker he was a ferocious tackler and made 20 interceptions.

He was playing mainly center in 1960 until an early-season injury to a linebacker forced Bednarik back to two-way duty. He played more than 50 minutes in three games, including 58 minutes in a 17-13 victory over the Green Bay Packers in the NFL championship game.

That game ended with Packers quarterback Bart Starr throwing a short pass from the Eagles' 22-yard line to fullback Jim Taylor, who tried to bulldoze the Eagles' defense. Rookie defensive back Bob Jackson made the initial hit and saved a touchdown; then Bednarik jumped in and sat on Taylor until time ran out. That marked the only time Lombardi's Packers were beaten in a championship game.

Bednarik, who missed only three games during his 14-year career and also sold concrete, was nicknamed "Concrete Charlie" by Philadelphia sports writer Hugh Brown. Bednarik, he wrote, "is as hard as the concrete he sells."

Opponents wouldn't argue. Hall of Fame quarterback Len Dawson was a Pittsburgh Steeler early in his career when he first became familiar with Bednarik. "You couldn't hurt him, but he could hurt you," Dawson recalled. "Some of those guys had an unbelievable threshold of pain."

Bednarik, who lives near his hometown, Bethlehem, Pennsylvania, said he never considered his double duty as anything special. He became accustomed to playing both ways at the University of Pennsylvania, and as his record shows, he never broke down.

13

PHILADELPHIA EAGLES
Years: 1949-62
Height: 6'3" Weight: 230
Number: 60
Nickname: Concrete Charlie
Hall of Fame: 1967
Born: May 1, 1925

The Eagles' Chuck Bednarik could also pose snapping the ball, because he was pro football's last two-way player. Here he takes his linebacker stance. Bednarik, of course, played with a helmet but not with a facemask in the early years of his career.
AP/WWP

"Mind over matter," he explained. "I was in good condition, and if you're winning, you never get tired and you don't want to get out of the game. It's when you get the hell kicked out of you that you're mentally and physically fatigued.

"It was part of my job. I never tried to do that figuring I'm going to do something extraordinary, something nobody else can do. As long as we were winning, I was happy."

Even when the Eagles were losing, from 1955-58, Bednarik didn't let up. He's no fan of today's NFL, which leaves Bednarik feeling shortchanged. His salary peaked at $22,000 his final season.

"That was football; today it's pussycat football," Bednarik said disgustedly. "These guys are making so much damn money. They're overpaid and underplayed. In my day, if a guy weighed 340 or 350, that was unusual. And you know what? It's impossible for anybody who weighs over 300 pounds to play both ways. That's why you don't see it. I have no desire or love for pro football. I live 15 minutes from Lehigh University. You've got scholar athletes and good football, and as far as pro football, I scratch that."

"You couldn't **hurt him**, but he could **hurt you**. Some of those guys had an unbelievable **threshold** of **pain**."

—Len Dawson

Bednarik scoffed at the notion that Deion Sanders was a two-way player for the Dallas Cowboys in 1996 because he played cornerback and wide receiver. He didn't enjoy Sanders's "Prime Time" persona, either.

"The positions I played, I made contact 100 percent on every play," Bednarik recalled. "I snapped on extra points and punts. Some of these guys who think they're playing both ways don't have to touch anybody. Deion Sanders? Talk about somebody claiming to be a two-way player? He never made a tackle and just came up and did a little dance."

Back in '96, Bednarik said, "I'm a Czech and we'd call what he does a polka step. That's nightclub entertainment, not sport. Nobody likes that kind of stuff. Besides, he does a bad polka step."

And don't even get him started on specialists.

"You have one guy come in just to hold the ball for a field goal, one guy just to kick and one guy just to snap the ball," Bednarik said. "At my age, if they'd pay me half of what they pay these guys, I'd make a comeback."

Bednarik played 18 straight seasons, in college and the NFL, for Philadelphia teams and remains a beloved figure there. He has no use for free agency because it severs a player's ties to a city.

"Loyalty will do you in high school, loyalty will do you in college," Bednarik said. "Where is the loyalty in pro football if a guy plays for three or four different teams? From the time I played, the Eagles have had five different owners. The Eagles today, they don't care about you, and you don't care about them."

The Eagles' first ownership group during Bednarik's career consisted of 100 buyers who each paid $3,000 to buy the team from Alexis Thompson. One of the new group's best moves was to draft Bednarik with the first overall pick in 1949, and the Eagles won their third straight Eastern Division title and second straight NFL title. The league back then allotted the top overall pick by luck of the draw.

"It's a **head-on collision** and I happened to get that forearm out and **hit** him high on the chest. That's when he **flipped**, his head's bent, the ball came out of his hands and he's **unconscious** for a minute or two."

—Chuck Bednarik

Chuck Bednarik hands his jersey and shoes to equipment manager Freddie Schubach after a December 16, 1962 game against the St. Louis Cardinals. The game was Bednarik's last—a 45-35 loss—but his jersey and shoes are now a part of the Hall of Fame.
AP/WWP

Bednarik's most recent association with the Eagles came during Dick Vermeil's stay as head coach from 1976-82. Vermeil hoped that having Bednarik around, even in an unofficial capacity, would set an example of toughness and success.

"I got a call and he said, 'Chuck, you're Mr. Eagle, I'd like you associated with my team.'" Bednarik recalled. "I stayed with him the whole time he was here. People in Philadelphia have been 100 percent for me. I never heard any nasty comments, nobody cutting me up."

Along with the Gifford photo, Bednarik has has a photo of his Hall of Fame class of 1967, which included eight inductees, including coach Paul Brown and quarterback Bobby Layne. Bednarik survived them all, which is especially impressive considering that after high school graduation he served as an air force gunner in World War II and was heavily decorated for flying dozens of bombing missions over Nazi Germany.

Bednarik remained feisty as he celebrated his 78th birthday but regretted that aches and pains have limited his golf to several fundraising tournaments a year. His fingers are disfigured from years of blocking and tackling, so he uses them to entertain youngsters.

"I've got two fingers that are pretty crooked, but I have a lot of fun with it," Bednarik said. "I'll shake the hand of a seven-, eight- or nine-year-old kid and tell 'em to squeeze as hard as they can. Then I'll say, 'Oh, oh, wait.'"

After a few moments of feigning pain, Bednarik will show the youngster his bent fingers.

"They look at me like, 'Did I do that?'" he said, laughing.

A grade schooler, understandably, doesn't realize what it takes to hurt an iron man.

SAM HUFF

T he Giants' fifth-year linebacker didn't know exactly what he was getting into when he agreed to wear a microphone during the 1960 preseason for a CBS television documentary, *The Violent World of Sam Huff*. Once that documentary was aired, Huff and other middle linebackers would never be viewed in the same light again.

"We were almost like offensive guards, which is what I came up as," recalled Huff, a longtime member of the Redskins' radio broadcast team after he retired as a player. "We were just there. The stars were the offensive people, like Charlie Conerly."

That all changed when a CBS microphone, run under Huff's arm and taped to the front of his shoulder pads, captured the speed and smack of pro football and the role of the middle linebacker at the intersection of mayhem.

"I did not like the title, but it was catchy," said Huff, who during eight years with the Giants played in six NFL championship games and won one. "Football is a violent game, but it's controlled, too. War is violent, and I guess football is war without guns.

"When they said, 'You're going to be wired for sound,' I said, 'What? You've got to be kidding. A microphone?' I did not realize what carrying an extra pound around would mean. I played all the defense and on the punt return team and kickoff team. I was very seldom out of the game. In practice and preseason, that one pound got a little heavy.

"We were playing the Bears up in Toronto and they had a wide receiver actually come and hit me after the play. I kind of knocked him down and said, 'What are you doing?' He said, 'I know if I hit you, I'm gonna get on TV.'

"I got a grand total of $500 for doing it and the rights to a rental car. I was the only one in camp who had a car. But I never got to use it. Everybody wanted to borrow it. Now they've got Cadillacs and SUVs."

Huff and the Giants' other defensive stars actually would've gotten plenty of attention even without the documentary. Though the Giants' offense had an impressive cast, the defense became the toast of New York.

"We were the first defensive team in the NFL to ever get introduced before the game," Huff said. "Our offense went a few games [in 1959] and never scored a touchdown, and when they introduced them, the hometown fans booed. They never booed the defense. We could just shut an offense down and we did. In order to stop the offense from getting booed, they introduced the defense and we got a standing ovation in Yankee Stadium.

"[Frank] Gifford walked by one time and said, 'You guys get all the recognition, but we get all the money.'"

Huff, to his chagrin, had to agree. He said he was so embarrassed by his low salary that he inflated it for the documentary, which was narrated by Walter Cronkite.

"It said, 'A great linebacker makes in the neighborhood of $12,000,'" Huff recalled. "I was making $9,000. I wasn't talking about a game. I was talking about a season. It's a different age, it's a game of entertainment. If somebody writes them a check for $10 million, they like that."

Though Huff was an All-America guard at West Virginia, once Giants coach Jim Lee Howell saw him at camp in Winooski, Vermont he doubted Huff was quick enough to be a pro guard or big enough for a tackle.

Huff, born in Edna Gas, West Virginia, a coal-mining camp near Morgantown, was struggling, hurt and homesick. He and his roommate, kicker Don Chandler, decided to quit and offered their playbooks to offensive coordinator Vince Lombardi. The temperamental coach snapped. "We've got two weeks invested in you guys. You may not make this ball club, but you're sure as hell not quitting

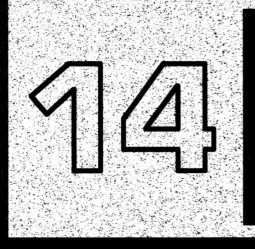

14

**NEW YORK GIANTS and
WASHINGTON REDSKINS**
Years: 1956-69
Height: 6'1" Weight: 230
Number: 70
Hall of Fame: 1982
Born: October 4, 1934

Sam Huff was experiencing a period of adjustment as he takes a break during a Redskins practice early in the 1964 season. Huff was shocked when Giants coach Allie Sherman traded him after the 1963 season, and Huff has never forgiven the Giants for that deal.

Huff and Chandler headed for the airport anyway. They were waiting for a flight when Lombardi stormed in and ordered them back to camp. When Huff returned, starting middle linebacker Ray Beck was injured, and Huff filled in so well that Beck retired. Huff became a star in coordinator Tom Landry's 4-3 defense, which dominated the Chicago Bears' offense in a 47-7 victory in the 1956 NFL championship game.

"It's **uncanny** the way Huff follows the ball. He ignores all the things you do to get him away from **the play,** and he comes after the **ball** wherever it's thrown or wherever the run goes. He seems to be **all over** the field at once."

—Vince Lombardi

Two of Huff's most memorable games came in '58. The Giants and Cleveland Browns, both 9-3, tied for the Eastern Conference title and met in a playoff game at Yankee Stadium. Jim Brown, arguably the best running back of all time, gained just eight yards on seven carries in a 10-0 Giants' victory.

"He was the greatest running back I ever laid eyes on," Huff said. "You talk about great defense—we had to be one of the best ever because we faced Jim Brown twice a year. To make the playoffs, you had to stop Jim Brown and stop the Browns. I remember in college, he broke my nose and knocked me out. The enamel popped off my teeth, he hit me so hard."

Beating the Browns earned the Giants a spot in the NFL championship game, but they were beaten, 23-17 in overtime, by the Baltimore Colts at Yankee Stadium. Nicknamed

"The Greatest Game Ever Played," that contest became the takeoff point for pro football's meteoric rise in popularity.

"They named it right," Huff said. "You had the two greatest teams in the NFL. We didn't have any fireworks, flyovers or sexy cheerleaders. We just went out and teed it up and played good football."

The Colts in 1959 beat the Giants again, 31-16, for the NFL title, but in the '60s the Green Bay Packers, coached by Lombardi, became the Giants' nemesis. They beat the Giants in the 1961 title game, and their rematch in '62 was played in conditions perhaps more frigid than the Dallas-Green Bay Ice Bowl five years later. That '62 game also featured constant collisions between Huff and fullback Jim Taylor.

"That was a street fight," Huff recalled. "Jimmy Taylor was one of the few backs who'd refuse the open field and try to run over you. I hit him so hard in that '62 game, I dented my helmet. It's in the Hall of Fame."

Taylor carried 31 times for 85 yards and the game's only offensive touchdown, despite Huff's best efforts to hit him, early and late, and taunt him. According to David Maraniss in the Lombardi biography *When Pride Still Mattered*, Taylor was at the bottom of a pile and supposedly bit Dick Modzelewski's leg. When the big tackle screamed, Taylor looked up and said, "Sorry, Mo, I thought you were Sam."

Both Huff and Taylor absorbed awful poundings that day.

"Every time he walked on the field, he had an **edge**. That much **dedication** requires extraordinary will. Sam's will and his brain made him one of the most **effective** middle linebackers in NFL history."

—Jim Brown

"I would watch Taylor come back, bent over and holding his ribs, after the Giants had hit him," Packers quarterback Bart Starr recalled. "We went after Huff, too. We had to if we wanted to make any headway. But no matter how hard we hit him, he never complained. It was all in a day's work."

Huff's ability to sniff out a play impressed some opponents even more than did his head-knocking.

"When Sam arrived in the NFL, he didn't bring a lot of pure skill, yet Sam was a unique individual because he was so addicted to detail," Brown said. "Every time he walked on the field, he had an edge. That much dedication requires extraordinary will. Sam's will and his brain made him one of the most effective middle linebackers in NFL history."

Sam Huff (70) was in the middle of some great Giants defenses and played in six NFL championship games, including this 37-0 loss at Green Bay in 1961. Cornerback Erich Barnes tries to prevent the Packers' Boyd Dowler from making the catch as Giants Hall of Fame end Andy Robustelli (81) and tackle Rosey Grier (76) trail the play.
VERNON J. BIEVER PHOTO

Lombardi, who brought Huff out of retirement to make him a player-coach for the Redskins in 1969, raved about Huff's nose for the ball.

"It's uncanny the way Huff follows the ball," Lombardi said. "He ignores all the things you do to get him away from the play, and he comes after the ball wherever it's thrown or wherever the run goes. He seems to be all over the field at once."

Huff, who made 30 interceptions, credited Landry's finely woven defense and meticulous game plans for helping him so often be in the right place at the right time.

"Tom Landry had a mind like a computer," Huff recalled. "He did tendencies of teams you were going to play. You knew Jim Brown was going to carry 30 or 35 times a game, so there was no need to look anywhere else.

"Plus, I knew where I was going to make the tackle as soon as I saw the back make his move because we played a team defense. The cornerback would come up and turn the ball inside; that's all he had to do.

"I used to make 15 to 20 tackles a game. I look at myself as the first designated hitter in all of sports."

Huff's last game with the Giants was a 14-10 loss to the Bears in the 1963 NFL championship game. Giants coach Allie Sherman considered Huff, 29, a declining player and traded him in 1964 to the Washington Redskins for defensive tackle Andy Stynchula and running back Dick James. Giants fans were shocked, but not as shocked as Huff.

"I never forgave the Giants for it, never to this day," Huff said nearly four decades later. "I played so hard against them. I wanted to prove that after trading me, they no longer had the great Giants' defense."

Huff made his point late in his third season at Washington in a 72-41 victory over the Giants. The score was 69-21 with the Redskins in field goal range and time running out, but Huff wanted more points.

"I sent the field goal unit in—it wasn't [coach] Otto Graham—to kick a field goal," Huff recalled. "That was one of the greatest days. That was revenge, and that's what a linebacker lives for."

Huff treasured his years with the Giants partly because they represented a special time, when he played in Yankee Stadium and shared Mickey Mantle's locker. The city was full of future Hall of Fame players and championship teams.

"When you're a coal miner's son and go to New York and find the trains run underground, that's really doing something," Huff recalled.

"It's just unbelievable when you look back at it, to have had Tom Landry coaching defense and Vince Lombardi coaching offense, and being around Kyle Rote and Frank Gifford—the glamour guys—and Pat Summerall. The Yankees were always in the World Series and we had to play our first three games away and practice at Fordham University. We all stayed at the Concourse Plaza Hotel, up the street from Yankee Stadium. We all went to Toots Shor's [restaurant in Manhattan] because Toots never charged us.

"That was a great time to be a player. That really was a golden age of sports."

BILL GEORGE

I t's hazardous in any sport to claim that any single athlete invented or defined a position, because new wrinkles tend to be more evolutionary than revolutionary. Yet Bill George stands as pro football's first true middle linebacker until somebody proves otherwise.

"Maybe we didn't invent the middle linebacker," George once said. "But the Bears, surely, were one of the first to try it."

When George arrived in Chicago in 1952, he was the middle guard in a 5-2 defense that was the NFL standard. Because most teams stressed their running attack, defenses needed a run stopper in the middle. In passing situations, the middle guard would bump the center, as if playing the run, then drop into coverage.

The popular story is that George invented his position out of necessity during the 1954 season when he got tired of seeing short throws completed just over his head. George supposedly remarked to George Connor, the left linebacker and defensive captain, that he could break up those passes if he didn't have to bump the center.

"What are you hitting him for, then?" Connor asked. "Why don't you go for the ball?"

The first time George dropped straight back, a pass hit him in the stomach. The next time, he made his first of 18 career interceptions.

But according to Ed O'Bradovich, a Bears defensive end from 1962-71, George's historic move wasn't made on the spur of the moment.

"I know for a fact that George Connor went to [assistant] Clark Shaughnessy and made the suggestion to put Bill George at middle linebacker," said O'Bradovich, who as a rookie played under Shaughnessy. "They revolutionized the defense. That really made Bill George and put the linebacker and the whole scheme where it is today."

When George was inducted into the Hall of Fame, Abe Gibron, then the Bears' coach and the one who hired George as an assistant in 1972, said: "He brought all the romance and charisma to the position."

George made eight straight Pro Bowls, and thanks to him, the middle guard was replaced by a third linebacker on the 1955 All-NFL teams named by the wire services. When Connor retired before the 1956 season, George replaced him as the signal caller for Shaughnessy's defense, so complicated that George had to learn hundreds of formations.

Coach George Halas tried to make George's job easier by putting a radio receiver in his helmet and transmitting defensive calls. NFL commissioner Bert Bell quickly outlawed that practice, but George did just fine on his own until Shaughnessy retired after the 1962 season. The Bears then switched defensive signal callers.

"John Unitas said he only feared one man in football and that was Bill George," O'Bradovich recalled. "Not because he was physical, but because of his intellectual prowess.

"I remember playing the Packers and I couldn't count how many times Bart Starr would be barking out signals and Bill would counter him with audibles. Bill would change the defense and say, 'O'B, they're coming inside! Jump inside!' Lo and behold, I'd come in there and he'd make me out to be a hero.

"And he did that many, many times. He was just a master at that game of defense.

"He was like a coach on the field. If you talked to people around the league, I don't know of too many players at any position who were respected more than Bill George."

George also is credited with figuring out how to stop the San Francisco 49ers' shotgun formation, briefly the offensive scourge of the NFL. The 49ers' offense was struggling in 1960 and hit bottom in a shutout loss to the Detroit Lions that dropped them to 3-4. But when coach Red Hickey installed the shotgun, his offense came alive and the 49ers won four of their last five games.

15

**CHICAGO BEARS and
LOS ANGELES RAMS**
Years: 1952-66
Height: 6'2" Weight: 230
Number: 61, 72
Hall of Fame: 1974
Born: October 27, 1930
Died: September 30, 1982

Bill George is best known as professional football's first true middle linebacker, but he's remembered for much more than that. He also made eight straight Pro Bowls, starred for the Chicago Bears' NFL champions in 1963 and was elected to the Hall of Fame in 1974.

The shotgun, with rookie Billy Kilmer at quarterback, hit its peak early in the 1961 season. The 49ers scored at least 35 points in four of their first five games before visiting Wrigley Field. George moved back to his old middle guard spot, lined up on the center's shoulder and blitzed repeatedly. The Bears held the 49ers to 132 yards in a 31-0 victory that prompted Hickey to cut back on the shotgun and play John Brodie at quarterback. O'Bradovich recalls that George was an exceptional blitzer and a master at getting a jump by correctly anticipating the snap count.

"John Unitas said he only **feared** one man in football and that was Bill George. Not because he was **physical**, but because of his **intellectual prowess**."

—Ed O'Bradovich

"We were the first team to really stress red dogs in the NFL," George said.

"You've got to put constant pressure on the good quarterbacks. One time, we went into a three-man line with eight players in the secondary to face Johnny Unitas, and he still picked us to pieces. You just can't let the good quarterbacks get set."

George was in his prime when he suffered two injured vertebrae in an auto accident after the 1961 season. He played despite a stiff neck for more than a season and in 1963 helped the Bears beat the New York Giants, 14-10, in the NFL championship game.

When Dick Butkus came along in 1965, George became a reserve. He asked Halas for his release after that season and finished his career in '66 with the Los Angeles Rams, coached by former Bears defensive coordinator George Allen.

George left Chicago with a lasting legacy. He invented a position that Joe Schmidt further glamorized and Sam Huff thrust into the national consciousness. George was among Huff's peers who liked to tease him about his famous documentary.

"Bill George and Joe Schmidt were the premier linebackers in the league and [reporters] asked Bill George what he thought of Sam Huff doing that TV show," O'Bradovich recalled.

"He said, 'I don't know, but they ought to get Joe Schmidt to play the part.'"

Bill George, who set a Bears record by playing 14 seasons, is shown here finishing his career as a Los Angeles Ram in 1966 under former Bears assistant coach George Allen. "I just thought I had some football left in my bones," George said. "The game gets in your system."
AP/WWP

TOMMY NOBIS

T ommy Nobis's first professional contract had to be the first one in any sport to make big news in outer space.

Frank Borman, command pilot of the Gemini 7 space mission, had two sons serving as ball boys for the AFL's Houston Oilers, and he was excited by one report in December, 1965 that Nobis, the top draft choice of both the Oilers and Atlanta Falcons, had agreed to become an Oiler. That report proved incorrect, though, and when Borman learned Nobis had signed with the Falcons, he radioed from space, "There's no joy in Mudville."

This attention was heady stuff for Nobis, a guard and linebacker who was named All-America at Texas and became the the first pick of the NFL draft. He also was the first pick ever for the Falcons, an expansion team about to make its debut in 1966.

"That was quite a thrill—someone who has his life on the line up there, thinking about the NFL and Houston Oilers," said Nobis, who's spent most of his post-linebacking days in the Falcons' front office. "That was one of the biggest moments of my whole career."

Nobis, like Borman, was brought down to earth soon enough. The Falcons enjoyed only two winning seasons during Nobis's career and never made the playoffs. He became to the Falcons what Archie Manning became to the Saints—a highly talented, much-admired player who became his franchise's signature player but never enjoyed the recognition he would've enjoyed with a winner. Nobis can see the parallels.

"I'm just a heck of a lot better-looking than he is," Nobis said, laughing.

"I certainly saw in Archie the tremendous athlete with a lot of talent who wound up taking a lot of hits. I think Archie would agree that timing is so important to all of our careers. That's what I say about the Hall of Fame. The Atlanta Falcons, after 37 years, didn't have one person in the Hall of Fame."

Nobis, arguably, was the best linebacker absent from the Hall of Fame as the 2003 season was about to start. Early in his career, he routinely was compared Dick Butkus and Ray Nitschke, both widely considered among the elite linebackers of all time.

Sport Magazine in 1968 asked five retired all-time greats to determine if Butkus, Nitschke or Nobis was the NFL's top linebacker.

The verdict was split, with Chuck Bednarik, the former Eagle, picking Nobis. Bednarik was partial to Nobis partly because both liked to freelance and had their fill of losing teams for most of their careers.

"I don't know if Atlanta lets Nobis go on every play, but I do know that he is just about everywhere at once," Bednarik said. "He's in on every tackle."

Pat Richter, discussing Nobis, added: "The only thing he's lacking is experience and a better ballclub. He can make 18 tackles in a game, but if they lose, everyone will write about the winners.

When he gets more experience, I would say that he probably has the tools to become the best in the business."

A few years later, Los Angeles Rams center Ken Iman, after facing the Falcons, said: "I've been in this league a long time and I've played against a lot of middle linebackers. You hear all this talk about Dick Butkus. In my opinion, Tommy Nobis is the best linebacker in the NFL this year."

Nobis said he wasn't so worried about the centers because they were right in front of him. He was far more worried about tackles and tight ends, whom he couldn't always see coming. Such tight ends as Baltimore's John Mackey, Chicago's Mike Ditka and St. Louis' Jackie Smith could pack quite a wallop.

16

Tommy Nobis takes a well-deserved break on the sidelines. As the first pick of the 1966 draft and first pick ever for the Atlanta Falcons, Nobis was called upon to make the lion's share of tackles as the expansion team struggled to assemble a respectable defense.
VERNON J. BIEVER PHOTO

"Those were guys who laid me out several times," Nobis recalled. "I saw my feet go over my head a few times, and that's a pretty good lick. You're moving, they're moving and it's those who have an angle on you and have some speed that will knock the fool out of you.

"I always thought I had good sensors, almost like radar. I could feel it coming. I'd step inside and out, then wonder, 'How'd I know to do that?'

"I was blessed with that and that's why I survived as long as I did. My body can take only so many good licks. People are going to get shots at you—not to hurt you, but maybe get you start thinking about them.

"It's still part of the game—the intimidation. I saw it work. Guys would get you talking and get you right out of your game plan. I didn't do that a lot, other than trying to stick somebody and let them know you're in the ballgame and they're not coming back in your hole."

All but three Hall of Fame linebackers had supporting casts strong enough to help them get to at least one league championship game or Super Bowl. Nobis had little help around him in his early years and the best team on which he played blew a playoff spot late in the 1973 season and finished 9-5.

"That should be a factor in evaluating [my career]," Nobis said. "However, you still have an assignment and you're still going to have opportunities."

The Falcons' poor defenses in their early years and major knee injuries to Nobis, which eventually reduced his range and left him limping, took an edge off his legacy. Yet Nobis,

---

"I don't know if Atlanta lets Nobis go on every **play**, but I do know that he is just about **everywhere** at once. He's in on every **tackle**."

—Chuck Bednarik

---

named to five Pro Bowls, insists he has no regrets about winding up with an expansion team. So fierce is his loyalty, in fact, that he still resents the ridicule heaped upon the Falcons for much of their history.

"The lack of respect this franchise has had, whether deserving or not, is the part that bothers me," he said. "I've worked with this franchise so many years and seen it kicked and slapped round, and not just on the field. Local writers for so many years made fun of the franchise. You don't like to have people throw sand in your face."

Nobis finally saw bouquets thrown at the Falcons in 1998, when Dan Reeves coached them to the NFC championship before a 34-19 loss to the Denver Broncos in the Super Bowl. As Nobis stood on the field in Miami before the Super Bowl, he could finally feel as if his immersion in the franchise had contributed to a major success.

"Down on the field, I got a little taste of it," he said. "I was a fan, attached to a team that was in it. It was everything I thought it was going to be."

Atlanta's Tommy Nobis was at the very top of his game in the early years of his career and waits here for Green Bay quarterback Don Horn to take the snap. Nobis routinely was compared to the greatest linebackers of his era before he was slowed by knee injuries.
VERNON J. BIEVER PHOTO

DAVE ROBINSON

Most of the College All-Stars were understandably nervous before facing the Green Bay Packers, defending NFL champions, at Chicago's Soldier Field in the summer of 1963. A few All-Stars wondered why Dave Robinson, a linebacker from Penn State, seemed so relaxed.

Robinson, the Packers' first-round draft choice, explained: "If we win, I'll party with you guys. If we lose, I'll party with the Packers."

The All-Stars won 20-17 and forever will remain the last All-Star team to win that annual game, discontinued after 1973. Robinson and two other Green Bay draftees were invited by a team official to visit the Packers at the Drake Hotel after the game, but the rookies didn't find a warm reception.

"We walked in and Lombardi wouldn't speak to us, and the players looked at us like we were lepers," Robinson recalled, laughing, from his home in Akron, Ohio. "Marie Lombardi was the only one who came over and talked to us."

Robinson, though, was looking forward to joining his new teammates and reviewing films of the All-Star game. He had, after all, played well and expected a compliment when the film showed him making a tackle at the expense of tight end Ron Kramer.

Instead, Lombardi berated Kramer for letting a rookie beat him and added, "That kid probably won't even make the team that drafted him!"

Robinson was startled and recalls that safety Willie Wood leaned over and teased, "Don't buy a house in town, kid." Robinson, with his wife, Elaine, back home pregnant, was worried now. He concluded Lombardi's oversight was due to Robinson wearing an unfamiliar number against the Packers. Not that it was of any consolation to him.

"Phil Bengtson got a funny look on his face," Robinson said, referring to the Packers' defensive assistant. "Vince, to the day he died, never apologized."

Robinson had no idea how strongly Lombardi detested that loss. The idea registered, however, during his first week of practice.

"He said that was the most discouraging loss of his career, and he worked the hell out of us," Robinson recalled. "He was a madman. We had to run extra laps, and [Ray] Nitschke missed the All-Star game and he didn't like to run."

The ferocious middle linebacker was just one of several Packers who that week told the first-round pick, "Thanks a lot, Robinson!"

Nitschke liked Robinson a lot better when he was able to get a raise, based on Robinson's rookie contract. Nitschke was a diligent negotiator and also benefitted from Lombardi's policy of not paying a rookie more than a veteran at the same position.

Nitschke left Lombardi's office, found Robinson and said, "I like you, kid!"

Robinson was determined to work and study hard enough that Lombardi would have no trouble identifying him now. He was eager to play on as many special teams as possible but found himself with one more assignment than he wanted. When Jerry Kramer wasn't booming kickoffs deep enough, Lombardi checked his scouting reports and realized that Robinson had kicked off at Penn State. He gave Robinson that job, too.

"I said, 'I'm studying my playbook, trying to become the best linebacker I can be,'" Robinson protested. "He put his arm around me and said, 'Son, your best chance to make this team is as a kickoff man.'"

Robinson didn't start until Nitschke suffered a broken arm in a Thanksgiving Day tie against the Lions in 1963. Robinson stepped in at right linebacker for Bill Forester, who moved to the middle. A year later, left linebacker Dan Currie was traded and Robinson replaced him. The trio of Robinson, Nitschke and Lee Roy Caffey would remain intact for the rest of the Lombardi era.

17

GREEN BAY PACKERS and
WASHINGTON REDSKINS
Years: 1963-74
Height: 6'3" Weight: 240
Number: 89
Born: May 3, 1941

Dave Robinson may have been the Packers' first-round draft choice in 1963, but it wasn't easy to make a name for himself in Green Bay. The summer after the draft, Coach Vince Lombardi misidentified Robinson on a game film as a sure-to-be-released rookie.

AP/WWP

Robinson, who made three Pro Bowls, was tough defending both the run and pass. When former New York Giants coach Bill Parcells was raving about Lawrence Taylor before their first Super Bowl, he was asked who rivaled Taylor for all-around ability.

"I think Dave Robinson and Ted Hendricks were the role models for the position Lawrence plays," Parcells said. "But I don't think either of them was any better than L.T."

Jack Christiansen, former San Francisco 49ers head coach, once said: "Trying to pass over Robinson, with his arms and reaction, is like trying to pass over the Empire State Building."

Robinson had a knack for making big plays in big games. In a 34-27 victory that put the Packers in the first Super Bowl, Robinson pressured Dallas Cowboys quarterback Don Meredith, rolling right near the end zone, into throwing a fourth-down pass that was intercepted by Tom Moore with 28 seconds left. Not that Lombardi was pleased. Robinson received the coach's lowest grade possible for freelancing on the play.

"I should've fronted the guard; instead I went behind him, and if Meredith gets in the end zone, it's because of me," Robinson said. "Even though I thought it was a great play, he gave me a minus two. He thought if you do things right every time, you win the war."

A few weeks earlier, the Packers clinched the Western Conference title in a 14-10 win at Baltimore, where Johnny Unitas had them on the ropes in the final 90 seconds. End Willie Davis came from behind Unitas and knocked the ball into the air, into the hands of Robinson.

The long arm of Green Bay's Dave Robinson was an unwelcome sight for any quarterback or running back. Robinson gets ready to wrap up Redskins running back Larry Brown, who was on his way to a 1,216-yard rushing season in 1972 that helped the Redskins reach the Super Bowl.
VERNON J. BIEVER PHOTO

Robinson received a degree in civil engineering from Penn State, which makes it easy to understand why Bengtson once said: "No one I've met in pro football has within him a higher degree of intelligence and a higher capability of aggressiveness than Dave Robinson."

The Packers may be remembered as the epitome of old-school football, yet Robinson often found them unconventional and even bizarre. In his first series at linebacker, late in a loss at Chicago, he was stunned to hear his teammates cursing and berating each other. And they proved as superstitious as they were quarrelsome.

"That came from Lombardi," Robinson recalled. "He was superstitious—not about black cats or walking under ladders, but it was a football thing. Nitschke always had to be next to Lombardi and followed him up and down the sideline.

"Jerry Kramer would never let anybody borrow his tape. My locker was next to his and he said one guy took his tape and he broke his leg. He'd use a roll of tape one time and throw it back in his locker. His locker was full of tape."

It didn't take Robinson long to get into the spirit of things.

"Before my first game, I got dressed in my full uniform and looked in the mirror," he recalled. "I looked great. We lost and I never looked in the mirror before a game again."

Lombardi refused to allow anybody except offensive linemen to wear gloves during games, but that had nothing to do with his superstition. This rule generally made sense because football gloves back then were heavy and made of leather and Lombardi didn't want anybody mishandling the ball. But surely he wouldn't enforce this policy for the Ice Bowl, the 1967 NFL championship game against the Cowboys in subzero temperatures. Of course he did. But Robinson, who is black, had an idea how to keep his hands warm.

"I told the equipment man, 'Give me a pair of brown gloves and Vince won't know the difference,'" he recalled, laughing. "But in passing situations, I took them off."

The way Robinson saw it, cold hands were a key to the Packers' 21-17 victory.

"Trying to pass over **Robinson**, with his arms and reaction, is like trying to pass over the **Empire State Building**."

—Jack Christiansen

"People said, 'How could we shut out Bob Hayes?'" Robinson recalled, referring to the wide receiver with world-class speed. "Bob Hayes never took his hands out of his pants unless he was going to be the primary receiver."

Because Robinson played with his brains as much as his brawn, he was a logical candidate to serve as the Packers' player representative, and he sat in on collective bargaining talks in 1968. The Players Association had a long wish list, including a non-discrimination clause, which was opposed by Lombardi, serving on the management team. Lombardi felt he was being asked to acknowledge past racial discrimination, which he felt did not exist, and put Robinson on the spot by asking him, "We don't have a problem, do we?"

"I told him, 'We don't have any problems, but we're winning; if we were losing, we might have a problem,'" Robinson recalled.

He reminded Lombardi that as a rookie, Robinson had his own hotel room on the road because he was the last of nine black players to report to camp. The others were paired up, and Lombardi saw no problem with this arrangement, though it surprised Robinson because he'd had a white roommate at Penn State.

"Because we were winning, we would laugh and joke about it," Robinson said. "If we were losing, it becomes an issue."

Robinson and his fellow negotiators gained significant concessions, but not before they were locked out of training camps until mid-July. Lombardi held no hard feelings, though. He congratulated Robinson for his union role and adopted an open policy on choosing roommates.

Robinson grew fond of the coach he'd once viewed as a madman.

"My wife always said that because my father died when I was in high school, maybe I was looking for a father figure," Robinson said. "He was like an old Italian father. He was hard on us. He believed in setting goals. As long as things were going good, he did everything first class. He treated us like kings."

When Lombardi died in 1970, Robinson attended his emotionally charged funeral.

"I told somebody it was the first time I ever cried at a white man's funeral," Robinson said. "I don't say that publicly because people may take the wrong reason."

That was Robinson's way of saying he felt as if a member of his own family had died. Their relationship had come a long way from the day Lombardi couldn't identify his own first-round pick. At the end, Robinson wasn't waiting for an apology, anyway.

"No one I've met in **pro football** has within him a higher degree of **intelligence** and a higher capability of **aggressiveness** than Dave Robinson."

—Phil Bengtson

CLYDE TURNER

When Bears coach George Halas saw a youngster named Dick Butkus, he said, "He's the greatest [linebacker] we've had here since Bulldog Turner."

Turner, actually, was inducted into the Pro Football Hall of Fame as a center, where he's considered among the top three of all time. But he was a two-way star on teams that played in five NFL championship games and won four of them.

The Bears finished Turner's rookie season with the most famous rout of all time, a 73-0 victory over the Washington Redskins in the NFL championship game. Turner contributed a 24-yard return of an interception for a touchdown and was so quick that in 1942 he led the league with eight interceptions.

One of Turner's favorite plays was a 96-yard touchdown return of an interception of Redskins quarterback Sammy Baugh in 1947. On that return, Turner sidestepped a bunch of Redskins and finally brushed off Baugh at the Washington 12. In his five title game appearances, Turner made four interceptions. He even served as an emergency running back in 1944 and scored on a 48-yard touchdown run in a 48-7 victory over Card-Pitt, a wartime combination of the Pittsburgh Steelers and Chicago Cardinals.

Turner also played guard for the 1945 Air Force Superbombers before he returned to the Bears in '46.

Turner, after his playing days, became a Bears assistant to Halas in 1953-58, then in 1962 replaced his old adversary, Baugh, as coach of the New York Titans of the American Football League. Turner was only 42 but ballooned to 280 pounds and wasn't nearly as successful as a head coach as he'd been as a player.

Bill Ryczek, in his book, *Crash of the Titans*, wrote: "Turner had a personality one would expect of a man nicknamed 'Bulldog': a gruff, hard-nosed temperament, with little concern for pomp and circumstance."

Turner went 5-9 in his only season before the franchise was sold. The new group, headed by Sonny Werblin, replaced Turner with Weeb Ewbank, changed the team's nickname to the Jets and brought badly needed stability.

Even an experienced head coach probably would've struggled in Turner's shoes. He was replacing Baugh, a more popular and outgoing coach, and had an owner, Harry Wismer, who behaved erratically, meddled in football decisions and was so financially strapped that on November 8, 1962, the league had to take over the team and cover the payroll for the rest of the season.

Turner responded to adversity with the kind of aggressiveness that served him so well as a player. That wasn't enough to make a winner of the Titans.

"I don't think he made the transition from playing to coaching," tight end Karl Kalimer told Ryczek. "He'd rather get out there and whup on somebody."

Added Ted Daffer, a Bears end while Turner was an assistant: "He was a hard charger. Bulldog's whole life had involved contact. Even when he was coaching, he'd haul off and knock the hell out of you. He'd get frustrated and would have to get rid of it that way."

Turner was joined in New York by another tough old Bear, former end Ed Sprinkle. He was anointed as "The Meanest Man in Pro Football," by *Collier's Magazine*.

"I think that Bulldog needed somebody to confide in—a friend," Sprinkle told Ryczek. "It was just a team that was in complete chaos. They wouldn't listen to Bulldog. I was sorry I ever went up there because I couldn't help."

Turner's involvement in a new league that battled the established NFL for talent seemed appropriate. After an exceptional career at Hardin-Simmons in Abilene, Tex., he was involved in the kind of intrigue that would be repeated decades later in the AFL-NFL signing wars.

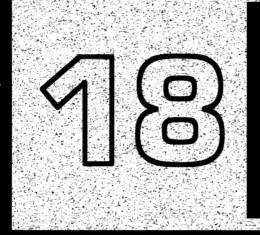

18

CHICAGO BEARS
Years: 1940-52
Height: 6'2" Weight: 235
Number: 66
Nickname: Bulldog
Hall of Fame: 1966
Born: March 10, 1919
Died: October 30, 1998

The 1942 Bears stood 11-0 when they lined up for this photo on the eve of the NFL championship game at Griffith Stadium in Washington. Clyde "Bulldog" Turner, a center and linebacker, is about to snap the ball to Hall of Fame quarterback Sid Luckman. The Bears beat the Redskins in the NFL title games in 1940 and '43, but lost 14-6 in '72.
AP/WWP

During Turner's junior year, a Hardin-Simmons fan told Bears scout Frank Korch to keep an eye on Turner. During an era in which scouting lacked sophistication, such a tip could be valuable. After watching Turner in the East-West Shrine game in San Francisco after his senior year, Korch recommended that Halas draft him. But the Detroit Lions also knew about Turner, and while he was still in college, owner George Richards invited Turner to his home in Beverly Hills, California. He treated him to hospitality, dental work and at least $100 if he'd refuse any other NFL offers.

Two-way star Clyde "Bulldog" Turner, far right, listens in 100-degree heat at the Bears' training camp in Collegeville, Indiana as owner and coach George Halas goes over a new offensive play before the 1947 College All-Star Game in Chicago. The play probably didn't pick up much yardage, because the Bears lost to the All-Stars, 16-0.
AP/WWP

When the Bears sent Turner their questionnaire for draft prospects, he responded: "I do not wish to play professional football."

The Lions still could have drafted Turner in the first round, but coach Gus Henderson had been assured by Richards that Turner was "in the bag." So he figured he could take Turner later in the draft, except that Halas suspected something fishy was going on. The Bears drafted Turner in the first round.

The Lions were penalized $5,000 by the league for tampering, and the Bears were rewarded with a player who helped them enjoy their greatest era.

"He was a **hard** charger. Bulldog's whole life had involved **contact**. Even when he was coaching, he'd haul off and **knock** the hell out of you. He'd get **frustrated** and would have to get rid of it that way."

—Ted Daffer

MIKE CURTIS

ike Curtis seemed so crazed on a football field that many who played with him or against him might be surprised to know how well he adjusted to polite society. Curtis, at age 60, was running a real estate firm in Washington, D.C.

"You have to buy from him, or else," joked Don Shula, who as the Colts head coach drafted Curtis in the first round in 1965.

Shula, as much as anyone, promoted Curtis's image as a madman. Before Super Bowl III, against the New York Jets in January 1969, Shula joked the Colts' were bringing Curtis down to Miami in a cage.

And even today, Curtis's words are as blunt as the tackles he made. But he never bought the perception that he hated opponents, and maybe the grass and trees, too.

"In order to perform in a physical business, if I was competitive, I wanted to perform correctly," Curtis explained. "You have to be aggressive and hit people and get them out of the way. If you give them a soft shot, it doesn't help. The idea that I was crazy or a mad dog…if you have people in the way, you have to get rid of them."

If some say Curtis played in a rage, he says he was just highly motivated. And that he should have been.

"You don't play a lot of games," he explained. "You played 14 games then and it shouldn't be hard to get up 14 times in one year. I didn't want to have any regrets about what I didn't do better, and I didn't.

"I was more intense than other people. I'm the same way in business. It's just my style, I guess."

The Colts' 1969 media guide quoted Curtis as saying, "I play football because it's the only place you can hit people and get away with it." He insists he never actually was interested in hitting people anyplace else.

"If I went to a bar and somebody wanted to put a notch in his gun because I'm Mike Curtis, I sat at the end of the bar or I left," he recalled. "I wasn't interested in the rooster chest-beating stuff that some people get into."

A national magazine story contrasting him with Colts defensive end Bubba Smith was entitled, "Beauty and the Beast." New York Giants general manager Ernie Accorsi, then the Colts' public relations director, said, "If Bubba had Mike's personality, he probably would've destroyed the league."

After Curtis was penalized once for a flagrant penalty against Shula's Miami Dolphins, he angrily explained: "That's football. Not that…stuff the referees are trying to put in the game."

During a 1971 game against the Dolphins in Baltimore, a fan ran onto the field and took the ball. Curtis registered a tackle, forced fumble and recovery that aren't in the record books. The fan was arrested, jailed and hospitalized, but Curtis insists he let the intruder off lightly.

"Everybody made a bigger deal about that than it was," he said. "I could've put his legs out permanently. I just gave him a forearm. He didn't bleed, I didn't hurt him. It was an important game and I didn't want a disruption, having him run around the field. He was a skinny little guy and I didn't use unnecessary force. I just wanted the ball back."

Curtis, a four-time Pro Bowl selection, excelled at getting the ball back. He made 25 interceptions, and his interception in Super Bowl V in January 1971 set up Jim O'Brien's 32-yard field goal that gave the Colts a 16-13 victory over the Dallas Cowboys.

Curtis especially relished that victory because two years earlier, he experienced a career low, a 16-7 Super Bowl loss to the New York Jets. Curtis spent much of the week before that game tolerating questions about his "animal" persona, then felt he played poorly in pro football's most famous upset ever.

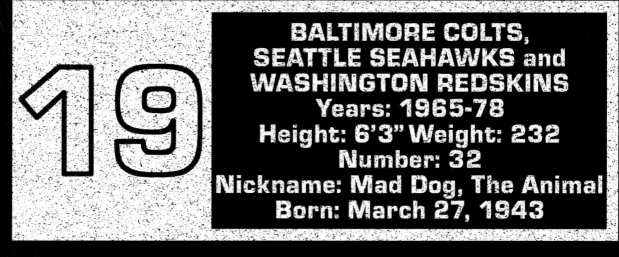

19

BALTIMORE COLTS, SEATTLE SEAHAWKS and WASHINGTON REDSKINS
Years: 1965-78
Height: 6'3" Weight: 232
Number: 32
Nickname: Mad Dog, The Animal
Born: March 27, 1943

Mike Curtis was a raging bull who played in two Super Bowls for the Baltimore Colts. He was not only ferocious, but quick, and his interception in the January 1971 Super Bowl set up Jim O'Brien's winning field goal with five seconds left for a 16-13 victory over the Cowboys.

"Even when we lost, I thought we were a lot better than the team that won," Curtis said. "We all brought down the wives and there were a lot of distractions. I think it contributed a lot to us being overconfident."

Overconfidence wasn't a problem for the Colts when they got their Super Bowl win two years later. They were led by rookie coach Don McCafferty, who said, "If we had 22 Mike Curtises, we could send them to the stadium and tell them to bring back a winner while we sat and watched the game on TV."

In a Super Bowl that included 11 turnovers, the Colts' defense held the Cowboys to 215 yards. Cornerback Rick Volk's interception set up the tying touchdown before Curtis's big play near the end.

"I was happy to get that ring," Curtis recalled. "Losing to the Jets was a pretty intense downer. Winning against Dallas was a pretty intense up. They were about equal."

Shula made a shrewd decision to draft Curtis. He recalls he wasn't quite as shrewd when he initially tried to play Curtis, a two-way player at Duke, on offense.

"One of the biggest mistakes I made was trying to make him a fullback," Shula said. "He was a great example of an offensive player with a defensive temperament. He could've been a great fullback, but he belonged on the defensive side of the ball.

"All his measurables were outstanding—the size, speed, strength and quickness. He just rewrote the charts."

Yet Curtis's achievements seem to have gotten lost in the shuffle. He was not in the Hall of Fame when the 2003 season rolled around, and *Pro Football Weekly* in 2002 didn't even include him on a list of its 26 top linebackers of all time.

"They don't know his athleticism as I know his athleticism," Accorsi said. "He was like Roberto Clemente on our softball team. You wouldn't know it to look at that body; he was stocky and square. I feel regretful he gets no consideration. There wasn't that much difference between him and [Willie] Lanier.

"He was making the Pro Bowl at outside linebacker, but we never had a great middle linebacker and moved Curtis to the middle [midway through 1969]. He just never got the acclaim. I don't think he'll ever get in the Hall of Fame unless I get on the old-timers' committee."

"All his **measurables** were **outstanding**—the size, speed, strength and quickness. He just **rewrote** the charts."

—Don Shula

Even then, Accorsi might not get much help from Curtis. He said: "I wouldn't want to form a committee and be a PR guy, going around trying to show people my stats. That would be embarrassing. If I got in, that would be super. I've seen some people get in who I think I'm a better player than, but that's my personal opinion."

Curtis said he doesn't follow the NFL much and was happy to see his sons concentrate on lacrosse and his daughter play soccer.

"I never watched football too much, maybe because I knew too much about it and I'd see people screw up and wouldn't enjoy it," he said. "I liked playing. I liked the camaraderie. When it was over, it was over, I don't like to see some players dwell on their careers like it was the highlight of their life. It wasn't the highlight of my life, I moved on to other things.

"Football's changed a lot, for the worse, because it seems to me it's more show business, as opposed to the boring plays."

Curtis was, of course, being sarcastic. Plays were never boring when he was making them.

This fan ran onto the field in Baltimore in 1971 to steal the ball, but instead found out why Mike Curtis was nicknamed "The Animal." Curtis quickly separated the intruder from the ball and sent him to jail and a hospital. Curtis and his defensive teammates were even tougher on the Miami Dolphins in a 14-3 Colts victory.
AP/WWP

LEE ROY JORDAN

As the Dallas Cowboys made the transition from expansion doormat to "Next Year's Champions" to "America's Team," there was one constant—Lee Roy Jordan, going from locker to locker after every game to compliment teammates for jobs well done.

Jordan wasn't the biggest star on the Cowboys' first three Super Bowl teams, but no teammate had more of an impact upon their rise to stardom.

When Jordan arrived in Dallas in 1963, the Cowboys showed little promise, and few in their locker room seemed to notice or care when something positive happened. Jordan, who'd starred for Bear Bryant at Alabama knew a winner, and a loser, when he saw one.

The Cowboys had won just nine games in 1960-62, their first three years in the NFL, and Jordan liked to tell a story from his rookie season that dramatized how little glamour came with being a Cowboy.

"I tried to cash a check that year and I said to the guy in the clothing store, 'Look, I'm a reputable guy, I'm with the Cowboys, you know,'" Jordan recalled. "And the guy looked at me and said, 'Really? I didn't know there was a rodeo in town.'"

Jordan decided to make sure the Cowboys got noticed, in their city and in their locker room. Shy by nature, he was reluctant to become a strong locker room presence. But Jordan disliked losing more than he disliked putting himself front and center, so he adopted the take-charge mode that would make him the Cowboys' inspirational leader.

"I've always had the sense of being a guy who found something positive in each game," he said from his redwood supply company in Dallas.

"I encouraged people to say, 'Hey, there are some things we did good. It's not enough, we've got to improve each week, but let's not get our heads down. Look at the optimistic part of it. Look at where we're going and let's set a goal.'"

The Cowboys in 1963 already included many of the defensive players who would help them reach the NFL championship game against the Packers in 1966. But they needed a better offense, which Coach Tom Landry and his front office provided. And they needed strong locker room leadership, which Jordan provided.

"Nobody went around when I got here," he once told Tom Callahan of the *Cincinnati Enquirer*. "In the beginning, I didn't have the guts to do it, to tell people how to play, how to do something or just to do something. But none of the veterans were doing it, and I made a decision one day that I was taking over."

Jordan didn't always throw bouquets, either. Upon his induction in the Texas Stadium Ring of Honor in 1989, Jordan told the *Dallas Morning News*: "If a guy was not giving 100 percent or was loafing or quitting a little bit on us, I felt like when it got to be a tough game that he would quit on us. If they were not giving their best effort, I wasn't really nice to them at all. I had battles with them in practice."

Jordan thrived on mixing it up in practice. Once, when backup quarterback Roger Staubach was scrambling, despite an injured back, Jordan ran by defensive coordinator Ernie Stautner and yelled: "Coach, can we hit this guy?"

It was Bryant who taught Jordan how to gun his engine.

"He instilled that back in college," Jordan recalled. "You play the game the way you practice. I practiced at full speed every day. You think you can turn it up an extra notch in a game, but you can't. You're missing something."

All Jordan missed, really, was another 25 pounds. He still made five Pro Bowls and intercepted 32 passes.

20

DALLAS COWBOYS
Years: 1963-76
Height: 6'1" Weight: 221
Number: 55
Nickname: Killer
Born: April 27, 1941

Green Bay's Elijah Pitts is out of running room as Lee Roy Jordan tackles him from behind in the NFC championship game in Dallas on New Year's Day, 1967. The Packers won 34-27 in their first of back-to-back championship game victories over the Cowboys.
AP/WWP

Added Staubach, who became the Cowboys' championship quarterback: "Lee Roy was smaller, but pound for pound, he was tougher than anybody who played. No player in Cowboys history meant more to the overall team than Lee Roy Jordan."

Jordan wasn't just tough. His dogged preparation and quickness enabled him to consistently beat blockers and bring down ball carriers. Philadelphia Eagles center Guy Morriss, after a 30-16 win over the Cowboys in 1973, said: "I'm glad we won, but I didn't contribute very much. I'll bet I didn't touch Lee Roy Jordan once. That man's as quick as a halfback."

Jordan's playmaking and inspiration helped the Cowboys persevere through repeated frustration. They were stopped short of the Super Bowl in the 1966 and '67 seasons by the Green Bay Packers. They were knocked out of the playoffs in '68 and '69 by the Cleveland Browns. They lost the Super Bowl in January 1971 to the Baltimore Colts on Jim O'Brien's 32-yard field goal with five seconds left. A year later, the Cowboys finally won a Super Bowl by beating the Miami Dolphins, 24-3.

Lee Roy Jordan used his quickness to make 32 interceptions, but this isn't one of them. Jordan can do little more than chase Steeler tight end Randy Grossman, who hauls in a Terry Bradshaw pass during the Steelers' 21-17 victory over the Cowboys in the January 1976 Super Bowl. It was the third and final Super Bowl of Jordan's outstanding career.
VERNON J. BIEVER PHOTO

"We had to struggle and get over this [reputation], 'We're a good team but can't win the playoff game,' " Jordan said. "We were so close, but we did lose. It took us a long time to feel the joy of our accomplishments. We did get recognized as a team that played exciting football—you didn't leave a game if we were down two touchdowns. We did take extreme pleasure when we became known as 'America's Team.' "

One of the Cowboys' most bitter losses came at Green Bay in the 1967 NFL championship game, better known as the Ice Bowl. Playing in subzero weather and on a frozen field, the Cowboys led 17-14 until quarterback Bart Starr scored from the one with 13 seconds left.

"The Ice Bowl really didn't let us show how good we were," Jordan said. "We were a speed football team, and on an ice rink you don't get to show your speed too much. No doubt we felt we should have beaten Green Bay up there, and in that game, we felt we'd arrived. But it's hard to have good memories of that, except getting warm after the game. That's the best memory of all. I thought we played really well on defense until that last drive."

From the Packer perspective, the 68-yard winning drive was an exercise in perfection. Jordan didn't see it that way, especially not after taking a second look.

"Looking at films, we were in position on every one of those plays on the last drive to make the tackle if we have decent footing," he said. "We had guys slip down at crucial times. Green Bay was pretty fortunate to win that game."

Jordan was the first-round pick of the Cowboys and, thanks to a bidding war with the AFL Boston Patriots, received a $5,000 signing bonus, a $17,500 salary and a $6,500 Buick Riviera. Gil Brandt, the Cowboys' player personnel director, told Jordan he would drive his car from Dallas to the Tuscaloosa campus. But the car didn't reach Jordan in quite the condition he expected.

"I was cruising along Highway 82, west of Starkville, Mississippi, and there were these little knolls in the road," Brandt recalled. "It was about 10 p.m. and I was going 40 or 45 and I come across a little knoll and see four cows. I try to swerve to the left and killed this cow and put a huge, huge dent in the car. Luckily, I didn't get killed."

Brandt got a ride into Starkville with another motorist and reported the accident to a local sheriff the next morning.

Brandt recalls being told, "I'm Sheriff Thompson and that's my daddy's cow you hit. How you want to take care of this?"

Brandt's only regret about Jordan is that he hadn't made the Pro Football Hall of Fame as the 2003 season was about to start.

"Everybody thinks their baby is the prettiest," Brandt said. "But I have a hard time understanding the workings of the Hall of Fame. Fortunately, he's in the Ring of Honor, so at least he's been recognized by the Cowboys."

Jordan talks as if he's received all the recognition he needs.

"I wish I was more involved in personal goals, like to be in the Hall of Fame, but it's not a concern of mine," he said. "I'd probably be just as happy to have my little grandgirls hug my neck."

RANDY GRADISHAR

W atching Randy Gradishar on videotape is like watching the practitioner of a lost art. On almost every tackle, Gradishar wraps up the ball carrier with as much precision as punishment. His primary aim was making the tackle, not a highlights hit, though Gradishar made more than his fair share of both.

In 10 years, he was credited with 2,049 tackles, including 286 in 1978. Though tackles are not an official NFL statistic, Gradishar by any estimation was one of the busiest and surest tacklers of his era.

"If I could grab on to you, usually I could get you down," he recalled.

Because of his strength, quickness and nose for the ball, Gradishar was the chief playmaker in coordinator Joe Collier's 3-4 defense. He played the right inside spot and was an every-down player.

"A typical game for Randy was 10 tackles, two tipped passes and a fumble recovery," teammate Tom Jackson said. "He did so many things well: run defense, pass defense, great goal-line defense and never missed a play in 10 years."

It's hard for anyone who grew up in Denver during the Broncomania era to realize that the Broncos were not always a point of civic pride. They misspent their youth as the doormat of the American Football League, and rooting for the Broncos was, for many years, more of a bad habit than a healthy passion. All that changed when the "Orange Crush" defense, named after a popular soft drink and led by Gradishar, gave Denver a Super Bowl team. That team bridged the bad old days and the John Elway era.

"When I go into the Village Inn, Marie Callender's or Denny's for the senior citizen's specials, they kind of know me," joked Gradishar, who remains in the Denver area.

"Everything was so orange, everybody was crazy, everybody was excited. I couldn't be any more proud being part of that era."

The Broncos enjoyed just one winning season, 1973, before coach John Ralston a year later drafted Gradishar, whom Woody Hayes called "the best defensive player I ever coached at Ohio State." In '77, the Broncos, led by their defense, finished 12-2 and won the AFC West for their first division title ever.

"That was the first time the Broncos ever went to the playoffs, let alone think we could win against the Steelers," Gradishar recalled. "But we knew we had something going. Our players and coaches knew we had a real shot at going to the Super Bowl."

First, the Broncos had to defeat the previous two Super Bowl champions in back-to-back games at Mile High Stadium. They beat the Pittsburgh Steelers, 34-21, as Jackson made two fourth-quarter interceptions and one set up Craig Morton's 34-yard touchdown pass to Jack Dolbin. Then the Broncos defeated the Oakland Raiders, 20-17, as Morton threw two touchdown passes to Haven Moses.

In the Super Bowl, however, the Orange Crush was overshadowed by Dallas's "Doomsday Defense." The Cowboys came up with four interceptions and four fumble recoveries in their 27-10 win. Linebacker Thomas "Hollywood" Henderson crumpled an orange cup after the game, tossed it at Denver fans and taunted, "There's your Orange Crush." But Gradishar and his teammates had spent 38 1/2 minutes on the field.

"We were going into the fourth quarter down 20-10 and still we had the thought that we had the passion and energy to still win this," Gradishar said.

"Our defense was the foundation of our team and that whole season we talked about, 'We're going to make turnovers, we're going to score points, we're going to make things happen.' And we did. That was a tradition our Orange Crush defense had."

21

in the 1977 AFC Championship game against the Oakland Raiders, Randy Gradishar keeps his eye—and the pressure—on quarterback Ken Stabler.
AP/WWP

Opponents scored only 148 points in 14 regular-season games, and none of the Broncos' five subsequent Super Bowl defenses were remotely as stingy. But the Broncos' Super Bowl champions in the 1997-98 seasons had far better balance.

"We had these old-fashioned reels of film and there were times our reels were overflowing and we couldn't get them started because we'd played so many darn plays," Gradishar said, chuckling. "Mentally, I might've played 11, 12 or 13 years because I played so many plays in 10 years."

Gradishar was especially effective in goal-line situations. George Hill, an assistant with the Dolphins, Colts and Eagles, said: "Coaches were happy with first and goal at the two yard line. But I'd say to my team, 'You'd better block Gradishar or we're not going to score.'"

Gradishar began acquiring his knack for short-yardage stops at Ohio State, especially on some big stands against Michigan.

> "Coaches were happy with first and **goal** at the two-yard line. But I'd say to my team, 'You'd better **block** Gradishar or we're not going to **score**.'"
>
> —George Hill

"If anybody remembers me or the Orange Crush, the short-yardage stuff was one of our trademarks," Gradishar said. "I had the opportunity to make the big hit because of the protection of the other 10 guys. My ability came from training and experience, film study and taking a chance. On a lot of plays, I'm going over the top when the running back was going to the outside.

"I'd see the offensive line's footwork, all those kinds of things. And a lot would depend on knowing the situation and the quarterback. Will they try a quarterback sneak? Ken Stabler never. Terry Bradshaw maybe. Roger Staubach probably.

"What is their bread-and-butter play? Is [Oakland's] Mark van Eeghen going to get it? [Pittsburgh's] Franco Harris? Fourth and half a yard, it's going somewhere between the tackles usually."

If Gradishar wasn't expecting a quarterback sneak in short-yardage situations, he'd stand back five yards, about a yard and a half deeper than most linebackers stood.

"That gave me the opportunity to adjust and read better," Gradishar said. "Who was actually getting the ball? If I did think incorrectly, I could still be part of the play. I could take one wrong step and with one other step I was back in the tackle."

Gradishar retired after the 1983 season, which marked his 10th season, seventh Pro Bowl appearance and a streak of 145 games played. He was just 31, had made 20 interceptions and 13 fumble recoveries, and likely could've played a few more years. He was a Pro Football Hall of Fame finalist in 2003 but wasn't elected.

"I wanted to leave the game at the height of my career instead of losing a step and going out on a down slope," he said. "There was some luck there, some of God's blessings that I didn't have the major injury. In seven out of the 10 years, I was in the hospital getting things fixed for the next year, but I didn't have an injury that slowed me down or eliminated me from continuing to play.

"I've heard some people say that if I played a couple of more years, it would've gotten me into the Hall of Fame. I had a 10-year career, gave 110 percent and haven't looked back."

Randy Gradishar (53) wasn't always the first member of the "Orange Crush" defense to crush the ball carrier. But he used his quickness, knack for sniffing out plays and flawless technique to average more than 200 tackles a season during his 10 years with the Denver Broncos. Gradishar led a defense that ranks among the best of the 1970s.
KANSAS COLLECTION, U. of KANSAS

NICK BUONICONTI

Members of the 1972 Dolphins keep champagne chilled each fall until the NFL's last unbeaten team finally loses. Then they pop their corks and toast to their continuing status as the only unbeaten and untied team in modern NFL history. No team had yet canceled their celebration as the 2003 season got under way.

This team, so famous for perfection, had a defense, oddly enough, best known for its anonymity. Before the January 1972 Super Bowl, Dallas Cowboys coach Tom Landry said of the Dolphin defenders: "I can't recall their names, but they are a matter of great concern to us."

Thus was christened the "No-Name Defense," and though the Cowboys beat the Dolphins 24-3, hardly anyone else beat them for the next two years. The 1972-73 Dolphins had regular-season records of 14-0 and 12-2 and two Super Bowl wins.

A 14-7 Super Bowl victory over the Washington Redskins in January 1973 completed the Dolphins' 17-0 season. Were it not for kicker Garo Yepremian's panicky pass that was intercepted and returned for a late touchdown, the Dolphins would have posted the first Super Bowl shutout.

Buoniconti was the No-Name Defense's leader and middle linebacker. He was undersized but aggressive, quick, fiery and adept at thinking on his feet.

"When he sees something, it doesn't take long for it to go from his mind to his feet," Dolphins coach Don Shula once said. "If he had the size of a Nobis or a Butkus, they'd have to outlaw the guy. He'd be too good to play."

When Shula went to Miami in 1970, he had to rebuild the defense but inherited a handful of standouts, including linemen Manny Fernandez and Bill Stanfill, safety Dick Anderson and Buoniconti. George Wilson, who preceded Shula, obtained Buoniconti from the Patriots in 1969 after he fell out of favor with new coach Clive Rush.

Buoniconti played in five AFL All-Star games for the Patriots, but Rush considered him a clubhouse lawyer. Buoniconti, actually, is a licensed one.

"I want Buoniconti traded, I don't want him on my football team," Rush declared before starting his 5-16 stint in Boston.

Wilson, learning of the linebacker's availability, told his front office: "Get Buoniconti down here. I don't care how long it takes. Get him any way you can. He's what this club needs."

The Dolphins acquired Buoniconti for linebacker John Bramlett, quarterback Kim Hammond and a fifth-round draft choice. This may not have been quite as disastrous as selling Babe Ruth to the Yankees, but, still, this was not a good deal for Boston.

It was, however, a momentous deal for the Dolphins and Buoniconti. The Dolphins made the playoffs for the first time in 1970, their fifth year of existence, and reached the Super Bowl in each of the next three seasons.

Despite the deserved recognition for their perfect season, the Dolphins were in many respects more dominant in the 1973 season. They won three postseason games by a combined score of 85-33 and did not allow a touchdown in six of the first 10 games.

"We took on the No-Name label, which meant 11 players playing [exceptionally well] instead of one or two superstars," Shula said. "We took a lot of pride in that team concept of defense. I think that's one of the big reasons our individuals are late in getting recognition."

The No-Name Defense included safeties Jake Scott and Anderson, Stanfill and Buoniconti—all Pro Bowl players. But the unit's success seemed to prove that, given excellence in talent and coaching, a defense doesn't need a bunch of Hall of Famers to reach a championship level.

Buoniconti has always claimed, though, that coordinator Bill Arnsparger's defense was so finely woven that even the brightest threads were often overlooked.

22

BOSTON PATRIOTS and
MIAMI DOLPHINS
Years: 1962-76
Height: 5'11" Weight: 220
Number: 85
Hall of Fame: 2001
Born: December 15, 1940

Nick Buoniconti had never been in a playoff game when he reported for the 1970 season with the Miami Dolphins. His luck was about to change, though, because the arrival of coach Don Shula marked the birth of a unit that would become known as the "No-Name Defense" and play in three consecutive Super Bowls.

AP/WWP

"Nobody stands out, but that is the way it is with the type of defense we play," Buoniconti said. "Every player has an initial responsibility to fill at a particular place and everything he does is integrated into what somebody else does. Even our pass rush works that way. And as far as talent, we have as much as anybody."

The Dolphin defense highlighted the "53," a 3-4 alignment named for the number of Bob Matheson, who came in as the fourth linebacker. That defense was especially effective against the pass, and Buoniconti made 32 career interceptions, which tied Jack Ham for most among Hall of Fame linebackers.

The Boston Patriots made a great choice when they took Nick Buoniconti from Notre Dame in the 13th round of the 1962 AFL draft. He's shown here in 1963, his first of five seasons as an AFL All-Star. He was traded to Miami in 1969, continuing a long history of ill-fated deals for Boston's professional franchises. AP/WWP

"He's too much," New York Jets quarterback Joe Namath once said of Buoniconti. "First, he's coming in at you, and the next time, he's right on top of your receiver. He covers so much ground."

Given his size, Buoniconti had to keep moving to thrive and survive.

"I've always been the sort of linebacker who kind of sneaks around, plugging up this, cutting off that," he once said. "I've often wondered what it could be like to just rip into some of those backs head on.

"It's a big man's game, but there's room for a little guy. You have to use your quickness as much as possible, though, and try to get around them. If you keep banging up against a 270-pound lineman all day, he'll destroy you."

Because of his size, Buoniconti, a star at Notre Dame, wasn't drafted until the 13th round of the 1962 AFL draft and wasn't drafted at all in the NFL. He was considered by many a smart player, though Oakland Raiders coach John Madden didn't agree.

"He was always a bright guy, but he didn't play like a bright guy," Madden wrote in his book, *One Knee Equals Two Feet*. "Not that he was dumb, but he was reckless, the most reckless player I've ever seen. When he saw a play developing, he just ran and dived. Just threw his body, whoom. I never saw a guy play with that much disregard for his body. He wasn't that big, he wasn't that strong. But he just bounced up. On the next play, he threw his body again."

Matheson preferred to view Buoniconti as instinctive. "Nick played with a great deal of intensity and 100 percent confidence," Matheson once said. "He was known for his gambling on the field and he won most of the time. I used to ask Nick how he got the quick key. He didn't know. It was all by instinct."

Buoniconti played 14 seasons and avoided major injuries until he spent the 1975 season on injured reserve. He always suggested too much was made of his size.

"When Dick Butkus hits you, you fall the way he wants you to fall," Buoniconti said. "When I hit you, you fall the way you want. But there's no difference. You still fall."

"When he **sees** something, it doesn't take long for it to go from his **mind** to his feet. If he had the size of a Nobis or a Butkus, they'd have to **outlaw** the guy. He'd be too good to **play**."

—Don Shula

HARRY CARSON

H arry Carson, for the biggest game of his career, is best remembered for what he did before the game even started.

It was time for the coin toss before the Giants and Denver Broncos met in the January, 1987 Super Bowl, and the Broncos sent out a posse of captains to the middle of the field. Giants coach Bill Parcells sent out only Carson. He was also sending the Broncos a message.

"My great vision of him was when they had about 11 captains and he walked out…captain of the Giants," recalled Giants general manager Ernie Accorsi. "When he went out there, he was in charge."

That's also what Carson remembers best about the Giants' 39-20 victory. Not that he stuffed Gerald Willhite on a key goal-line stand in the first half, when the Giants were clawing to stay in the game. Carson, the right inside linebacker, shared captain honors with quarterback Phil Simms and defensive end George Martin, but for the Super Bowl, Carson was designated as the chip on the Giants' shoulder.

"When Parcells and I had a little conversation before the coin toss, I asked, 'Is Phil going with me?'" Carson recalled. "He said, 'No.' I said, 'Go out by myself?' He said, 'Yeah, go out by yourself.'

"It was designed by Bill to sort of send a message. I could see 10 or 12 players walking towards me from the Broncos' side. It looked like the lone gunman going against a whole gang. It was ominous going out there, with [John] Elway, [Karl] Mecklenburg and all those guys. I've had a number of people tell me that's one of the things that stood out in their minds in that game."

What also stood out in Carson's mind that day was how long a journey he'd taken with the Giants. He came to them when their once-proud tradition was in shambles and it depressed him. He asked to be traded and even quit the team twice. Now, before that Super Bowl appearance in Pasadena, California, Carson was glad he'd stayed.

"I remember thinking of all the players with the Giants who should have been there and for whatever reasons weren't," he recalled. "I felt I was representing all those guys. I was carrying a different set of weights than other people. I was thinking about all those guys who didn't make it and all the fans who stuck with the team. They burned their tickets and voiced their displeasure with the team and we finally got to the top of the mountain.

"I'm one of those players…one of the chosen ones who helped push the team all the way to the top. And I hadn't wanted to stay in that situation. It was especially gratifying to have persevered through all the bad times to the point where things were great. My taste of winning was probably sweeter than for many of the other players."

Carson was in his third season when the Giants bottomed out. They just needed to take a knee to beat the Eagles at Giants Stadium in 1978, but a handoff from Joe Pisarcik to Larry Csonka was mishandled and the fumble was returned by cornerback Herman Edwards for a game-winning touchdown. For the Eagles, that was the "Miracle of the Meadowlands." For Giants fans, that was "The Fumble," as well as the last straw.

Before a December 10 home loss to the St. Louis Cardinals, some fans lit a fire in a trash barrel outside Giants Stadium and tossed in their tickets. During the game, a single-engine plane flew over the stadium, pulling a banner that read: "15 Years of Lousy Football, We've Had Enough."

Carson took the hard times hard. A *Gameday Magazine* profile recalled he would park his car far from the players' entrance at Giants Stadium so fans wouldn't recognize him and even saw a psychologist to help him deal with being a Giant.

The franchise's deterioration, and especially a stony silence between owners Tim and Wellington Mara, was of such concern to NFL commissioner Pete Rozelle that he stepped in and strongly suggested they hire George Young as general manager in 1979.

23

NEW YORK GIANTS
Years: 1976-88
Height: 6'2" Weight: 245
Number: 53
Born: November 26, 1953

Harry Carson was best known as a run stopper, but he could rush the passer, too. Here he takes down St. Louis quarterback Neil Lomax in a 27-7 victory as the 1986 Giants neared the end of a 14-2 season, the prelude to a Super Bowl victory over the Broncos. The Giants' defense did not allow a touchdown in two NFC playoff victories.
AP/WWP

"I came from a winning tradition in college, and the losing started to eat away at me," Carson said. "It was frustrating to play professional football and the team sucked."

Carson quit the Giants after a 35-3 loss to the Eagles in the third game of the1980 season. He asked to be traded after a 3-12-1 season in 1983. He left training camp in '84. But the Giants weren't about to lose a player who'd wind up with nine Pro Bowl berths.

"One year coming back from the Pro Bowl, I stopped in Los Angeles and got a California Angels cap," Carson recalled. "I thought if I wore the cap long enough, it would send a subliminal message to trade me somewhere on the West Coast. Once George Young took over, he said he was not going to trade me."

Accorsi was Young's assistant before replacing him in 1998. He saw Carson play with almost no supporting cast and with a powerful one. He saw Carson exasperated by losing, then become a locker room leader who showed teammates how to win.

"He was a great tackle-to-tackle inside linebacker with great leadership and probably suffered a little bit being in the shadows of Lawrence Taylor," Accorsi said. "When people say that, I say, 'Yeah, but he played on great teams because of Taylor.'"

Carson implies he and other Giants defenders were overshadowed more than they should have been by Taylor, a Hall of Fame outside linebacker. Carson had already played five seasons and made two Pro Bowls before Taylor arrived in 1981 and became one of the league's great pass rushers.

"I think I helped Lawrence become the player he was," Carson said. "Lawrence was a great player outright, but he learned a lot from me and the other guys who were there. He learned about our work ethic, he learned about playing as a team…about knowing the big picture as opposed to just what was going on in his little world.

"Lawrence could not have done the things he was able to do had it not been for the people around him: George Martin setting him up, working games with him; Leonard Marshall working games with him, allowing Lawrence to be one on one with an offensive player; Jim Burt solidifying the middle, making the running back bounce outside to Lawrence. We all had a responsibility. Lawrence was able to do much of what he did because we did our job.

"I had my own reputation before Lawrence got there. Lawrence was a Ferrari, whereas I was a hard hat vehicle. You weren't going to get anything spectacular out of me, but I wasn't going to break down, I was going to be reliable. My role was as a run defender, being solid…keeping things together…maintaining that level head…reminding guys what was taking place.

"Plus, I was the captain. I had to make sure to keep things in order. Lawrence was more of a fiery kind of guy. I was more cerebral and had to think about things going wrong and not get too emotional."

Carson and Taylor had a public spat the winter before Taylor's induction into the Hall of Fame in 1999. Carson, however, surprised Taylor at the induction ceremony by attending, which Taylor called "the classiest thing I've ever seen in my life."

Carson should've been accustomed to being compared with famous linebackers by then. He was scouted by Marty Schottenheimer, then the Giants' linebackers coach, who told Carson his size and speed could enable him to become as good as Willie Lanier, the Chiefs' Hall of Fame middle linebacker. Then, Carson was assigned No. 53, he recalled, because Giants coach Bill Arnsparger wanted him to emulate Bob Matheson, whose number designated the Miami's famous "53 defense." Matheson was the fourth linebacker in the 3-4 alignment used by Arnsparger as the Dolphins' coordinator.

"He wanted somebody who could play the rush but also defend against the pass," Carson said. "Bob Matheson was that kind of player in the 53 defense. They gave me 53 in hopes I could be the same kind of player."

Carson, however, became best known as a punishing run stopper, though he was versatile enough to catch a 13-yard touchdown pass on a fake field goal attempt against the

Eagles. He played defensive end at South Carolina State, and Schottenheimer lobbied for the Giants to draft him in the fourth round.

"He had no training as a linebacker, but he had the instincts," Schottenheimer recalled. "We wound up standing him up and after four or five games he had a chance to exceed the learning curve because of his instincts."

Carson became the starting middle linebacker midway through the 1976 season and was named to the NFL All-Rookie team. During 1979, his first Pro Bowl season, the Giants were on the verge of a loss in Kansas City when Carson scooped up a fumble and scored for a stunning 21-17 victory. He recovered 17 fumbles during his career.

Carson went into broadcasting after retirement, but sensed he might have a neurological problem. He was diagnosed with postconcussion syndrome in 1990.

"I felt somewhat off," he recalled. "When I was on TV, I'd lose my train of thought on the air. I had sensitivity to light and loud noises. I took a physical and said I'd been having headaches occasionally. I had two days of tests and the results came back as mild post-concussion syndrome. I asked, 'Is this something that's going to kill me?'"

Carson was shocked to read that a similar condition contributed to the death of Hall of Fame center Mike Webster in 2002. Partly because of the deaths of Webster and Minnesota Vikings lineman Korey Stringer, Carson planned to write a book contending, in part, that an NFL player's excessive pride can become self-destructive.

Carson doesn't much care if this viewpoint is accepted. He's become accustomed to standing out there by himself.

Losing weighed heavily upon Harry Carson during the New York Giants' lean years. But he picked up the Giants, and loose balls, when he could. The 1979 Giants seemed assured of yet another loss before Carson scooped up this fumble late in a game at Kansas City and scored to pull off an improbable 21-17 victory. KANSAS COLLECTION, U. of KANSAS

GEORGE CONNOR

T he most famous tackle of George Connor's career was, according to the victim, an accident. An extremely painful one.

Veryl Switzer of the Green Bay Packers was returning a kickoff against the Bears at Wrigley Field on November 6, 1955, when Connor hit him so hard that he knocked off Switzer's helmet and forced a fumble that linebacker Bill George recovered for a touchdown.

"After five minutes, there was a roar from the crowd," Connor once said.

"I asked [quarterback] Johnny Lujack what happened and he said, 'Switzer just got up.'"

Switzer suffered a torn sternum, the result of a hit, he said, that was delivered because teammates forming his wedge ducked out the way when they saw all 240 pounds of Connor, head down, hurtling at them. Switzer said game film of the Bears' 52-21 victory clearly showed what happened.

"He didn't do it on purpose, it was a blind hit," he recalled from his home in Manhattan, Kansas "I saw him coming and they got out of the way to stop from getting hit themselves. I ran right into him and didn't know what was happening, and neither did he.

"He was aiming his head like a spear and when they got out of the way, he put his helmet right into my sternum and tore it loose. When he made contact, it was like an explosion. There was a lot of internal bleeding. But I wound up going back in five or 10 minutes later.

"They scored again and kicked off. My players wanted to bring the ball up the middle again, and I shook it off and said we should go left. I didn't take the ball that time, but I went looking for George Connor. Nothing happened. I brushed up against him and he brushed up against me and that was it because the play was on the other side of the field."

That season was Connor's last, and one of his best, with the Bears, though he didn't make the Pro Bowl. Perhaps that was because there was no room left for him after seven teammates, including George, made the Western Conference team. Connor had played in the first four Pro Bowls, starting in January 1951 and, like Hall of Fame pitcher Carl Hubbell, is best remembered by many for his performance in an All-Star game.

That was the 1952 Pro Bowl, between the American Conference, coached by Cleveland's Paul Brown, and the National Conference. The National Conference won 30-13 and yielded just 15 total yards, thanks partly to a fourth-quarter possession dominated by Connor. On first down, he threw Dub Jones for a loss. On second down, he stopped Eddie Price on an end run. On third down, he sacked Otto Graham for a 10-yard loss and on fourth down dropped into coverage and batted a pass.

Connor also played offensive and defensive tackle for the Bears but left a legacy as the NFL's first big and mobile linebacker. He was playing tackle in 1949 when the Bears were preparing for the Philadelphia Eagles, who were running over opponents with fullback Joe Muha and two guards leading halfback Steve Van Buren on sweeps.

Bears defensive assistant Hunk Anderson suggested to coach George Halas that they move Connor to linebacker, where his speed and aggressiveness could stop the sweep. Thanks to the switch, the Bears gave the Eagles their only loss of the season on their way to a second straight NFL championship. Connor stayed at linebacker and set a new standard for size and athleticism at the position.

No wonder he got along so well with Halas, who also owned the team and was notoriously tough and crusty. Connor chipped a tooth his rookie season while playing without a facemask and told Halas he wanted the team to pay for his dental work.

24

CHICAGO BEARS
Years: 1948-55
Height: 6'3" Weight: 240
Number: 81
Hall of Fame: 1975
Born: January 21, 1925
Died: March 31, 2003

George Connor was the first of the big, mobile outside linbackers. When he joined the Bears in 1948, he had a 48-inch chest and a 37-inch waist and was so muscular that sports writer Grantland Rice called Connor "the closest thing to a Greek god since Apollo."

AP/WWP

Connor gave this account of his request to Cooper Rollow of the *Chicago Tribune*:

"He reached into a file and pulled out an envelope. He always wrote notes on envelopes, you know, like Abraham Lincoln. He looked at it and said, 'Well now, George, let's see how you chipped that tooth. It says here it was third down and we were playing the Steelers. It says here the runner [Joe Geri] made the first down right through you. And you want to get your tooth fixed?'

"I said, 'Yes, sir, Coach.' I went out and got them all fixed and he paid for them."

Connor, who had a huge chest and a tapered physique, was described by sports writer Grantland Rice as "the closest thing to a Greek god since Apollo." He'd come a long way since he came into the world prematurely as a three-pound baby. His parents gave him constant care and plenty of boiled cabbage juice.

Connor had grown to only five feet four and 135 when he began playing high school football in Chicago, but filled out by his senior year. He began his college career at Holy

"He was **aiming** his head like a **spear** and when they got out of the way, he put his helmet right into my sternum and tore it **loose**. When he made contact, it was like an **explosion**."

—Veryl Switzer

Cross in 1943 but was sent to Notre Dame by the navy for its college training program. Connor became an All-America player for the Irish in 1946 and '47, and in '46 became the first winner of the Outland Trophy, awarded annually to the nation's best college lineman.

Connor's career was shortened by a knee injury in 1954, and though he bounced back in '55, he felt as if his skills were declining. He was only 31 when he retired in the summer of '56.

"After a few days in camp, I realized I couldn't do the job any more," he said. "I was determined I would never be content just to hang on. I wanted to leave while the cheers were still ringing."

hat should have been the sweetest stretch of Junior Seau's career in San Diego was played in pain.

The Chargers were rolling towards an AFC West title in 1994 when Seau suffered a pinched nerve in his neck during a November loss at New England. For the rest of the season, contact often caused him searing pain and numbness in his left arm. Seau was in such obvious pain during a December loss to San Francisco that 49ers tackle Harris Barton told him to save himself for the playoffs. Seau had too much pride to accept that advice, but couldn't ignore the pain.

"To know every day, going to work, if someone hit that shoulder it could go numb and you would be worthless was an obstacle that I had to overcome mentally and physically," Seau told Jim Trotter in the book; *Junior Seau: Overcoming the Odds.*

"To know that there was a player that you were facing that you had beaten so many times, and come to find out now you're an average player—that is something I've always been afraid of, being average. There were plays I could see happening before they happened and there was nothing I could do about it.

"[Opponents] were talking about me, knowing that I'm hurt and knowing that I'm not all there, and it was tough. You picture them talking about you while you're down and mentally jot down names for the next time we come back around. I definitely did that. I'm not naming names, but there was a time where they took advantage of it. I still remember them today."

The Chargers ended their 1994 regular season with a 37-34 home win over the Pittsburgh Steelers and faced a rematch three weeks later at Pittsburgh in the AFC championship game.

The Chargers were underdogs and many, especially some Steelers, attributed their December loss to coach Bill Cowher resting his regulars because they'd clinched home-field advantage in the AFC playoffs. Some Steelers had a party the night before the title game, and several mimicked the 1985 Bears by recording a Super Bowl rap video. Defensive tackle Ray Seals claimed the Chargers wouldn't score.

This was all the ammunition Chargers coach Bobby Ross needed to send his players out with fire in their eyes. Seau and his teammates acknowledged after their 17-13 upset win that they had felt belittled. Seau made 16 tackles and set the tone on the Steelers' first play by throwing running back Barry Foster for a loss.

Seau totaled 11 tackles and a sack in the Super Bowl, but the Chargers were trounced by the 49ers, 49-26. A season later, Seau appeared in his last Chargers playoff game, a loss to the Indianapolis Colts. Still hunting for a Super Bowl ring, he forced a trade to the Miami Dolphins on April 16, 2003. The Chargers received a 2004 draft choice.

"This is a definite move that I wanted to take part in due to the fact that the opportunity of winning a Super Bowl ring is here in Miami," Seau said.

During his 13 years in San Diego, Seau earned 12 Pro Bowl berths and became the franchise's centerpiece. In addition to routinely leading the team in tackles, he totaled 47 sacks and 15 interceptions. He even caught two passes when used as an H-back in short-yardage and goal-line situations in 1999.

"He did everything well," said Marty Schottenheimer, who coached Seau for one year in San Diego and coached against him for nine years in Kansas City. "He could blitz, he could run and tackle. He was very disruptive and a good pass defender. When you look at the era Junior falls into, he'd certainly be one of the best."

The Dolphins were a consistent winner during Dave Wannstedt's first three seasons but had just one playoff win and were hoping Seau, at age 34, could bring enough talent and leadership to push

25

SAN DIEGO CHARGERS and MIAMI DOLPHINS
Years: 1990-
Height: 6'3" Weight: 255
Number: 55
Born: January 19, 1969

The Chargers were off to a fast start in 2002, and Junior Seau celebrates before the hometown fans after making one of his seven tackles in a 24-3 victory over the Houston Texans. Seau also had a sack and an interception that set up a touchdown.
AP/WWP

Junior Seau is not about to let a couple of Raiders block his path to quarterback Rich Gannon late in the 2001 season. Gannon looked before Seau could leap on him, however, and escaped for a first down in the Raiders' 13-6 victory.
AP/WWP

them over the top. Wannstedt said he welcomed the chance to acquire a player with such "passion" for football.

"Junior is not going to come over and be a leader and take over the Miami Dolphins," Seau insisted. "Junior is going to play alongside the leaders that you have here. I just have to come in and be the fluff. I'm the glitter, I'm the fanfare."

Seau reminded everyone how long he'd been around when he recalled signing a poster for Zach Thomas when the Dolphin middle linebacker was still in school. Seau was expected to play next to Thomas, on the weak side.

"He is definitely going to bring enthusiasm to our team and it can take us to another level," Thomas said. "I know with the way we have been playing on the road, we needed just a little more energy and hopefully he will bring that and turn us into a great team.

"He is not a guy that will sit there and look back at what he has done. He is one of the hardest workers in the league."

If Seau's reputation had a downside in San Diego, it was his tendency to free lance.

"Junior would be phenomenal if he paid attention to defenses," said Hall of Fame quarterback Len Dawson, who as a radio analyst for Kansas City Chiefs' games has seen plenty of Seau. "He looks like he improvises a lot. Sometimes he blitzes and maybe he wasn't supposed to. I've talked to people in San Diego and they said he doesn't go by what was called sometimes.

"But if you're talking about talent, tenacity and competitiveness, my God, he's tremendous."

As Seau moved to Miami, he knew many would wonder if he could still perform at a Pro Bowl level and how he'd physically hold up after 200 regular-season games.

"Funny thing about football, you have to prove yourself every day," he said. "Whether or not they're praising you, saying you lost a step, it doesn't matter. Every day that you come to work, you're going to be judged."

Nor did Seau seem concerned with how he might fit the Dolphins' defensive scheme. "You just give me a helmet," he said. "I've seen it all."

"...if you're talking about **talent, tenacity** and **competitiveness**, my God, he's **tremendous**."

—Len Dawson

THE TOP TRIOS

Any team considers itself fortunate to have even one top-flight linebacker. On rare occasions, three star linebackers arrive on one defense, and when they do, a Super Bowl title can't be far behind.

There are just a handful of elite trios and two in particular stand out—the Pittsburgh Steelers' unit of Jack Ham, Jack Lambert and Andy Russell, and the Kansas City Chiefs' unit of Bobby Bell, Willie Lanier and Jim Lynch. Both trios include two Hall of Famers and a less heralded player who excelled nonetheless.

A posed photo hardly does justice to the fast and fluid motion of Kansas City outside linebacker Bobby Bell. Teammates routinely called him the best all-around athlete they ever saw, and he is arguably the best player in the history of the Chiefs' franchise.
© Bettmann/CORBIS

Jim Lynch (51) was the unsung linebacker of an extraordinary trio. Though he didn't make the Hall of Fame, as did Bobby Bell and Willie Lanier, Lynch got his uniform just as dirty as either of them did. Lynch comes from his right-side spot to hold Minnesota fullback Bill Brown to a three-yard gain on the Vikings' opening possession in Super Bowl IV.
© Bettmann/CORBIS

Ham and Bell are among the most versatile outside linebackers of all time, and the comparisons between the Steeler and Chief trios don't stop there.

"Andy Russell reminds me of Jim Lynch; each was very knowledgeable about the game and did his homework," Bell recalled. "Lambert was like Lanier—a head hunter."

Russell is quick to point out that Lambert was much more than a head hunter, and Lynch makes the same case for Lanier.

Kansas City linebacker Willie Lanier brings down Buffalo's O.J. Simpson but couldn't stop him from gaining 157 yards on 39 carries in the Bills' 23-14 Monday night victory in 1973. Simpson passed the 1,000-yard mark that night on his way to the first 2,000-yard rushing season in NFL history.
© Bettmann/CORBIS

"Willie Lanier was punishing and extremely physical, but he was quick and could cover," Lynch said. "He was very analytical about things; it almost belies how physical he was. He was not a knock-somebody's-head-off-and-that-makes-me-happy player, though he did do that."

Lynch and Russell, who both played the weak side, were more than third wheels.

"To me, Lynch is an underrated player," Russell said. "I watched him on film and thought he was superb. The poor guy was stacked up next to a guy who was so good. I had the same situation. I agree they were a terrific group."

Which unit was better? The Steeler group was more accomplished—each player earned at least seven Pro Bowl berths.

"We were three guys who made very few mistakes and wanted to be the best," Lambert said.

But the Steeler's trio lasted just three seasons, until Russell retired after 1976. The Chiefs' trio played together seven seasons, 1968-74. The Steeler's unit had the more successful tour. The Chiefs' unit was the longer-playing band.

Russell can tell you off the top of his head that his trio, with a combined 24 Pro Bowl berths, had six more than the Chiefs' trio. The Bears' trio of Mike Singletary, Wilber Marshall and Otis Wilson, intact from 1985-87, combined for 14 Pro Bowl berths. The Packers' Ray Nitschke, Dave Robinson and Lee Roy Caffey, together from 1964-69, combined for just five Pro Bowl berths.

"Football's all about **gaining** square footage. You can get yourself in a certain **position** and it doesn't matter if they **knock** you down. You've **screwed up** the play."

—Andy Russell

"It's difficult to compare trios, because there aren't stats you can really use," said Russell, a seven-time Pro Bowl pick. "The only thing I've seen that's compelling is cumulative Pro Bowls, and that put us at the top by a fairly good margin."

But Nitschke, an all-time great, made just one Pro Bowl, and the Packers' group claims the most championships—an NFL title in 1965 and victories in the first two Super Bowls. The Steeler's trio helped win two Super Bowls, and Ham and Lambert were around for two more. The Chiefs' and Bears' trios each helped win one Super Bowl.

Russell had been a star in the lean years before Chuck Noll began rebuilding the Steelers in 1969. Noll quickly shook up the Steelers, Russell included.

"I used to think being a good linebacker was a result of how many big plays you made," recalled Russell. "I made my first Pro Bowl in the '68 season and I was quite proud of that. Noll was hired in '69 and he called me in. I thought he was calling me in to congratulate me.

Steelers linebackers Andy Russell, Jack Ham and Jack Lambert made a total of 24 Pro Bowls, and Russell and Ham were among six Steelers to represent the AFC in the wake of their Super Bowl win in January 1975. That's Russell in the second row, with running back Franco Harris to the left and defensive end L.C. Greenwood, Ham and kicker Roy Gerela to the right. Defensive tackle Joe Greene lounges in front.
© Bettmann/CORBIS

"Instead, he said, 'Russell, I don't like the way you play. You're far too aggressive, you're trying to make big plays and I don't want that. I don't want any heroes. I want consistent players who do their jobs. I don't want you to cherry-pick and make big plays on somebody else's responsibilities.'

"As an athlete, you want to make big plays. I was playing on losing teams and I wanted to make things happen. When we got really good in the '70s, I didn't want to make any

"We were three guys who made very few mistakes and wanted to be the best."

—Jack Lambert

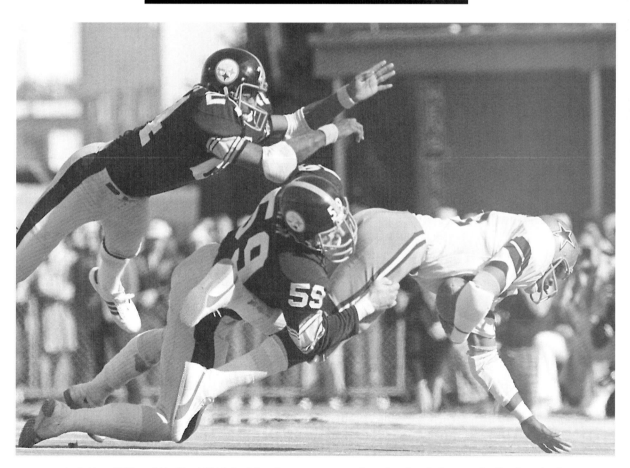

Jack Ham (59) and his Steel Curtain defensive mates came down hard and often on the Cowboys in the Steelers' 21-17 victory in Super Bowl X. Ham drags down Dallas running back Doug Dennison, who's trying to run after the catch, as defensive back J.T. Thomas dives in to help.
AP/WWP

mistakes. I'd do things by the numbers. Then your game's not as visible to the fan, but other teams are saying, 'Russell's always where we don't want him.'

"Football's all about gaining square footage. You can get yourself in a certain position and it doesn't matter if they knock you down. You've screwed up the play."

Football's also about knowing what your teammates are doing, and the great linebacking trios developed special chemistry.

"We knew each other like the backs of our hands," Bell recalled. "We knew where we'd get help from and we capitalized on each other."

If you see any footage of the Chiefs' trio late in their careers, you might notice strings dangling from their pants. That tradition began one summer when the Chiefs' linebackers had more of training camp in Liberty, Missouri than they could stand.

The calendar was running out on Jack Lambert's Hall of Fame career as he brought down Minnesota running back Tony Galbreath in a 17-14 Steeler loss to the Vikings late in 1983. Lambert retired a year later after playing for nine playoff teams, including four Super Bowl champions, and anchoring the Steel Curtain Defense for 11 seasons.
AP/WWP

"It was a pretty boring existence and was the start of some goofy things," Lynch recalled. "Lanier started wearing a shoestring on his belt and next Bell and I started wearing a string. We called it the Sacred Order of the Secret String. We did it until the end."

Even then, the Chiefs' linebackers kept their personal ties tight. They remain close today.

"It was based on human beings who shared some important times in their lives but also came to know each other as young men with growing families and growing respect of their entire lives," Lanier said. "Football was what created the knowledge of each other. Human beings enjoying the fullness of each other enables us to have the dialogue we do today."

LINEBACKERS, CHICAGO STYLE

When Hall of Fame coach Marv Levy was growing up in Chicago, he played for the Junior Bears, a 14-and-under team that played abbreviated games during halftime of Bears games at Wrigley Field.

"I think I led the league in rushing with nine yards," Levy recalled, laughing. "The Bears would send different guys to our practice each day for about 15 minutes. 'Bulldog' Turner came over to visit, gave me a few hints and he was gone."

Clyde "Bulldog" Turner was just coming into the NFL then, and though he's best remembered as a center, he was a two-way player and started a grand tradition of Chicago linebackers. Of the 25 linebackers ranked in this book as the best of all time, five were Bears, and all are in the Pro Football Hall of Fame.

Turner (1940-52) was succeeded in Chicago by George Connor (1948-55), Bill George (1952-65), Dick Butkus (1965-73) and Mike Singletary (1981-92). Over 53 seasons, the Bears lacked a Hall of Fame linebacker only from 1974-80.

"The 'Monsters of the Midway' were all two-way players," recalled Levy, who coached the Buffalo Bills to four straight Super Bowls. "First, I remember Red Grange and Bronko Nagurski. I was also aware, 'The Bears, boy do they have linebackers!'

Middle linebacker Brian Urlacher made the Pro Bowl in each of his first three seasons and is widely considered a worthy successor to the Chicago Bears' five Hall of Fame linebackers. Urlacher forces Denver Broncos quarterback Brian Griese to cough up the ball in a 2002 preseason game.
AP/WWP

"Connor was a magnificent athlete. He grew up in my neighborhood, the south shore of Chicago. He could run and was one of the great kick coverers."

While Levy was head coach at New Mexico in 1958-59 and California from 1960-63, he didn't have to be a Chicago native to be aware of Butkus.

"I was one of 10,000 coaches who came through Chicago Vocational High School and tried to recruit him," Levy recalled.

"He had this unbelievable thirst to play. He was dominating. You see a sport and say, 'These guys are at the very top of the business.' With that said, one person stands out leaps and bounds beyond that.

"Cornelius Bennett was as good an athlete as I ever coached. The first time [Bills general manager] Bill Polian saw Cornelius, he said, 'Why don't they all do it that way?' That's also my reaction with Butkus."

Butkus replaced George, who's credited with becoming, in 1954, the first true middle linebacker in pro football. After Butkus retired, the Bears had to wait eight years for Singletary. He became the leader of the "46 defense," which led the Bears to a 46-10 victory over the New England Patriots in the Super Bowl of January 1986. The Bears tied a Super Bowl record with seven sacks and set a record by yielding minus-seven yards rushing.

"It felt good to be part of it, and I was very excited to go to a place where playing linebacker was special," Singletary said.

Butkus credits the Bears' linebacking tradition chiefly to George Halas, their founder and longtime coach. Under Halas, both Connor and George were switched from linemen to linebackers.

"I think they had a jump with the old man, he'd been in the game so long," Butkus said. "He was an innovator of a lot of defenses. Other people started catching up because he didn't change. But we had [great] linebackers and running backs."

Ed O'Bradovich, a Bears defensive end from 1962-71, suggested some of their outside linebackers deserve mention, too.

"Joe Fortunato [a five-time Pro Bowler] and Larry Morris, they were no slouches," O'Bradovich said, referring to teammates of George and, briefly, Butkus. "Wilber Marshall [of the "46" defense] was almost in a class by himself as an outside linebacker, the way he'd get from point A to point B. The Bears have always had great linebackers, and now we've got Urlacher. I don't know where they get that water. It must be out of the same darn well."

Brian Urlacher, the Bears' first-round choice in 2000, made the Pro Bowl as a middle linebacker in each of his first three seasons. He's big enough, six feet four and 254, to play the middle, yet quick enough to have also played safety at New Mexico.

"This guy is no nonsense, he's there to take people down," O'Bradovich said. "He's very much a private person—as Bill was, as Dick was. They were all very knowledgeable and serious people on the field."

Butkus, too, considers Urlacher a worthy torch bearer for Bears' linebackers. But he said he'd like to see Urlacher separate opponents from the ball more often.

"He's great and everything else," Butkus said. "But he'd be numero uno in my mind if he'd start punishing people."

One who didn't make the cut...

There's not enough room in this book to list all the outstanding linebackers who've played pro football, but this book would not be complete without mentioning an extraordinary linebacker with a most unusual story.

THOMAS "HOLLYWOOD" HENDERSON

Thomas Henderson can't believe he's not one of this book's top 25.

"All the people I played with said I was the greatest," Henderson said from his home in Austin, Texas. "Lawrence Taylor told me he picked number 56 because he thought I was the best linebacker in the game. Not only did I talk, but I'd knock your head off. I also had speed and skill.

"When they started using the nickel package, they'd put me in the game to cover the best receiver out of the backfield. I covered, man to man, O.J. Simpson, Chuck Foreman, Terry Metcalf, Walter Payton and Tony Galbreath—all the best running backs of the '70s, including [teammates] Tony Dorsett and Preston Pearson. And no one could beat me.

"I set the standard for the new linebacker with speed. I don't think there's been a player like that since myself. There are no more Hendersons in the league now."

Henderson would, undoubtedly, be ranked among the best linebackers ever had his career not flamed out so early. Every profession has its shooting stars, and in pro football, none was brighter than Henderson. He still had a career most players can only dream about—three Super Bowls and a Pro Bowl berth as a Dallas Cowboy from 1975-79—but who knows how much more he might have achieved had he avoided drug and alcohol addiction?

"Hollywood Henderson had Bobby Bell's skills," recalled Gil Brandt, the director of player personnel when the Cowboys made Henderson a first-round pick out of Langston, Oklahoma College in 1975. "He was a great, great player. He was athletic, tremendously fast. He would've been one of the best of all time had he not gone astray. Unfortunately, he went astray."

Henderson is bugged that anyone would hold his career's brevity against his legacy. "I was not a flash in the pan," he said. "Seven years is a pretty good career. I won the Super Bowl. I was voted by my peers to the Pro Bowl. So I don't know how much longer I have to play."

The Cowboys had the second and 18th picks in 1975 and used their first pick for defensive tackle Randy White from Maryland. Henderson held a press conference to announce: "I haven't had White's publicity because I played at a small college, but you can write this down: I'm just as good a player as he is and maybe better."

Henderson as a rookie returned a kickoff 97 yards for a touchdown. He and White were among the "Dirty Dozen," an exceptional rookie crop that gave the 1975 Cowboys the depth and energy to reach the Super Bowl. After becoming a starter at strong-side linebacker in 1977, Henderson boasted, "I have decided I am the best linebacker ever to play pro football. Dick Butkus was just a lineman standing up."

Henderson said he flapped his gums so much because that was the quickest way for a small college player to get noticed. Teammates nicknamed him, "Hollywood" because of his fast lifestyle, though few realized how fast it really was. Henderson's trash talking could

Thomas "Hollywood" Henderson, shown here at a farewell press conference, said he "always wanted to be remembered as a Cowboy" and announced his retirement after facing his release late in the 1979 season. Henderson kept playing until 1981, but a broken neck ended his career and drug addiction sent his life spinning out of control.
AP/WWP

be obnoxious but also entertaining. Before the Cowboys' 35-31 loss to the Steelers in the January 1979 Super Bowl, Henderson made fun of Pittsburgh's folksy quarterback when he said: "Terry Bradshaw couldn't spell 'cat' if you spotted him the 'c' and the 'a.'"

He also made a remark after his second Super Bowl, against the Denver Broncos in Jan., 1978 that was unfortunately prophetic. "You know, they say the average playing time for a pro football player is four and a half years," he said. "That means I only got a year and a half left, so I figure I got to make the most of it."

Sure enough, Henderson didn't make it through five years as a Cowboy. He'd inhaled cocaine on the sideline during his last Super Bowl, he later admitted, and a career killing explosion wasn't long in coming. Henderson threw a tantrum in November 1979 and was released by the Cowboys. He was picked up in 1980 by the San Francisco 49ers and Houston Oilers, but wasn't productive.

Henderson finally admitted his addiction and asked the NFL to put him in rehabilitation. The Miami Dolphins didn't know he'd relapsed when they signed him in 1981, and his career ended when he suffered a broken neck in the last exhibition game.

The news about Henderson kept getting worse. He was arrested in 1983 for having sex with two minors and also was charged with bribery when he tried to pay them to drop the charges. He was sentenced to four years, eight months in prison and served half his term.

Henderson kicked his drug habit while in prison and returned to his hometown, Austin, Texas. He established Thomas Henderson Films and a charity, the East Side Youth Services & Street Outreach. He speaks about drug prevention, addiction and sobriety on his national tours and also in films for the prison community. Henderson's donations, fundraising and bare hands built a football stadium and track, completed in 1999, on the grounds of his long-closed high school in East Austin.

While in prison, Henderson began his autobiography, *Out of Control*, with Peter Knobler. While promoting the book in 1987, he told *The Houston Post* he at times considered suicide and added: "There's no reason why I'm alive. There is no reason that Larry Bethea, Don Rogers or Lenny Bias should have perished due to cocaine use. I probably did 10 times, probably 20 times, the dope they did. I just think I'm here for a reason.

"I'm happier now than I have ever been in my entire life. I have regrets, I wasted myself. But I'm more successful now with myself. I'm not a people pleaser anymore. I'm not a management pleaser anymore. I'm sober. I'm in the Sober Bowl. I've been in three Super Bowls, but the Sober Bowl is more important."

The welcome attention Henderson once attracted returned in March, 2001. He hit a Texas Lottery jackpot, which brought him almost $14.5 million. Henderson had been avidly buying lottery tickets once the jackpots accelerated and estimated he'd spent $20,000 on tickets during the five years before his big hit.

"When I won the lottery, I, of all people, wasn't surprised by the gift because there'd been tens of thousands of hours with my hands in the dirt and a shovel in my hand and planting grass and picking up trash," Henderson said, referring to his field of dreams.

"When that happened, everybody in my community said, 'You deserved that.' Life is a strange machine."

In addition to being a Pro Bowl linebacker, Thomas "Hollywood" Henderson excelled on Dallas's special teams. He shakes his fist in celebration after helping tackle Pittsburgh Steeler kick returner Larry Anderson during the Cowboys' 35-31 loss during Super Bowl XIII.
AP/WWP

THE MEAT EATERS

CERATOSAURS

The earliest carnivorous dinosaurs evolved in the Late Triassic, about 220 million years ago. Contrary to popular belief, few of these meat eaters were giants, but what they lacked in size they made up for in speed and agility. Sprinting on their back legs and balancing with their long tails, lightweight species called ceratosaurs could snap at animals on the ground or even leap after insects in the air. Many had beaklike jaws armed with small but needlelike teeth, and slender hands with sharp claws—ideal implements for gripping and holding down struggling prey.

△ Procompsognathus *(above left and center) and* Compsognathus *(above right) lived over 50 million years apart, but they had many features in common. Among these were a slim body, a long, stiff tail, and a slender head on a flexible neck. Both dinosaurs would have had good eyesight, essential for catching fast-moving prey.*

PROCOMPSOGNATHUS
One of the oldest theropods discovered so far—and one of the earliest dinosaurs—*Procompsognathus* is known from a single skeleton, which is far from complete. However, judging from the remains of its badly crushed skull, it seems to have had a long, pointed snout and sharp teeth. It probably lived on a diet of insects and small lizards, which it caught either in its jaws or with its large, five-fingered, clawed hands.

MAXIMUM LENGTH	4 ft. (1.2m)
TIME	Late Triassic
FOSSIL FINDS	Europe (Germany)

COMPSOGNATHUS
Lightly built and highly agile, *Compsognathus* probably weighed up to 6.6 lb. (3kg), about as much as a large chicken. Its name means "elegant jaw"—a flattering description of a narrow mouth that was packed with small but sharp teeth. Like its relatives, it was birdlike in appearance, with long back legs, three-toed feet, and hollow bones. Fossilized stomach remains show that it ate lizards, and it also may have been cannibalistic.

MAXIMUM LENGTH	4.6 ft. (1.4m)
TIME	Late Jurassic
FOSSIL FINDS	Europe (Germany, France)

SALTOPUS
Saltopus is one of the smallest dinosaurs known, weighing about 2.2 lb. (1kg)—the same as a large domestic cat. Fossil evidence is scant, making an accurate reconstruction impossible, but remains show that this tiny hunter had five-fingered hands—a primitive feature that changed as theropods evolved. Some scientists have suggested that *Saltopus* may have hopped like some rodents and marsupials do today, but this interesting idea cannot be proven. Given its small size, insects were probably an important part of its diet, although it may also have scavenged animals killed by larger dinosaurs.

MAXIMUM LENGTH	2.3 ft. (0.7m)
TIME	Late Triassic
FOSSIL FINDS	Europe (Scotland)

COELURUS
Another small predatory dinosaur of similar stature and behavior to *Compsognathus*, *Coelurus* lived in the swamps and forests of Jurassic North America. Unlike earlier theropods, it had only three fingers on each hand, each armed with a sharp, curved claw. Its head was relatively small—about the size of a human hand—with a narrow but blunt-ended snout. When fully grown, *Coelurus* probably weighed up to 44 lb. (20kg).

MAXIMUM LENGTH	6.6 ft. (2m)
TIME	Late Jurassic
FOSSIL FINDS	North America (Wyoming)

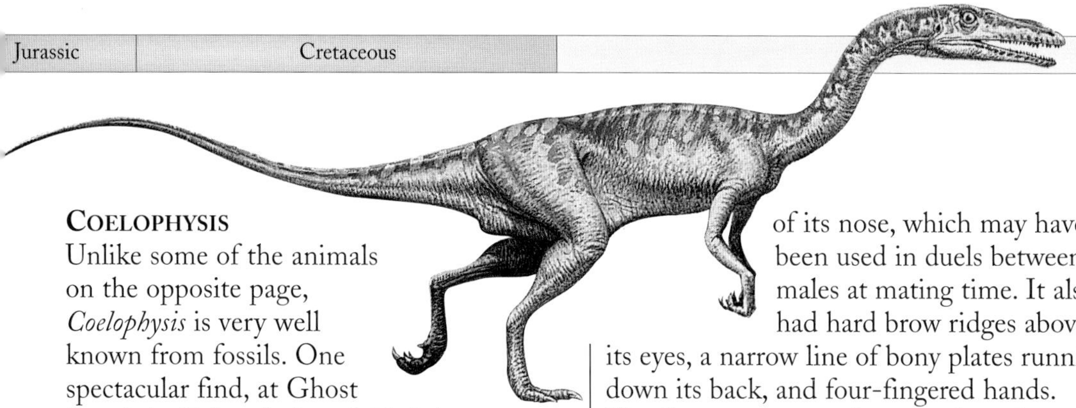

COELOPHYSIS

Unlike some of the animals on the opposite page, *Coelophysis* is very well known from fossils. One spectacular find, at Ghost Ranch in Colorado has yielded the remains of about 1,000 specimens, from juveniles to adults, making this one of the best-known Triassic dinosaurs. This mass grave strongly suggests that *Coelophysis* was sociable, although the discovery of fossilized bones inside larger specimens may well mean that they were not averse to eating each other's young. From this wealth of fossils two types—known as robust and gracile forms—have been identified. Paleontologists think that these are males and females, rather than members of two separate species.

MAXIMUM LENGTH 10 ft. (3m)

TIME Late Triassic

FOSSIL FINDS North America (Arizona, Colorado, New Mexico)

CERATOSAURUS

Weighing up to one ton, *Ceratosaurus* was a sizable hunter, although not as large as the true giants of the theropod world. Its most characteristic feature was a horn on the top of its nose, which may have been used in duels between males at mating time. It also had hard brow ridges above its eyes, a narrow line of bony plates running down its back, and four-fingered hands. The first nearly complete remains of *Ceratosaurus* were found alongside those of *Allosaurus* in a quarry in Colorado in 1883. Fossilized footprints discovered since then show that it may have hunted in packs. Unlike packs of smaller theropods, *Ceratosaurus* packs would have been able to attack and kill plant eaters weighing many tons.

MAXIMUM LENGTH 20 ft. (6m)

TIME Late Jurassic

FOSSIL FINDS North America (Colorado), Africa (Tanzania)

◁ Coelophysis *was a medium-sized predator, standing about as high as an adult man. When running quickly, it probably would have stabilized itself by lowering its neck and holding its tail almost horizontal. Its small, serrated teeth were designed mainly for dealing with prey smaller than itself.*

▽ Ceratosaurus *attacks a* Brachiosaurus. *On its own* Ceratosaurus *would have been a serious threat to large sauropods, but it would have been deadly if, as seems likely, it also hunted in packs.*

117

MOVING ON TWO LEGS

THE WORLD'S LARGEST DINOSAURS WALKED ON FOUR LEGS, BUT THE FASTEST AND MOST AGILE SPECIES—INCLUDING ALMOST ALL OF THE HUNTERS—WALKED OR RAN ON TWO.

Dinosaurs evolved from reptiles that walked and ran on all fours, but many of them moved on their back legs alone (pages 64–65). This way of moving brought three advantages: two-legged reptiles could often run faster, they could see farther, and because their front legs were not needed for moving, they became free to carry out other tasks instead. The disadvantage of this way of moving was that, at high speed, a single misplaced step could send a dinosaur crashing to the ground.

△ *Moving at full speed, tyrannosaurs held their tails high to balance the weight of their heads. When standing still, they kept their bodies upright.*

BIPEDAL DINOSAURS
Two groups of dinosaurs walked partly or wholly on two legs: the theropods (both light- and heavyweight hunters) and the plant-eating ornithopods (pages 91–112). Many of the ornithopods were facultative bipeds. This means that they walked on all fours most of the time, but could switch to two legs to get to food, to defend themselves, or to get away from danger. Their front and back legs differed in size, but their front legs were strong enough to support their body weight.

In theropods the two-legged lifestyle went much further. Most of these dinosaurs always stood on their back legs and were incapable of walking on all fours. Their front legs were much less powerful than their back legs, but they often had long fingers armed with sharp claws, which could be used for unearthing eggs, gripping food, or slashing at their prey.

Tyrannosaurs—the largest of these bipedal hunters—had back legs that could be twice the height of an adult human, but front legs that were not much longer than a human arm. These tiny front legs could have played no part in moving around and would not have been much use for feeding. Some experts think that they may have been used as props when lying down, or perhaps when mating, but they remain a mystery.

SPRINTERS AND PLODDERS
Moving on two legs made small hunters fast and very maneuverable. One of the speediest of them all, the bird mimic *Dromiceiomimus*, had very long bones in the lower part of its back legs—the ideal shape for running. It could reach a speed of over 40 mph (60km/h), fast enough to overtake most land animals today.

But not all two-legged dinosaurs were good long-distance runners. With its massive back legs and seven ton body, *Tyrannosaurus* was probably too heavy to keep up the chase for long, and when it was running, it would have found it almost impossible to twist and turn after its prey. Many paleontologists believe that it was more likely to have been a stand-and-wait predator, lurking among vegetation and bursting out of cover once its prey was within striking range.

△ *On the inside of each hind foot* Deinonychus *had a retractable toe armed with a giant, sickle-shaped claw. The claw swiveled downward when the animal was about to launch an attack.*

STAYING BALANCED

For animals that move on two legs, staying balanced is vital. This would have been true for large hunters like *Tyrannosaurus*, because once it was in motion, it developed an almost unstoppable momentum. If it tripped, it risked a dangerous accident, with only its tiny front legs to break its fall. For lightweight hunters, such as *Deinonychus*, falls were less critical.

The human body is vertical, so our center of gravity is above our legs—the right position for staying balanced. In theropods the head and trunk leaned forward in one direction and the tail in another. To keep their center of gravity above their back legs, they had to make sure that these two parts of the body were balanced. For the largest hunters having a huge head was a problem— it threatened to destabilize them and make them fall over. So they probably leaned forward only when they ran.

▷ *At about 13 ft. (4m) long,* Deinonychus *was a middleweight bipedal hunter, but one with well-developed front legs. Like other theropods, it used its tail partly as a counterbalance and partly as a stabilizer to absorb energy—like kangaroos do today.*

BACK TO ALL FOURS

Many paleontologists believe that sauropods—the largest planteaters of the dinosaur world—evolved from bipedal ancestors. But as they evolved and grew in size this two-legged lifestyle was soon abandoned. Some sauropods could probably stand on their hind legs, propped up by their tails, but with their huge and heavy digestive systems, it is highly unlikely that they could have taken a single step on their back legs alone.

STUDYING DINOSAUR TRACKS

BECAUSE DINOSAURS DIED OUT SO LONG AGO, WE HAVE VERY LITTLE IDEA OF HOW THEY BEHAVED. FOSSILIZED TRACKS ARE VALUABLE EVIDENCE IN THIS AREA OF RESEARCH.

Although fossilized dinosaur tracks have been found all over the world, they are rarer than fossilized bones. This is because footprints are preserved only when conditions are exactly right. The ground must be soft, but not so soft that the prints soon fill in, and the prints must be covered by something that protects them—such as sediment or sand—not long after they are made. Most dinosaur tracks belong to single animals, but in some places entire herds have left their imprint on the ground.

◁ Tracks at Lark Quarry, in Australia, show the world's largest fossilized stampede. About 150 small theropods and ornithopods seem to have been running for their lives from a large carnosaur. The tracks do not show if the predator managed to make a kill.

IDENTIFYING FOOTPRINTS

With living animals it is often easy to match footprints with the animals that made them. But with dinosaurs it is usually more difficult. From a print's shape experts can generally tell what type of dinosaur left it. For example, the prints left by sauropods and theropods look different because sauropods had rounded or oval feet, and theropods had birdlike feet, with long toes and large claws. However, deciding which kind of sauropod or theropod left a set of prints is much harder. To avoid guesswork, tracks are often given their own scientific names.

▽ Walking slowly in the heat of the midday sun, a small herd of Iguanodon make their way along a beach. Damp sand sometimes produced clear fossil prints, whereas sticky mud would blur the shape.

GAUGING SPEEDS

As well as showing where a dinosaur went, tracks can often give an idea of its speed. To calculate this, a track expert needs to know two measurements—the length of the dinosaur's leg and the length of its stride. These measurements show that ornithomimids—the fastest dinosaurs—could probably reach about 40 mph (60km/h), and because they were light, they would have been able to accelerate and stop quite quickly. The largest sauropods and carnosaurs were much slower and would have taken longer to build up speed. They probably had a maximum speed of about 20 mph (30km/h)—roughly twice as fast as a human can run. For giant sauropods, such as *Seismosaurus*, true running is likely to have been impossible, because it would have put immense strain on their legs. These animals probably broke into an accelerated walk if threatened, moving one foot at a time, with the other three in contact with the ground.

Like other animals, dinosaurs did not waste energy unnecessarily, so tracks that show running are rare. Lark Quarry, in Queensland, Australia, is one of the few sites where the track makers—a group of small theropods and ornithopods—seem to be moving at top speed. It is believed that the animals were escaping from a predator.

TRACKWAYS

Collections of footprints—called trackways—can reveal a lot about dinosaurs on the move. Some trackways contain prints formed by several animals in a herd, but occasionally trackways contain prints from more than one species. One of the most famous examples, at the Paluxy River in Texas, shows the three-toed footprints of a large predatory theropod apparently stalking its sauropod prey. Trackways also indicate social interactions, such as the large adult dinosaurs walking on the outside of a herd to protect the young in the middle.

Like today's animals, dinosaurs gathered at particular places to feed or to drink. Where this happened, the ground became trampled, leaving a confusing jumble of tracks. Track experts, or ichnologists, call this kind of trampling dinoturbation. Dinoturbation is common in rocks that have formed from ancient lake shores where dinosaurs left their footprints in the mud. In other places, called megatrack sites, dinosaurs have left telltale footprints across huge areas of ground. Some paleontologists think that these were migration routes—prehistoric dinosaur paths that may have been used for thousands of years.

FOSSIL EVIDENCE

This collection of footprints in Utah was left by several dinosaurs walking over the same patch of damp ground. Dinosaurs sometimes stepped in each other's prints, so track experts can often tell the order in which the tracks were made. This provides useful evidence about whether the dinosaurs were interacting with each other at the time. Utah is rich in fossilized tracks. Some prints, left by a hadrosaur, hold the world record at 4.4 ft. (1.35m) long.

△ *Closing in on a slow-moving sauropod, a theropod moves in for the attack. This scene—and events leading up to it—is recorded in tracks discovered in the bed of the Paluxy River in Texas. The predator left the typical three-toed footprints of a theropod; the sauropod's prints were rounded, with small claw marks visible at the front. Shortly after the attack the prints were covered by sediment. Millions of years later they were revealed as fossils.*

THE MEAT EATERS

▷ *With its long neck and slender body and back legs,* Dromiceiomimus *bears a startling resemblance to a present-day flightless bird. Birds evolved from close relatives of these animals (page 134).*

BIRD MIMICS

Bird mimics, or ornithomimids, were long-legged, slender-bodied dinosaurs that probably lived and hunted in small packs. They fed on smaller reptiles and insects as well as plants and eggs, and they behaved like today's large flightless birds, running up to 45 mph (70km/h) to escape danger. Bird mimics had beaklike jaws without teeth, and slender arms for picking up food. They were quick-thinking, and had large brains relative to their size.

▽ *Running for their lives, a herd of* Struthiomimus *quickly outpace a lumbering* Tyrannosaurus.

DROMICEIOMIMUS
Studies of *Dromiceiomimus* fossils show that this animal must have been one of the most intelligent dinosaurs of its time. Its large eye sockets make it likely that it hunted at night, and its relatively long lower leg bones show that it would have been exceptionally swift, perhaps reaching speeds of 40 mph (65km/h). Its jaws were weak, and it probably snapped up insects and other small items of food, perhaps digging them out with its three-fingered hands. Its wide pelvis could be a sign that it gave birth to live young or laid very large eggs.

MAXIMUM LENGTH	44.5 ft. (13.5m)
TIME	Late Cretaceous
FOSSIL FINDS	North America (Alberta)

STRUTHIOMIMUS
Struthiomimus means "ostrich mimic"—an appropriate name for a dinosaur with slender legs and large, birdlike eyes. It had long, gangly arms and well-developed claws on its fingers. It also had a remnant fourth toe on its hind feet. Its tail kept it balanced as it ran and as it swerved to avoid attack. *Struthiomimus* was probably carnivorous, but its lack of teeth would have restricted it to small prey. This dinosaur was originally classified as a form of *Ornithomimus*, and some experts think that as more fossils are found it may prove to be the same animal. All bird mimics look very similar—apart from the giant *Deinocheirus*—so classifying them has proven difficult.

MAXIMUM LENGTH	13 ft. (4m)
TIME	Late Cretaceous
FOSSIL FINDS	North America

BIRD MIMICS

ORNITHOMIMUS

Bird mimics were built for speed, and *Ornithomimus* was no exception to this rule. It had light, hollow bones and long, powerful, birdlike legs with clawed feet. With good eyesight and quick reactions, it was

◁ Ornithomimus *was a typically athletic member of the bird mimic family, running quickly whenever food beckoned or danger threatened. It would have run with its head held high, giving it a good view of its surroundings. Its long, stiff tail acted as a counterbalance.*

▽ *Running with its head up,* Gallimimus *was like a mobile lookout post with a far-reaching view of its surroundings. Its eyes were on the sides of its head, like those of ostriches and other flightless birds. This arrangement is not good for judging depth, but it is ideal for spotting possible danger from any direction.*

probably an efficient hunter and a successful scavenger. However, recent studies of this dinosaur's skull suggest that it—and perhaps other bird mimics—were cold-blooded, which means that they would have been able to run only in short bursts. *Ornithomimus* was initially identified from only feet and leg bones—the first complete skeleton was found 30 years later, in 1917.

MAXIMUM LENGTH 13 ft. (4m)

TIME Late Cretaceous

FOSSIL FINDS North America (Alberta, Colorado, Montana), Asia (Tibet)

ANSERIMIMUS

All that is known about *Anserimimus*— a name that means "goose mimic"—comes from one fossilized skeleton found in Mongolia. Even though this lacks part of its head, the species seems to have been a typical ornithomimid, although one with particularly strong, short arms and long-fingered claws. This suggests that *Anserimimus* may have relied on digging for finding food.

MAXIMUM LENGTH 10 ft. (3m)

TIME Late Cretaceous

FOSSIL FINDS Asia (Mongolia)

GALLIMIMUS

Despite its name, which means "chicken mimic," *Gallimimus* may have been the largest member of the ornithomimid family. It stood about twice as high as an adult man, but even so was relatively light for its size, allowing it to run at fast speeds. Its face and beak were elongated, and its hands were shovellike, indicating that it dug for food.

MAXIMUM LENGTH 20 ft. (6m)

TIME Late Cretaceous

FOSSIL FINDS Asia (Mongolia)

DEINOCHEIRUS

Known only from a pair of arms and some shoulder bones, *Deinocheirus* is one of the great mysteries of the dinosaur world. If it was an ornithomimid, it was certainly the giant of the family, because its arms were over 8 ft. (2.5m) in length. They were armed with claws over 10 in. (25cm) long, which could have made formidable weapons.

MAXIMUM LENGTH 33–66 ft. (10–20m)

TIME Late Cretaceous

FOSSIL FINDS Asia (Mongolia)

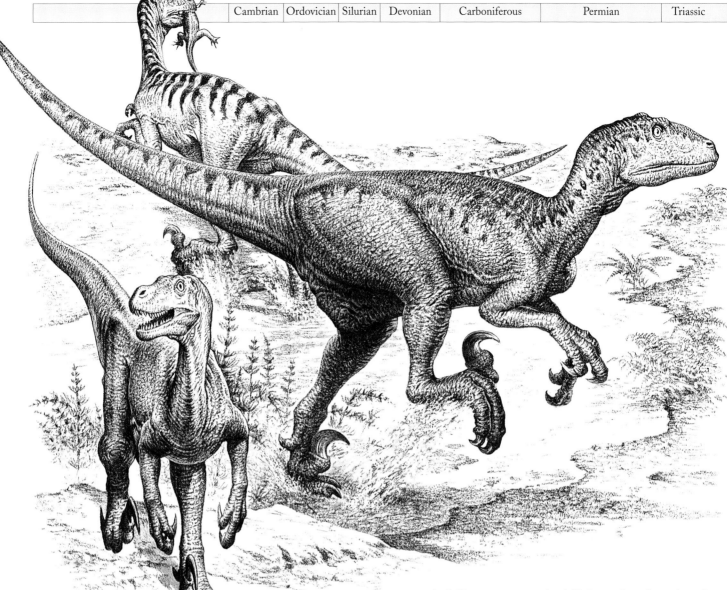

△ Dromaeosaurus *(top)*, Deinonychus *(center)*, and Velociraptor *(bottom) were highly efficient predators, all armed with a single retractable claw on each foot. The claw stayed off the ground when the animal was moving, keeping its point needle-sharp.*

DROMAEOSAURS

Fast and ferocious, dromaeosaurs were killers of other dinosaurs. They were perfectly built for speed and slaughter, with light bodies, athletic legs, and sharp, sicklelike claws. Their heads were relatively large, and their long jaws were armed with sharp, curved teeth. They had well-developed brains, and they often worked in packs to hunt down animals several times their own size.

DEINONYCHUS
Although it was far smaller than many other predators that lived during the Cretaceous Period, *Deinonychus*, meaning "terrible claw," was a serious threat even to the largest plant-eating dinosaurs. By operating in packs, like modern wolves, it would harass and exhaust its prey before closing in for the final attack. When the moment came to make the kill the members of the pack would jump at their victim and slash it with their retractable sickle-shaped claws—formidable weapons that were up to 5 in. (12cm) long. As the pack members leaped and ripped into their prey they used their stiff tails as counterbalances to prevent themselves from becoming destabilized. Like other dromaeosaurs, *Deinonychus* had a large brain for its size. This gave it the intelligence and rapid reactions needed in a

hunter that operated in groups. *Deinonychus* was such an active and energetic predator that some experts think it may have been warm-blooded (pages 148–150), a theory that has yet to be proven.

MAXIMUM LENGTH   13 ft. (4m)

TIME	Early Cretaceous
FOSSIL FINDS	North America

DROMAEOSAURUS

Half the size of *Deinonychus*, but built along very similar lines, *Dromaeosaurus* was another fast-footed predator, probably able to reach speeds of around 40 mph (60km/h). It also had a sicklelike claw on the inner toe, which could be retracted when not in use. Fossils of this animal were discovered 50 years before its larger relative, which is how the dromaeosaur family got its name. These early remains were only partial, and paleontologists could not interpret them fully until they had studied *Deinonychus* and seen the similarities.

MAXIMUM LENGTH   6 ft. (1.8m)

TIME	Late Cretaceous
FOSSIL FINDS	North America

VELOCIRAPTOR

Similar in size and body shape to *Dromaeosaurus*, although with a longer and flatter head, *Velociraptor* was first discovered in Mongolia in the 1920s. Its way of life was vividly illustrated when many years later an expedition uncovered the fossilized remains of a *Velociraptor* that had been killed while attacking a *Protoceratops* (page 155). *Velociraptor* means "speedy thief"—a good description of a small, fast-moving, and intelligent hunter that could probably reach speeds of 40 mph (60 km/h). Although it could run at this speed only in short bursts, *Velociraptor* may have been second only to the bird mimics (page 122) in top speed. Like other dromaeosaurs, little is known about its breeding habits and whether it laid eggs.

MAXIMUM LENGTH   6 ft. (1.8m)

TIME	Late Cretaceous
FOSSIL FINDS	Asia (Mongolia, China)

SAURORNITHOLESTES

Uncertainty surrounds *Saurornitholestes*, because knowledge of it is limited to remnants of a skull, some teeth, and arm bones found in Alberta, in 1978. Based on this slender evidence, paleontologists have classified it as a dromaeosaur, but it may have been a "bird lizard," or saurornithoid (page 126). An agile hunter, it had large hands with grasping fingers.

MAXIMUM LENGTH   6 ft. (1.8m)

TIME	Late Cretaceous
FOSSIL FINDS	North America (Alberta)

▽ *Like other predatory dinosaurs, Deinonychus could not slice into its prey. Instead, it used its backward-curving teeth to rip away chunks of flesh. It also had large eyes, and it would have relied mainly on its sharp eyesight to spot potential prey when hunting. Its sense of smell was probably less important for finding food.*

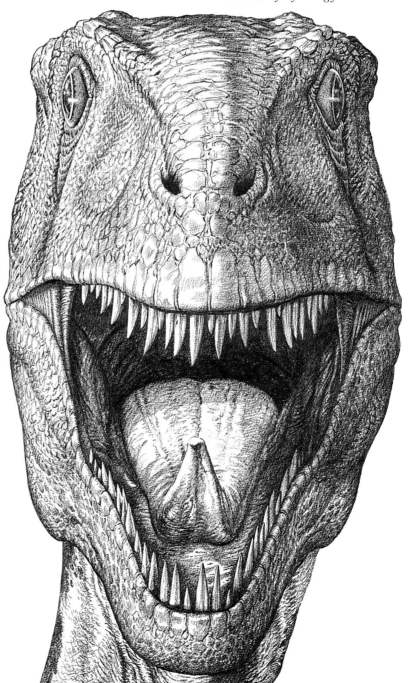

THE MEAT EATERS

TROODONTS

The animals on these two pages belonged to several families, but most were lightweight theropods with unusually large brains. The troodonts in particular were highly intelligent by dinosaur standards, with large eyes that suggest they hunted at night. Fast and agile, some of them may have been warm-blooded, retaining their body heat with a layer of insulating feathers. *Baryonyx* was a much larger animal and probably not much brighter than other theropods of its time.

▷ Oviraptor *made up for its lack of teeth by having sharp shearing edges on its beak. Because its beak was short, it would have closed with considerable force— enough to break bones. The size of the crest probably varied according to sex and age.*

▽ *Lean and energetic,* Troodon *was one of the most intelligent land animals of the Late Cretaceous. This artist's impression shows it with bare skin, but it is possible that it had a covering of downy, heat-retaining plumage.*

OVIRAPTOR
With its birdlike head and short, toothless beak, *Oviraptor*, meaning "egg thief," was an unusual and distinctive animal. Standing about the same height as an adult man, it had thin but well-developed arms, and fingers that were equipped with slender claws. Its beak was hooked and had sharp edges for slicing through food. Recent fossil discoveries show that, although it may have eaten other dinosaurs' eggs, it was careful with its own (page 109).

MAXIMUM LENGTH 8.2 ft. (2.5m)
TIME Late Cretaceous
FOSSIL FINDS Asia (Mongolia)

TROODON
From a distance, *Troodon* looked like a bird mimic (pages 122–123), but it shared the same kind of weaponry as the dromaeosaurs— a lethal claw on each of its second toes, which could be swiveled upward when it ran. Some paleontologists think it may actually have been a dromaeosaur, but it is possible that these swiveling claws evolved more than once. It also had large, serrated teeth, grasping hands, and eyes that faced partly forward—a combination that would have made it a very effective hunter. If *Troodon* did hunt after dark, as the size of its eyes suggests, its main prey might have been mammals, which were almost all nocturnal in the Cretaceous. *Troodon* teeth were first discovered nearly 150 years ago, but nothing was known about the animal itself until the 1980s.

MAXIMUM LENGTH 6 ft. (1.8m)
TIME Late Cretaceous
FOSSIL FINDS North America (Alberta, Montana, Wyoming)

SINORNITHOIDES
Another member of the troodont family, *Sinornithoides* is the only one known from a complete fossil skeleton. It was a small and very slender animal, weighing perhaps just 6.6 lb. (3kg) when fully grown, and its food is likely to have consisted of insects and other small animals that it may have found by scratching with its front claws.

MAXIMUM LENGTH 8.2 ft. (1.2m)
TIME Early Cretaceous
FOSSIL FINDS Asia (China)

BARYONYX
Discovered in an English clay pit in the early 1980s, *Baryonyx*, meaning "heavy claw," is one of the most intriguing European dinosaurs to surface in recent times. For a theropod its skull had a very unusual shape, ending in a flattened, crocodile-like snout. Its teeth were conical rather than bladelike and packed in dense rows along its jaws. It had at least two very large claws, about 12 in. (30cm) long. No close relatives of this animal have been found yet, and it is classified in a family of its own.

MAXIMUM LENGTH 29.5 ft. (9m)
TIME Early Cretaceous
FOSSIL FINDS Europe (England)

TROODONTS

*Standing in shallow water, Baryonyx uses its
extra-large front claws to grab unsuspecting fish.
Two Brachiosaurus in the background know that
this specialized predator does not present a threat.*

DINOSAUR BRAINS

DINOSAURS WERE THE
PROVERBIAL DIMWITS OF THE
PREHISTORIC WORLD. BUT IS IT
A REPUTATION THEY REALLY DESERVED, AND
IF SO, HOW DID THEY MANAGE TO SURVIVE?

Myths abound about dinosaurs' rumored stupidity:
one is that they had two brains; another is that
their lack of brainpower helped make them extinct.
But as living animals prove, large brains are not essential
for biological success. Research shows that brain size and
intelligence varied greatly from one group of dinosaurs
to another. Some were slow to grasp situations, but others
were just as intelligent as many
mammals alive today.

NERVOUS SYSTEMS
Because dinosaurs
were vertebrates,
their nervous systems
would have been similar to
those of today's vertebrates. In a vertebrate
the control center of the system is the brain,
which merges with the spinal cord—a
multistranded filament of nervous tissue
that runs through the hollow core of

△ Stegosaurus *had a brain about the size of a*
walnut, weighing roughly 2.6 oz. (75g), but some of its
nerve cells supplying distant parts of its body were over
10 ft. (3m) long. How fast its nerves worked would
have depended on whether or not it was cold-blooded.

the backbone. Nerves lead away from the
spinal cord to all parts of the body, collect
information from the sense organs, and
send signals to trigger muscles into action.

In all vertebrates the brain plays a key role
in initiating movement and making sure the
body works in a coordinated way. But some
movements, called reflex reactions, are
triggered without the brain being directly
involved. If you step on something sharp,
for example, your leg will immediately
pull back, because an automatic response
has been triggered by your spinal cord.

Reactions like these are potential
lifesavers, and they have to be fast—but the
larger an animal is, the farther the signals
have to travel. In today's reptiles, signals
move along nerves at up to 130 ft. (40m) per
second—quick enough to produce an almost

◁ *This diagram (above left) shows the brain cavity of a* Stegosaurus *and other*
structures close to it. The ear opening is shown in black; the circular objects above
it are part of the inner ear, which played a part in controlling balance.

◁ *Dome-headed dinosaurs, or pachycephalosaurs, looked as though they had large*
brains, but this was because their small brain cavity was covered by a mound of bone.

instant response. But in large dinosaurs nerve signals would often have had to travel many feet, creating a significant time lag.

This time-lag effect may help explain what is called the "second brain," which is seen in stegosaurs and some other dinosaurs. Instead of being a true brain, this was actually an enlarged relay center that controlled these automatic reactions.

RELATIVE BRAIN SIZE

Dinosaur skulls often contain the remains of a brain cavity. This allows their brain volume to be measured by computerized imaging or by the more simple technique of filling the cavity with fluid and then measuring the fluid when it is poured out.

Dinosaur brains varied between the size of a walnut and a grapefruit. But the size of the body also has to be taken into account, because the larger an animal, the more nerves were needed to control it.

With living animals researchers have made detailed studies of the ratio between brain weight and total body weight. For humans the figure comes out at about 1:40; for an average dog it is about 1:125. For a stegosaur the figure was about 1:50,000—indicating that these animals were not very

bright. But body size and brain size do not always correlate. In small birds the ratio can be 1:12, which would appear to make them brighter than humans.

In gauging the relative intelligence of related animals, a more useful figure is an encephalization quotient, or EQ, which gives an idea of relative brain development. As the chart below shows, sauropods had the lowest figure among dinosaurs, with values of about 0.2, whereas small theropods did well, with scores above 5.5. Among mammals humans have an EQ of about 7.4, but this does not tell us much about dinosaur brainpower, as figures from very different groups cannot be directly compared.

INSTINCT AND LEARNING

Given their way of life, it is no surprise that plant-eating dinosaurs are on the bottom of the EQ list. Unlike hunting species, these animals did not need to stalk or ambush their food, and their daily life consisted largely of eating and digesting. By contrast, small hunters such as *Dromiceiomimus* survived by learning from experience, which gave them the best chance of making successful kills. For them intelligence was essential for survival.

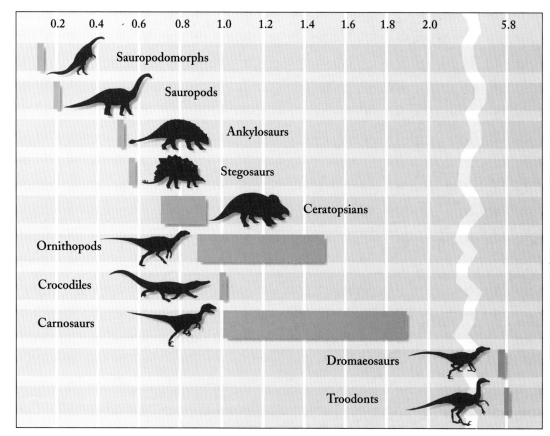

◁ This chart shows typical encephalization quotients, or EQs, for dinosaurs and crocodilians. EQ—not to be confused with IQ—is the ratio of actual brain weight to the expected brain weight given an animal's size and type. The expected brain weight for dinosaurs is based on measurements of living reptiles. EQ gives a general indication of brain development and therefore of an animal's intelligence. An EQ of more than 1 shows that an animal has a brain weight above average for its class, while an EQ below 1 shows the reverse.

EGGS AND PARENTAL CARE

AS FAR AS IS KNOWN, ALL DINOSAURS REPRODUCED BY LAYING EGGS. FOSSILIZED NESTS SHOW THAT SOME WERE CAREFUL PARENTS AND LOOKED AFTER BOTH THEIR EGGS AND THEIR YOUNG.

People have unearthed fossilized dinosaur eggs for centuries without realizing what they were. The first to be correctly identified were in France, just over 150 years ago. Since then many different types have been found, often exactly as they were laid. Dinosaur eggs were surprisingly small. The largest discovered is only about twice the length of an ostrich egg. They could not be larger, because the thick shells would have stopped the embryos inside from getting enough oxygen, and the baby dinosaurs would have been unable to break the shell when they hatched.

Dinosaur eggs came in a wide variety of shapes. Some of them looked like overstuffed sausages; others were round. Their shells could be pitted or smooth.
1 *Modern-day hen's egg—3 in. (7.5cm) long*
2 Maiasaura *egg—6 in. (15cm) long*
3 Protoceratops *egg—8 in. (20cm) long*
4 Hypselosaurus *egg—12 in. (30cm) long*

DINOSAUR EGGS
Many of today's reptiles lay their eggs in shallow holes, which they scrape out in loose soil or mud. Fossilized nests, which have been discovered in many different parts of the world, suggest that most dinosaurs behaved in the same way. By scraping the ground with their feet, or perhaps their snouts, they excavated hollows or craters that could be over 3.3 ft. (1m) across. Like modern reptiles, the number of eggs laid by the dinosaurs varied. Some laid fewer than 10 eggs at a time, but some giant nests discovered recently in China contain 40 or more eggs.

Complete dinosaur nests—like the one shown here—are a rare and exciting discovery. Most nests leave few remains, and for an entire nest to become fossilized before the young dinosaurs could hatch, something had to have gone badly wrong. This nest, which is being excavated by scientists in Argentina, was probably covered by a sudden sandstorm. The dinosaur embryos would have died from a lack of oxygen, allowing the whole egg clutch to be preserved.

INCUBATION
What happened after egg laying is more difficult to piece together. At one time paleontologists assumed that female dinosaurs covered their eggs and left them to develop on their own, but some fossils have shown that this may not always have been true. In the 1920s a fossil *Oviraptor* was found, apparently caught in the act of stealing eggs from a nest. However, more recent fossils (page 109) have shown *Oviraptor* sitting on its own eggs, probably to protect them and perhaps to keep them warm. If *Oviraptor* did incubate its eggs, it is unlikely to have been the only dinosaur that behaved in this way.

Some dinosaurs may have incubated their eggs by covering them with fresh vegetation. As the plants rotted they generated warmth like a compost heap. The warmth would

▷ *Dinosaur eggs were packed with nutrients, which would have made them a useful source of food for omnivores such as* Oviraptor. *Here, one has been caught trying to raid a* Protoceratops *nest, and the nest's owner has gone on the attack with its beaklike jaws.*

▽ *By nesting together, herd-forming species like* Maiasaura *had a better chance of fighting off nest raiders. Each female — perhaps helped by her mate—built a crater-shaped nest of mud up to 6.6 ft. (2m) wide. The female then laid about 20 eggs and covered the clutch with a mixture of foliage and sand. The eggs probably took about a month to hatch.*

have allowed the eggs to develop, even if the outside temperature was low.

LEAVING THE NEST

By examining the shells of empty eggs, researchers can figure out how young dinosaurs behaved immediately after they hatched. In many nests the shells are open at one end but largely intact. This suggests that the young moved out of their nest soon after hatching, or the empty shells would have been crushed by the young dinosaurs.

To leave the nest this early, these young animals must have been well developed. Their parents may have watched over them, but they were more likely to have been left to fend for themselves.

STAYING PUT

Other dinosaur nests tell a very different story. At a nest site in Montana crushed eggshells have been found with the fossilized remains of young nestlings. The nests were made by *Maiasaura*, a duck-billed dinosaur (page 104) that nested in groups. The recently hatched *Maiasaura* were still poorly developed, which makes it unlikely that they were about to leave the nest. They probably relied on their parents to bring them food. Once the young left the nest, they were protected by being part of a herd and by growing extremely rapidly. Even so, many young dinosaurs failed to survive their first year. This is why large families were an essential part of dinosaur life.

Carnivorous dinosaurs would have easily carried dead prey back to the nests. But plant food is harder to carry. *Maiasaura* probably brought plants back to its young, but other plant eaters may have fed their young with regurgitated semidigested food.

Longisquama's *featherlike scales may have been used for gliding, but they are unlikely to have had any direct connection with the feathers evolved by birds.*

THE ORIGIN OF BIRDS

MOST SCIENTISTS BELIEVE THAT BIRDS EVOLVED FROM SMALL THEROPOD DINOSAURS. THE KEY STEP WAS THE DEVELOPMENT OF FEATHERS, TURNING ANIMALS THAT COULD RUN OR CLIMB INTO ONES THAT COULD FLY.

The earliest true bird known to science is *Archaeopteryx*, which lived in the Late Jurassic Period, over 150 million years ago. Discovered in 1861, the fossil looked like a cross between a reptile and a bird, with a toothed beak, a long bony tail, and the unmistakable outline of feathers. In recent years other feathered reptiles have been found.

THE FIRST FEATHERS

Birds use feathers for two different things: to keep themselves warm and to fly. Feathers that are used for insulation are usually short and fluffy; those used for flight are much larger, with a curved surface, or vane. These two kinds of feathers are unlikely to have evolved at the same time. Insulating feathers most likely came first, and then, over millions of years, some developed into specialized feathers that could be used for flight.

No one knows when feathers first appeared. Some paleontologists have claimed that they can be seen in *Longisquama*, a reptile that dates back to Triassic times, but the majority of experts are not convinced. The best evidence for feather evolution comes from small theropods recently discovered in China. One of these, called *Sinosauropteryx*, had short downy plumage and a feathery crest running down its neck and back. It was a feathered dinosaur, but it would not have been able to fly.

INTO THE AIR

Sinosauropteryx lived slightly later than *Archaeopteryx*, so it could not have been its direct ancestor. However, its downy plumage shows what the forebears of flying birds may have looked like before they evolved fully feathered wings. But how did wings develop and, more importantly, why?

One theory is that the ancestors of birds evolved wings as an adaptation for hunting insects and other small animals. According to this idea these protobirds chased their

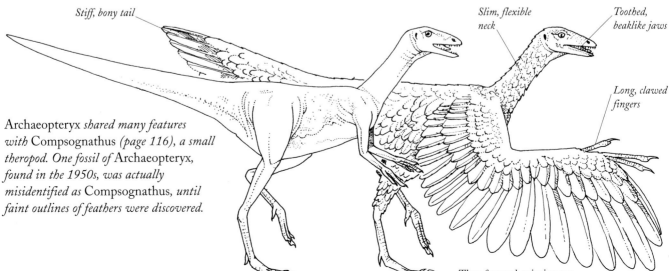

Stiff, bony tail

Archaeopteryx *shared many features with* Compsognathus *(page 116), a small theropod. One fossil of* Archaeopteryx, *found in the 1950s, was actually misidentified as* Compsognathus, *until faint outlines of feathers were discovered.*

Slim, flexible neck

Toothed, beaklike jaws

Long, clawed fingers

Three forward-pointing toes

prey across the ground, leaping into the air to catch small animals as they tried to escape. Over a long period of time they developed extra-large feathers on their front legs to help them stay balanced and also perhaps to help them scoop up their prey. The feathers gradually became longer as the muscles that worked the front legs became stronger. Eventually this created animals that could flap their way off the ground.

GLIDERS IN THE TREES?

This ground-based theory is supported by some features shown by *Archaeopteryx*, such as its strong legs. But most paleontologists believe that birds actually evolved from reptiles that lived not on the ground, but in trees. By evolving extra-large feathers, these animals would have developed the ability to glide so that they could travel through woodlands and forests without having to touch the ground. From this, flapping flight would gradually have developed.

Gliding is something that has cropped

Avimimus

up many times in reptile evolution. It was used by *Coelurosauravus* (page 170) and a range of other tree-dwellers, and it can be seen in several species of lizards alive today. For supporters of the tree-based theory, this makes it all the more likely that birds began in a similar way.

LIGHT FOR FLIGHT

Gliding uses up very little energy, but flapping flight is strenuous. To stay airborne, early birds had to undergo some important

design changes that made them increasingly different from their dinosaur ancestors. Evolution cannot look ahead, so these changes were not preplanned. Instead, they built up slowly over a long period as birds spent more and more of their time in the air.

Many of these changes helped birds lose the weight that made it harder for them to stay aloft. Many of their bones fused, and their skeletons became lighter. Like their theropod ancestors, they had hollow, air-filled bones, but the air spaces became larger and more extensive, reaching most of the way down their wings and legs.

Archaeopteryx

They also developed enlarged breastbones, which anchored the powerful chest muscles that were needed for flight, and a V-shaped furcula, or wishbone, that braced the chest during flight.

These changes proved to be a winning combination. Birds became increasingly common in Cretaceous times, and when the Age of Reptiles came to its cataclysmic end, they were the only dinosaur descendants that managed to survive.

▷ Archaeopteryx *had assymmetrical or "lopsided" wing feathers, like those of modern birds. Feathers like these generate lift when air flows over them, and they are evidence that* Archaeopteryx *could fly.*

▽ Avimimus *(far left) was a feathered theropod that could not fly.* Archaeopteryx *(center) was smaller and lighter with well-developed flight feathers.*

Pigeon

△ *Unlike* Archaeopteryx, *modern birds like this pigeon have no teeth, short tails, and—with a handful of exceptions, such as the hoatzin—they have no wing claws.*

THE MEAT EATERS

EARLY BIRDS

Despite the discovery of many fossils, there are still plenty of unanswered questions about how early birds evolved. Some researchers think that they may have split into two groups early in their history. According to this theory the first group contained *Archaeopteryx* and other long-tailed species; the second contained short-tailed birds—the direct ancestors of the ones alive today. Not all paleontologists are convinced, but one fact is certain: by Late Cretaceous times, birds were very successful and lived all over the Earth.

△ *Apart from its toothed beak,* Ichthyornis *looked like a modern tern, and it probably had a very similar way of life. The evidence for* Ichthyornis' *diet comes from large numbers of fish bones found near its fossilized remains.*

▷ Hesperornis *swam by paddling with its webbed feet while using its stubby wings to steer. Compared to flying birds, diving species like* Hesperornis *have fewer air-cavities in their bones. This helped them stay submerged.*

ARCHAEOPTERYX

Archaeopteryx is probably one of the most famous prehistoric animals known. Only six fossil specimens have been found—all from Solnhöfen in southern Germany—but in most of them the imprint of feathers can clearly be seen. *Archaeopteryx* was about the size of a crow, but had toothed jaws and a long, reptilelike tail. Its legs were long, and its wings had three claws at their elbows, which might have been used for climbing. Like today's birds, it probably reproduced by laying and incubating eggs, although no fossils of these have been found.

MAXIMUM LENGTH 13.8 in. (35cm)
TIME Late Jurassic
FOSSIL FINDS Europe (Germany)

ICHTHYORNIS

With a name meaning "fish bird," *Ichthyornis* was similar to some of the seabirds alive today, although it still had one primitive feature—a beak lined with sharp teeth. Unlike *Archaeopteryx*, the bony part of its tail was very short, and its wings did not have claws. Internally it had two other features that are found in all modern flying birds: many of its bones contained large air spaces, which helped reduce its overall weight, and it also had a narrow, forward-pointing flap called a keel that protruded from its breastbone. This flap, which is missing in *Archaeopteryx*, anchored the large chest muscles that powered its wings.

MAXIMUM LENGTH 14 in. (35cm)
TIME Late Cretaceous
FOSSIL FINDS North America (Kansas, Texas)

HESPERORNIS

The earliest true birds were flying species, but as birds evolved some species lost the power of flight. One of them was *Hesperornis*—a large, fish-eating diver with tiny wings and legs placed far back along its body, near its tail. On land *Hesperornis* may have lumbered along like a seal, but its streamlined shape and webbed feet made it fast and maneuverable underwater like today's grebes. Becoming flightless may seem like a step backward, but during bird evolution many other species have followed this path. They include many land-dwelling species, including the largest birds that have ever lived (page 213).

MAXIMUM LENGTH 5.7 ft. (1.75m)
TIME Late Cretaceous
FOSSIL FINDS North America (Kansas)

▷ Archaeopteryx *is a classic example of an evolutionary link between two groups of animals. It was discovered just two years after Charles Darwin published his theory of evolution.*

134

GIANT MEAT EATERS

During the Jurassic and Cretaceous periods, predatory theropods evolved along with their prey. Some species, such as *Deinonychus*, tackled large animals by hunting in packs, but others relied on their individual size and power to make a kill. These giant meat eaters were the superpredators of the reptile age, able to topple plant eaters that could weigh over 30 tons. *Tyrannosaurus* is by far the most famous among them, but recent discoveries have shown that in Cretaceous times other predatory theropods may have been larger.

PACK ATTACK

Launching a deadly ambush, a group of Deinonychus *attack a plant-eating hypsilophodont several times their own size. For Cretaceous plant eaters packs of these small and highly agile hunters would have been just as dangerous as much larger predators that stalked prey on their own.*

CARNOSAURS

AT ONE TIME ALL LARGE PREDATORY
DINOSAURS WERE CLASSIFIED IN A GROUP
CALLED THE CARNOSAURS, MEANING "FLESH
REPTILES." SINCE THEN RESEARCH HAS
SHOWN THAT GIANT MEAT EATERS WERE
NOT NECESSARILY CLOSE RELATIVES.

Unlike the smaller theropods, which often used their claws to attack their prey, the largest meat eaters of the dinosaur world used their teeth to attack their victims. Their arms were often puny, but their skulls were huge—a feature that *Carcharodontosaurus* (page 160), shows in a particularly chilling way. For hunting, this kind of anatomy proved to be lethally effective, and it probably evolved separately in several different theropod groups.

▽ *This cladogram shows the possible links between tetanurans, or advanced theropods. Each branch forms a clade, which includes an ancestral species and its descendants.*

FAMILY FEATURES
At first glance giant theropods, such as *Allosaurus* and *Tyrannosaurus*, look very similar. All of them had powerful hind legs, small arms, and narrow skulls with immense, tooth-filled jaws. They may not have been as fast on their feet as paleontologists once supposed, and it is likely that some of them were scavengers as well as hunters, but their reputation as the ultimate terrestrial killers is still well deserved.

It seems only logical that these massively built hunters were as closely related as, for example, tigers and lions are today. But for paleontologists trying to work out the evolutionary history of dinosaurs outward similarities can cause problems. Animals often develop similar adaptations if they have similar lifestyles through convergent evolution. If they are already similar to begin with, convergence can make true family relationships extremely difficult to unravel. This is true of large theropods.

UNRAVELING THE PAST
To get a true picture of how closely different species are related, paleontologists and biologists use a system called cladistics. This involves comparing animals in detail and seeing how many derived features they share. A derived feature is one that develops in an ancestral species and that is then handed on to all of its descendants. Because ancestors have ancestors themselves, derived features steadily build up as time goes by. The more derived features two species share, the more closely they must be related. This information can be used to construct a cladogram, a chart that shows the branches in evolution that divide one group of species from another.

The cladogram on this page shows one idea of how all the advanced theropods might have been related. The allosaurs and tyrannosaurs are far apart and belong to two separate "clades": the carnosaurs, a group that contains some of the largest theropods, and the coelurosaurs, which contains some of the smallest. Through convergent evolution

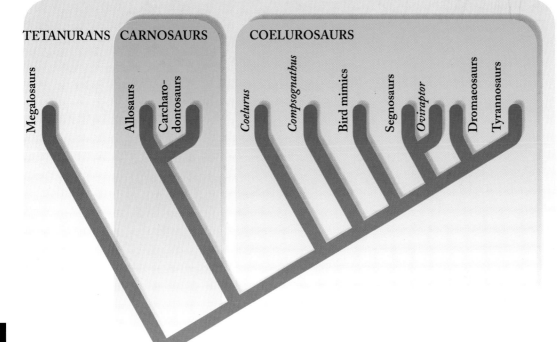

TETANURANS   CARNOSAURS   COELUROSAURS

Megalosaurs

Allosaurs

Carcharo-dontosaurs

Coelurus

Compsognathus

Bird mimics

Segnosaurs

Oviraptor

Dromaeosaurs

Tyrannosaurs

tyrannosaurs developed giant bodies and tiny arms, just like the allosaurs, which had appeared 50 million years earlier.

LIMITS TO GROWTH

Like the plant-eating sauropods (page 84), giant theropods enjoyed some obvious advantages because of their size. Weighing up to six or seven tons, and with bodies up to 46 ft. (14m) long, they would have developed a nearly unstoppable momentum as they slammed into prey. As sauropods increased in size these hunters did as well, although the increase happened at different times in different groups, with the megalosaurs being the first to enter the heavyweight class.

But if large size was such an asset, why did theropods stop growing at seven tons, when plant-eating dinosaurs evolved bodies that were perhaps ten times heavier? The main reason is that, unlike plant eaters, predators rely on speed and agility to survive. Compared to smaller theropods, animals like *Allosaurus* were already slow and lumbering, and it is likely that if they had evolved much larger bodies, they would not have been able to function as predators that pursued their prey.

▽ *Large theropods like* Tyrannosaurus *evolved extreme differences in size between the front and back limbs. Their heads were the largest of all the dinosaurs, apart from some ceratopsians.* Tyrannosaurus *may have ambushed animals rather than chasing them. It may also have obtained a proportion of its food from carrion, which is an efficient form of nutrition.*

MEGALOSAURS AND SEGNOSAURS

The megalosaurs were the earliest of the giant bipedal hunters. Megalosaurs had small front legs with three-fingered hands, massively built skulls, and in some cases horns or crests. Segnosaurs, also known as therizinosaurs, are known only from fragmentary remains. They were unrelated to megalosaurs, and experts have had great difficulty deciding where they fit into the dinosaur world. Some believe they were plant-eating sauropods, but others think they were highly specialized large theropods.

DILOPHOSAURUS

The earliest known megalosaur, *Dilophosaurus* was an agile hunter, despite weighing up to half a ton. Its most conspicuous feature was its double crest, which was positioned over its forehead and muzzle with a central furrow running down its length. Its function is unclear. It may have been used in courtship displays and is likely to have been larger in males than in females. The remains of three *Dilophosaurus* found together in Arizona suggest that this species may have hunted in packs. Some scientists have concluded from its long, thin teeth that *Dilophosaurus* was more likely to have used its clawed hands, rather than its teeth, to grab its prey and tear it apart.

MAXIMUM LENGTH	19.7 ft. (6m)
TIME	Early Jurassic
FOSSIL FINDS	North America (Arizona), Asia (China)

△ Dilophosaurus' *double head crest was partly hollow, so it is unlikely that it was used for self-defense. It may have been for display and unique to males.*

▷ Eustreptospondylus *was first mistaken for* Megalosaurus, *since the two animals were similar in many ways. However, it was about 6.5 ft. (2m) shorter, with a much smaller body weight.*

EUSTREPTOSPONDYLUS

Only one specimen of *Eustreptospondylus* has ever been found. Unusual for a land animal it was discovered in marine sediments, leading scientists to conclude that its carcass was washed out to sea. It may have reached the sea by a river, but it is possible that it lived on the shore, perhaps scavenging food from the remains of animals left stranded by the tide. Although incomplete, the fossil is still the best-preserved carnosaur yet found in Europe. It had a typical megalosaur build, with large back legs, three-fingered hands, and a head without a crest. Some of the bones show signs of not being fully developed, which makes it likely that it was not fully grown when it died.

MAXIMUM LENGTH	23 ft. (7m)
TIME	Mid Jurassic to Late Cretaceous
FOSSIL FINDS	Europe (England)

MEGALOSAURUS

Standing 10 ft. (3m) tall and weighing about a ton, *Megalosaurus*, meaning "great lizard" was an animal that lived up to its name. A *Megalosaurus* thighbone, found in England in 1676, was the first dinosaur bone to come to the attention of European scientists. At the time no one correctly guessed what it was, and over 150 years passed before Richard Owen, the pioneering anatomist and paleontologist, included *Megalosaurus* in a new category of extinct reptiles—the dinosaurs. Since then *Megalosaurus* remains have been found in several different countries, although none of the remains are complete. However, they show that it was one of the largest predators of the Jurassic, with a head around 3 ft. (1m) long. Fossilized trackways found in southern England show that it had a pigeon-toed gait and held its

a feature of *Nanshiungosaurus* and its relatives. One species, called *Alxasaurus*, had finger claws that were up to 27.6 in. (70cm) long, making them probably the largest of any dinosaur.

MAXIMUM LENGTH 16.4 ft. (5m)
TIME Mid to Late Cretaceous
FOSSIL FINDS Asia (China)

PROCERATOSAURUS

The most unusual feature of *Proceratosaurus* was the horn on the top of its snout. This was thought to be evidence that it was a forerunner of the ceratosaurs (page 116), which is how it got its name. It is often classified as a megalosaur, but its place is open to doubt because the only remains found so far have been part of the skull and jaw. Apart from its horn, *Proceratosaurus* seems to have been a typical Mid Jurassic hunter, although a fairly small one with a maximum weight of perhaps 220 lb. (100kg).

MAXIMUM LENGTH 13.1 ft. (4m)
TIME Mid Jurassic
FOSSIL FINDS Europe (U.K.)

◁ *Megalosaurus was a successful prototype version of the giant bipedal predator. The same body form was seen among various groups of theropods right until the Age of Reptiles ended.*

◁ *Proceratosaurus is known from a single skull, which makes it difficult to judge exactly how it looked. This reconstruction shows it as a typical theropod, with small front legs.*

▽ *Looking more like a sauropod than a theropod, Nanshiungosaurus is a mystifying animal. It may have led an amphibious existence, feeding on fish, but its large size, long neck, and small head make it just as likely that it was a grazer.*

tail off the ground when moving quickly. It was probably a fairly rapid runner, although it was not built for a long chase.

MAXIMUM LENGTH 29.5 ft. (9m)
TIME Jurassic
FOSSIL FINDS Europe (France, U.K.), Africa (Morocco)

ERLIKOSAURUS

Erlikosaurus belonged to the segnosaur, or therizinosaur, family—an obscure group of less than a dozen known species, all from central Asia or the Far East. Although segnosaurs are generally classified as theropods, *Erlikosaurus*'s skull—the only segnosaur example discovered so far—looks unlike those of other predatory dinosaurs, with small teeth overall but an upper jaw that ends in a toothless beak. It had unusually large claws and probably stood on two legs. From studies of its teeth and skeleton, it seems possible that *Erlikosaurus* and other segnosaurs may have been fish eaters.

MAXIMUM LENGTH 19.7 ft. (6m)
TIME Mid Cretaceous
FOSSIL FINDS Asia (Mongolia)

NANSHIUNGOSAURUS

Like *Erlikosaurus*, this animal was also a segnosaur, but knowledge about it is based on a handful of very incomplete remains. Nothing is known about its head, because its skull has not been found, but it had a long neck and tail. Its front legs were well developed, and it may have moved on all fours. Enlarged finger claws seem to have been

141

GIANT MEAT EATERS

ALLOSAURS

Appearing 50 million years before the tyrannosaurs, the allosaurs may have included the largest carnivores ever to have lived on land. Found throughout the world, they were bipedal predators, with immense heads, very large back legs, but relatively short arms with three-fingered hands. No dinosaur—no matter how large—would have been able to withstand allosaur packs.

▽ *An* Allosaurus *attacks a* Diplodocus *several times its own size.* Allosaurus *may have hunted individually—on their own they would have been fearsome—or in packs.*

CARCHARODONTOSAURUS

Meaning "shark-toothed lizard," *Carcharodontosaurus* was first discovered in the 1920s. These remains were destroyed during World War II, but some new ones have only recently been unearthed (pages 160–161). This massively built hunter (and possible scavenger) may have weighed as much as eight tons, and had teeth up to 8 in. (20cm) long. Its skull measured about 5.2 ft. (1.6m) from front to back, and it is possible that the entire animal may have been larger than *Tyrannosaurus* (page 144), even though its brain was only about half the size.

MAXIMUM LENGTH	44.3 ft. (13.5m)
TIME	Early Cretaceous
FOSSIL FINDS	North Africa

ALLOSAURUS

Allosaurus was a common and widespread predator 150 million years ago. It hunted or scavenged for a living, and weighed up to three tons. Scientists are still debating how a predator this large would have moved or whether it would have been able to chase and catch fast-moving prey. Despite its powerful hind legs, it is unlikely that it would have been able to run faster than 18 mph (30km/h), and skeletal injuries in some *Allosaurus* remains suggest that it was often injured while hunting —either in falls or by its prey fighting back.

MAXIMUM LENGTH	39.5 ft. (12m)
TIME	Late Jurassic
FOSSIL FINDS	North America (western U.S.A.), Australia

ALLOSAURS

NEOVENATOR

Discovered on England's Isle of Wight in 1978 but not excavated until the 1980s, *Neovenator*, meaning "new hunter," was a smaller and more agile predator than its cousin *Allosaurus*. The single fossil found so far shows that *Neovenator* has a strongly curved forehead and large nostrils, indicating a good sense of smell. During Cretaceous times it was probably the largest flesh-eating dinosaur in what is now northern Europe.

MAXIMUM LENGTH	42.6 ft. (13m)
TIME	Early Cretaceous
FOSSIL FINDS	Europe (England)

△ *Striding across a marshy landscape,* Neovenator *sniffs the air for prey. This recently discovered allosaur had a muzzle shaped like a giant beak.*

GIGANOTOSAURUS

Found in 1994 by an amateur paleontologist in Patagonia, *Giganotosaurus* may have been the largest predatory dinosaur ever. Its skull alone was nearly as long as a man is tall, and its body was as long as a bus. Estimates of its weight vary, with the highest figure— about eight tons—putting it among the real heavyweights of the theropod world. Unlike *Tyrannosaurus*, *Giganotosaurus* had a relatively narrow head and teeth that were shaped for slicing through flesh, rather than for breaking bones. Its name means "giant southern lizard."

MAXIMUM LENGTH	42.64 ft. (13m)
TIME	Late Cretaceous
FOSSIL FINDS	South America (Argentina)

◁ *With its right shoulder seriously injured, the* Apatosaurus *risks crashing to the ground. If it does, it cannot escape, and the* Allosaurus *can make an easy kill.*

143

		Cambrian	Ordovician	Silurian	Devonian	Carboniferous	Permian	Triassic

GIANT MEAT EATERS

◁ *Two young* Albertosaurus *race past a* Daspletosaurus *that has waded into water to eat a carcass. If the* Daspletosaurus *had been on land, the smaller animals would not have risked venturing so close.*

TYRANNOSAURS

Although they existed for only 15 million years, the tyrannosaurs are among the most fascinating and awe-inspiring animals from the dinosaur age. Their huge heads were armed with immense, serrated teeth, and they stood on pillarlike back legs that could be twice as tall as an adult man. Their front legs were even smaller than those of the allosaurs, and they ended in two-fingered hands not much larger than our own. Tyrannosaurs were undoubtedly meat eaters and probably lived mainly by hunting. They may also have scavenged for dead remains.

ALBERTOSAURUS
Weighing about three tons, *Albertosaurus* was small compared to its relatives, but still much larger than any predatory land animal alive today. It had the typical tyrannosaur build, with an outsized head, long hind legs, and a muscular tail that helped it balance. Each of its jaws had a single row of serrated teeth, which were gradually shed and replaced throughout its lifetime. It shared its habitat with plant eaters such as hadrosaurs (pages 104–107) and ankylosaurs (pages 164–165), which would also have been its prey.

MAXIMUM LENGTH	26.5 ft. (8m)
TIME	Late Cretaceous
FOSSIL FINDS	North America (U.S.A., Canada)

▽ *For tyrannosaurs life was a constant balancing act. As it strides along this* Tarbosaurus *holds its tail high so that it acts as a counterbalance for its enormous head.*

DASPLETOSAURUS
Only a handful of specimens of this dinosaur have been found, but its fossilized remains suggest that it may have been a direct ancestor of *Tyrannosaurus*. It probably weighed up to three tons, and would have been about 16.5 ft. (5m) tall. Like other tyrannosaurs, *Daspletosaurus* had an extra set of ribs called gastralia between its true ribs and its pelvis. These helped support its intestines and may have protected them when resting on the ground.

MAXIMUM LENGTH	26.5 ft. (8m)
TIME	Late Cretaceous
FOSSIL FINDS	North America (Alberta)

TARBOSAURUS
This Asian tyrannosaur looks very much like *Tyrannosaurus*, but had a longer skull and was not so heavily built. Like *Tyrannosaurus*, it was unlikely to have survived solely by hunting and probably scavenged dead remains. It lived in Asia, where it would have been the largest land predator. Fossil remains of *Tarbosaurus* were first discovered in 1948 and since then experts have been divided on exactly where it fits into the tyrannosaur family. Because it is so similar to *Tyrannosaurus*, some experts think that it might actually be the same animal.

MAXIMUM LENGTH	46 ft. (14m)
TIME	Late Cretaceous
FOSSIL FINDS	Asia (Mongolia)

▽ *With a menacing lunge of its head, a Tyrannosaurus threatens a Troodon that has just stolen part of its meal. The subject of the feast is a hadrosaur, which has died from natural causes. Remains like these probably made up an important part of Tyrannosaurus' diet. Like scavengers today, Tyrannosaurus would have found this type of food partly by smell and partly by looking to see where other scavengers had gathered.*

TYRANNOSAURUS

After *Carcharadontosaurus* (page 142), this huge animal was probably the largest land-based predator that has ever lived on Earth. Several superbly preserved fossil skeletons have been found, most notably "Sue" (page 147), which was discovered in 1990. These fossils show that *Tyrannosaurus* weighed up to seven tons and towered up to 20 ft. (6m) high. It took strides nearly 16.5 ft. (5m) long—farther than most long-jumps—and dealt with its food using 6 in. (15cm)-long teeth with serrated edges like steak knives. Some scientists have suggested that it was too large to pursue its prey in the open, because its tiny arms could not have broken its fall if it tripped and fell. Instead, it may have hunted by lurking among trees, launching an attack when its prey was close.

MAXIMUM LENGTH	46 ft. (14m)
TIME	Late Cretaceous

FOSSIL FINDS North America (U.S.A., Canada), Asia (Mongolia)

ALIORAMUS

Most tyrannosaurs had deep skulls, and jaws that were flattened from side to side. *Alioramus* and its relatives were different, because their skulls had elongated snouts with weaker jaws. *Alioramus* also had about six bony knobs located between its nostrils and eyes. These knobs were too small to have been weapons, and it is possible that they played a part in courtship, like the "horns" some lizards have today. If this is true, they may have been present only in the males.

MAXIMUM LENGTH	16.5 ft. (6m)
TIME	Late Cretaceous
FOSSIL FINDS	Asia (Mongolia)

FOSSIL HUNTING IN NORTH AMERICA

THE FIRST DINOSAUR FOSSILS WERE FOUND IN EUROPE, BUT NORTH AMERICA IS THE PLACE WHERE "DINOMANIA" REALLY GOT UNDERWAY —PARTLY AS A RESULT OF A BITTER FEUD BETWEEN TWO LEADING PALEONTOLOGISTS.

In 1858 the zoologist Joseph Leidy described the first dinosaur skeleton found in North America as *Hadrosaurus*. But during the late 1800s two much more forceful characters dominated the fossil-hunting stage: Edward Drinker Cope (1840–97) and Othniel Charles Marsh (1831–99). They discovered huge numbers of fossils, and their rivalry ignited public interest in North America's fascinating prehistoric life.

Dry places are particularly good for finding fossils. Over millions of years wind and rain scour the surface of the ground, revealing fossils entombed in the underlying rock. This tree trunk is one of hundreds in Arizona's Petrified Forest National Park. This particular trunk has broken into sections as the rock that supported it has slowly crumbled away.

COLLECTING THE PAST

By the time Cope and Marsh died, they had accumulated an extraordinary variety of fossil remains. These included the first reconstruction of a giant plant-eating sauropod—*Apatosaurus* (known at the time as *Brontosaurus*)—and a wide array of others, including predators such as allosaurs and tyrannosaurs, as well as the horned dinosaurs, or ceratopsids, which were unique to North America. They also helped trace the path that evolution had followed. Marsh, for

△▷ *Edward Drinker Cope (above) and Othniel Charles Marsh (right) were pioneering North American paleontologists.*

example, assembled a complete series of fossil horses, showing how these animals had slowly adapted to life on North America's open plains.

TREASURE TROVES

Because of its size and varied geography North America is a paleontologist's paradise. Many of the best finds have been made in the Badlands and deserts of the midwestern U.S.A., where ancient sedimentary rocks have been slowly eroded by rivers, rain, and wind. Some of these sites have produced an enormous number of fossils. At Ghost Ranch in New Mexico, for example, the remains of over 1,000 *Coelophysis*—a small bipedal predator—are convincing evidence that these agile animals hunted in packs. Another site, the Red Deer River in Alberta, Canada, has produced more types of dinosaurs than any equivalent area in the world. Farther west—and further back in time—Canada was also the site of one of the most important fossil formations revealing early animal life: the Burgess Shale (page 32–35).

Not all North American fossil finds consist of remains that were once buried in rock. The famous La Brea tar pits, in Los Angeles, are deposits of sticky tar that has seeped up from natural springs since prehistoric times. From these treacherous pools the fossilized remains of thousands of trapped animals have been recovered (page 212).

△ *Paleontonlogists work on the fossilized skeleton of a* Tyrannosaurus, *cleaning and stabilizing the remains before they are removed from the site where the have lain for over 60 million years.*

RECENT DISCOVERIES

North America is famous for giant fossils, and in recent years there have been spectacular discoveries. One of the most exciting came in 1990, when the remains of a gigantic

Tyrannosaurus rex were found in South Dakota. The fossil—named Sue after its finder Sue Hendrickson—is now displayed in the Field Museum, Chicago, and is the largest and most complete *Tyrannosaurus* on display anywhere in the world. Unlike previous finds, Sue's skeleton includes a wishbone, or furcula—evidence that supports the widespread belief that birds evolved from predatory dinosaurs.

Some finds are accidental. In 1979 two hikers in New Mexico came across the fossilized tail of *Seismosaurus*. The tail led paleontologists to the rest of this plant eater's skeleton, which is still being unearthed.

▽ *Soft sedimentary rocks are a prime source of fossils. These rocks in Arizona were laid down during the Triassic.*

△ *Excavating fossils is a delicate business. A wooden frame is used to protect the pelvis of a* Tyrannosaurus *before it is winched away from the surrounding bedrock.*

◁ *The completed mount of Sue's fossilized skeleton is displayed at the Field Museum in Chicago. This massive animal weighed about 6.5 tons and was nearly 42.7 ft. (13m) long.*

WERE DINOSAURS WARM-BLOODED?

BECAUSE DINOSAURS WERE REPTILES IT IS EASY TO IMAGINE THAT THEIR BODIES WORKED LIKE MODERN REPTILES'. BUT IN ONE KEY AREA THEY MAY HAVE BEEN DISTINCTLY DIFFERENT.

At one time, scientists assumed that dinosaurs were cold-blooded, which means that their temperature depended on their surroundings. But in the early 1970s an American biologist, Robert Bakker (page 84), argued that they might have been warm-blooded, like mammals and birds. This controversial theory has radically altered ideas about dinosaur biology.

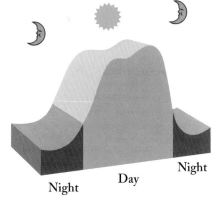

Lizards are cold-blooded. Their temperature rises as the day warms and then falls at night.

Walruses are warm-blooded. Their body temperature always remains at 95°F (35°C).

WARMTH FROM WITHIN

Living vertebrates (animals with backbones) can be divided into two overall groups. Animals in the first group—amphibians, fish, and reptiles—are cold-blooded, or ectothermic. Their body temperature rises and falls according to the temperature around them. Birds and mammals, on the other hand, are warm-blooded, or endothermic. An inbuilt thermostat keeps their body temperature almost constant—and usually much higher than that of their surroundings. Warm-blooded animals generate more heat by breaking down more food, and they retain it by having an insulating layer of feathers, fat, or fur.

These two different systems have some far-reaching effects on the way animals live, because bodies work more efficiently at high temperatures. When it is hot, cold-blooded animals are also hot, and they can move quickly. But when it becomes cool, the same animals become slow and sluggish. In really cold conditions they have difficulty moving at all. Warm-blooded animals stay warm whatever the conditions are outside, so birds and mammals can remain active and busy during the coldest winters; some of them are even comfortable on polar ice.

WRAPPING UP

Dinosaur remains do contain some clues that hint at a warm-blooded lifestyle. For many paleontologists one of the most convincing is feathery insulation—something that has only been seen in the very recent past. The first feathered dinosaur, *Sinosauropteryx*, was discovered in northeast China in 1996, revealing patches of feathery filaments around its fossilized skeleton. In 2000 an even clearer example of primitive plumage—this time in a dromaeosaur—was unearthed in the same region (page 111). Neither of these Chinese dinosaurs could fly, and the only conceivable function for their feathers was to retain body heat. Both were small predatory theropods, and if they had feathers, it is quite likely that other theropods did as well. They were not the only insulated reptiles of prehistoric times. Some pterosaurs, such as

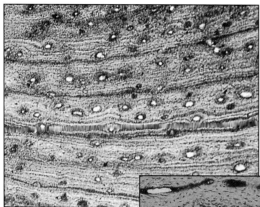

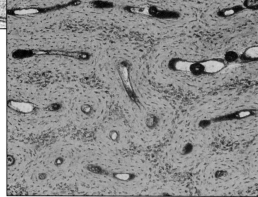

Sordes (page 174), seem to have had the equivalent of close-cropped fur.

Another factor that points to warm-bloodedness was their way of life. Like other small theropods, *Sinosauropteryx* had a relatively large brain, and its skeleton shows that it would have been an agile and fleet-footed hunter. This kind of lifestyle would have called for rapid reactions—a characteristic feature of warm-blooded animals.

EVIDENCE IN BONE

Some experts also believe that signs of warm-bloodedness can be seen in dinosaur skeletons. In the 1970s Robert Bakker pointed out that when looked at under a microscope, dinosaur bones show signs of sustained rapid growth. This feature is common in warm-blooded animals, but rarer in cold-blooded ones, except in times when there is a particularly good supply of food.

But many paleontologists today find this evidence doubtful, and recent research into dinosaur breathing has prompted different conclusions. The paleontologists looked at dinosaur noses with X-ray scanners, searching for turbinal bones inside the nasal cavity. In birds and mammals these bones form a complicated collection of paper-thin scrolls that allow warmth and moisture to be collected and recycled from outgoing air. But if dinosaurs were cold-blooded, their breath would also have been cold, so there would have been no warmth to recycle and probably no turbinal bones. The results so far show that dinosaurs did not have them.

DINOSAUR HEARTS

If dinosaurs were warm-blooded, their circulatory systems would have been modified to produce a higher rate of oxygen flow. They would have needed larger hearts than their cold-blooded relatives, and their blood would almost certainly have flowed in a figure-eight circuit. This double circulation system allows oxygen-rich blood to be pumped at high pressure and high speed.

Unfortunately, soft organs, such as dinosaur hearts, hardly ever fossilize, but in 2000 the remains of what looked like a heart were found in a fossil of *Thescelosaurus*, a small plant-eating hypsilophodont. Using medical scanning techniques, researchers concluded that it did have a double circulation system, meaning that it could have been warm-blooded.

◁ *The photograph (far left) shows growth rings in dinosaur bone. Growth rings like these are usually found in cold-blooded animals, and they show spurts of growth that occur during warm conditions, when there is plenty of food.*

◁ *Dinosaurs also have fibrolamellar bone (center), which is found in warm-blooded animals. This kind of bone grows quickly, and is not usually found in cold-blooded animals, although there are some exceptions to this rule.*

DOUBLE CIRCULATION SYSTEM

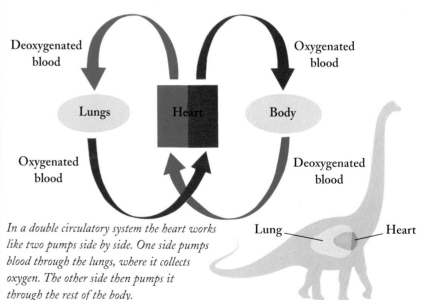

Deoxygenated blood · Oxygenated blood · Lungs · Heart · Body · Oxygenated blood · Deoxygenated blood · Lung · Heart

In a double circulatory system the heart works like two pumps side by side. One side pumps blood through the lungs, where it collects oxygen. The other side then pumps it through the rest of the body.

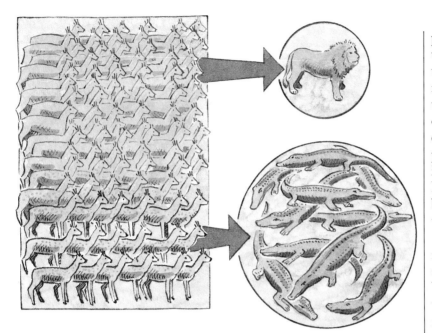

△ A warm-blooded predator needs about ten times as much food as a cold-blooded one, so 100 antelope could keep one lion, or 10 crocodiles, fed for a year.

▽ Warm-blooded hunters need a high intake of food to keep their bodies working, and to make up for heat loss.

ENERGY FROM FOOD

In the debate about whether dinosaurs were warm-blooded, the search for anatomical clues continues. But paleontologists also have another line of evidence—the relative numbers of predators and their prey.

Cold-blooded predators, which include all of today's reptiles, can survive on a small amount of food. Crocodiles, for example, can go for weeks between meals, because they need only a small amount of energy to keep their bodies running, and some snakes can last over a year. Warm-blooded predators, on the other hand, use up about ten times as much energy simply running their bodies and keeping them warm, which means that they need to take in about ten times as much food per kilogram (2.2 lb.) of body weight. A lion can survive without eating for a few days, but if this hungry period stretches to much more than a week, it runs the serious risk of starving to death. For smaller warm-blooded animals things become critical even more rapidly, because their body warmth quickly drains away.

This difference means that the same numbers of prey can support ten times as many cold-blooded hunters as warm-blooded ones. Assuming that hunters and their prey fossilize at the same rate (which may or may not be true), paleontologists should be able to tell if a predatory dinosaur was warm-blooded simply by counting fossils, and doing some simple arithmetic.

At present, this work on prehistoric ecology is still underway. Some researchers claim to have found a warm-blooded ratio, but the overall picture is far from clear.

MIX AND MATCH

Faced with this confusing and sometimes contradictory evidence, paleontologists have come to a variety of conclusions. Some think that all dinosaurs were warm-blooded, while others believe that they were cold-blooded, like modern reptiles. But a growing number are convinced that different groups of dinosaurs worked in different ways.

According to this idea, small highly active predators, such as *Sinosauropteryx*, were fully warm-blooded, like birds, while some of the smaller plant eaters may have been cold-blooded, like modern reptiles. But the largest dinosaurs—particularly the sauropods—may have been somewhere in between, simply because they were so big. Like giant fermentation tanks on legs, these animals would have absorbed heat energy as their internal microbes broke down their food, but their massive bulk would have meant that this heat would have been very slow to drain away. They would have been "lukewarm-blooded"—a curious situation that has no equivalent in animals alive today.

ARMORED DINOSAURS

In the early stages of dinosaur evolution, plant-eating species often relied on their great size to protect them from predators. But during the Jurassic Period, different ways of protecting herbivores from attack evolved. One of these was body armor, a defensive system that allowed plant eaters to stand their ground. Most armored dinosaurs belonged to the ornithischian, or bird-hipped, branch of the dinosaur world. They included animals with massive head shields and gigantic horns, as well as ones that carried their own armor plating on their backs.

DINOSAUR DEFENSES

FOR PLANT-EATING DINOSAURS, RESISTING
ATTACK RATHER THAN RUNNING AWAY WAS
A HIGH-RISK STRATEGY. IN A WORLD FULL
OF PREDATORS THEY NEEDED THE BEST
DEFENSES THAT EVOLUTION COULD PROVIDE.

It is hard to imagine what it feels like to be approached
by a hungry carnivore weighing six or seven tons. In
normal circumstances most plant-eating dinosaurs did
their very best to prevent this from happening by being
constantly alert for danger and being ready to walk or run
away. But for armored dinosaurs different instincts applied.
These animals evolved a strategy that meant standing their
ground. Their bodies were designed to withstand a direct
assault, but to increase their chances of survival, many of
them tried to land the first blow by going on the attack.

*Dinosaur defenses are not always what
they seem. Stegosaurus had a row of bony
plates along its back, which were once thought
to be armor against attack. However, detailed
examination of fossilized plates—like the one
shown here—has revealed that they were made
of relatively soft bone. Instead of being a form
of armor, they are more likely to have been
used to control body temperature.*

JAWS AND CLAWS
Unlike predatory theropods, most plant-
eating dinosaurs were unable to do much
damage with their teeth. This was either
because they did not have any or because
their teeth were shaped for collecting and
crushing plants, rather than for stabbing
flesh. Some armored species had toothless
beaks that could deliver a dangerous
bite (page 155), but jaws played little
part in plant eaters' self-defense.
Feet and claws were another
matter. Many sauropods could
rear up on their hind legs
to stamp on an attacker—
something that was
made even more
effective by a single
sharp thumb

claw on each front foot. Although they were much smaller, many ornithopods also had these claws, and because they often moved on only their hind legs, they would have been able to carry out hand-to-hand combat. These thumb claws were especially large in iguanodonts (page 100).

WHIPS AND CLUBS

But with some plant eaters the part that a predator had to watch out for was the tail. The 33-ft. (10-m)-long tail of an adult *Diplodocus* had the same sort of strength and flexibility as tire rubber reinforced by strands of steel wire. If it was given a sudden flick, the tip would reach supersonic speeds, wrapping around an enemy's body like a whip. A well-aimed blow against a predator's eyes or legs would leave it temporarily blinded or reeling on the ground.

Some sauropods, such as *Shunosaurus* (page 75), had tails with bony tips, which turned them into clubs. The real specialists at this form of defense were the ankylosaurs (page 165). Their tails were not particularly long by dinosaur standards, but they carried a more substantial weight. In *Euoplocephalus*, one of the largest species, the tail could probably reach a speed of over 30 mph (50km/h) by the end of a 180-degree swing, landing with enough force to inflict a skull-cracking blow.

SPINES AND HORNS

Clubbing the enemy was one way to fight back—stabbing it was another. Stegosaurs and nodosaurs both used this kind of defense, one group fielding spines on their tails and the other having them on their shoulders. It is not always easy to distinguish true weapons from ornaments (pages 162-163), but a sideways slant is often a clue that a spine could be used in earnest—vertical ones were more likely to be for show.

Ceratopsians, which include *Triceratops* and its relatives, often had giant head shields and horns projecting from their muzzles and brows. These were probably used partly for impressing rivals and partly for self-defense.

ARMOR PLATING

If all else failed and a predator continued its attack, armored dinosaurs relied on their body plating to save them. This consisted of flat pieces or raised nodules of bone, which developed in the skin rather than being attached directly to the skeleton. Bony growths like this, called osteoderms, also formed the ankylosaurs' clubs. Interestingly, osteoderms are one of the oldest forms of self-defense in the vertebrate world, dating back to the first armored fish, 400 million years ago. Unfortunately, osteoderms—and the spines attached to them—usually become scattered when an animal dies, so it is often difficult to decide exactly how they would have been arranged in life. However, they were usually separated by small areas of skin, which allowed the armored layer to bend. Many armored dinosaurs had well-protected backs but relatively vulnerable undersides—a weak point that their enemies would have exploited if they had the opportunity.

△ *These three tails show different adaptations for defense. In* Ankylosaurus *(left) the tail ends in a body club.* Stegosaurus' *tail (center) is armed with spikes.* Diplodocus' *tail (right) had neither, but was extremely strong and could be slapped at an enemy like a whip.*

◁ *A* Stegosaurus *fossil from the Morrison Formation, in Wyoming, shows what look like defensive plates. The true function of these plates may actually have been very different.*

◁ *Crouching down to protect its vulnerable underside (far left), a* Euoplocephalus *lashes out at a* Tyrannosaurus *with its tail club. To be really effective, the blow needed to be well aimed —not easy to do because the animal was inevitably facing the other way.*

		Cambrian	Ordovician	Silurian	Devonian	Carboniferous	Permian	Triassic

ARMORED DINOSAURS

CERATOPSIDS

Often known as horned dinosaurs, most members of this family were distinguished by armor-plated skulls and formidable horns. Their armor would have been used for defending themselves against predators and perhaps in courtship, much as rhinoceroses use theirs today. The ceratopsids were one of the last families of dinosaurs to evolve before the great extinction 66 million years ago. They were plant eaters and ranged from the size of a large dog to larger than a bull elephant. They almost certainly foraged in herds and lived across the Northern Hemisphere.

PSITTACOSAURUS

Named "parrot lizard" because of its parrotlike beak, *Psittacosaurus* walked on two legs and was once classified as an early iguanodont. However, it is now thought to have been a primitive ceratopsid. It lacked the horns and frills of true horned dinosaurs, but it did have a ridge of bone at the top of its skull to which its jaw muscles were attached, and small horny projections on its cheeks. *Psittacosaurus* stood about

▽ Psittacosaurus *ate cycads and other tough plants, and it balanced itself with its tail.*

◁ Leptoceratops *would probably have been able to move on either two or four legs. Its front feet had five clawed, prehensile fingers for grasping vegetation and pulling it toward its beak.*

3.3 ft. (1m) high at the shoulder and probably had a lifespan of 10 to 15 years.

MAXIMUM LENGTH 8.2 ft. (2.5m)	
TIME Early Cretaceous	
FOSSIL FINDS Asia (China, Mongolia, Thailand)	

LEPTOCERATOPS

This small dinosaur represents a halfway stage between the parrot dinosaurs, such as *Psittacosaurus*, and the later horned dinosaurs. Like *Psittacosaurus*, it had a parrotlike beak, although with some teeth in the upper jaw. However, the fringed projection at the back of the skull is more evident, without being as exaggerated as it was in later ceratopsids. Unlike its later relatives, it did not have any horns. With its well-developed back legs, *Leptoceratops* was a good runner—an essential feature for a plant eater with no other way of defending itself. It probably ate on all fours, but reared up when it needed to move at any speed.

MAXIMUM LENGTH 9 ft. (2.7m)	
TIME Late Cretaceous	
FOSSIL FINDS Asia (Mongolia), North America, Australia	

MICROCERATOPS

The midget of the ceratopsid family, *Microceratops* was lightly built and probably quick on its feet, judging from its long, athletically built hind legs. However, it would almost certainly have grazed on all fours, keeping an eye out for potential predators and running away if one was spotted. The back of its skull had the raised fringe typical of this dinosaur family.

MAXIMUM LENGTH 31.5 ft. (80cm)	
TIME Late Cretaceous	
FOSSIL FINDS Asia (China, Mongolia)	

BAGACERATOPS

Bagaceratops represents another step along, or divergence from, the evolutionary line for the ceratopsids. It was small but heavily built, with a solid body and stout legs, and it would have moved on all fours. It had the beginnings of a skull crest, with bony ridges leading up from its sharp, birdlike beak. It also had a blunt, stubby horn on the top of its nose and earlike horny projections on each cheek. It would have used its beak to tear off vegetation and its cheek teeth to grind it up. Well-preserved fossils of *Bagaceratops* have been found. From their posture it seems some may belong to animals that were in underground nests when they died.

MAXIMUM LENGTH 3.3 ft. (1m)

TIME Late Cretaceous

FOSSIL FINDS Asia (Mongolia)

PROTOCERATOPS

Some excellent fossil finds have given paleontologists a good picture of what *Protoceratops* looked like and how it lived. It was a heavily built creature, weighing about 440 lb. (200kg), although it stood less than 3.3 ft. (1m) tall. It normally moved on all fours, but it may have been able to raise itself up and run on two. It had a pronounced shieldlike projection at the back of its head, which anchored some of the muscles that worked its powerful beak. When this dinosaur was discovered, in the 1920s, paleontologists also found nests and fossilized eggs. The eggs had remarkably thin shells and were laid in groups of over a dozen in spirals in the sand.

MAXIMUM LENGTH 9 ft. (2.7m)

TIME Late Cretaceous

FOSSIL FINDS Asia (Mongolia, China)

▽ *The fossilized remains of a fight to the death between a* Protoceratops *and a* Velociraptor *were found in 1971.* Velociraptor *had vicious claws to slash its prey, but despite being a plant eater,* Protoceratops *was able to hit back with its powerful beak. The desperate duel seems to have ended in a stalemate, leaving both dinosaurs mortally wounded. Their remains were probably engulfed by sand.*

ARMORED DINOSAURS

STYRACOSAURUS

The most formidably armed of the horned dinosaurs, *Styracosaurus* fully lived up to its name, which means "spiked lizard." It was actually far larger than any lizard alive today, with a single 2-ft. (60-cm)-long horn on the tip of its nose and a ring of equally impressive spikes around its head shield. It weighed about three tons, and it probably defended itself like a modern-day rhinoceros, using its horns and spikes to inflict serious injuries. Studies of this dinosaur's body shape and fossilized tracks indicate that it ran on all fours at speeds of up to 20 mph (32km/h). A find of about 100 fossilized specimens in Arizona makes it look very likely that *Styracosaurus* lived in herds.

The dinosaurs probably ate cycads and palms, grinding the tough leaves with their cheek teeth.

MAXIMUM LENGTH 18 ft. (5.5m)

TIME Late Cretaceous

FOSSIL FINDS North America (Alberta, Arizona, Montana)

PACHYRHINOSAURUS

Scientists are unsure whether or not this ceratopsid had a nose horn because the fossil evidence consists of about a dozen incomplete skulls. The skulls have a thick ridge of bone between the eyes. This may have formed the base of a horn that later fell away, or it may have been a weapon in its own right. However, both sexes certainly had a large, frilled head shield, which was armed with horns and spikes. *Pachyrhinosaurus* weighed over 2.5 tons, and its

▽ *During their relatively short history ceratopsids developed an amazing variety of head shields and horns. From the left the trio shown below are* Styracosaurus, Pachyrhinosaurus, *and the massively built* Triceratops. *These animals' shields and horns had a dual purpose —they were used to fend off predators, but they were also used in real or mock fights with rivals. The horns and frills may also have been used to help them cool down when necessary.*

arched back was almost twice the height of an adult human being.

MAXIMUM LENGTH	23 ft. (7m)
TIME	Late Cretaceous
FOSSIL FINDS	North America (Alaska, Alberta)

TRICERATOPS

The most famous of the horned dinosaurs, *Triceratops* gets its name from its three-horned head. It was the giant of its family, weighing up to ten tons. The two horns on its brow were 3.3 ft. (1m) or more in length, while its entire skull was up to 10 ft. (3m) long, making it one of the largest of the dinosaurs. Its skull shield was remarkable because of its size and because it consisted of a solid sheet of bone. Hundreds of fossils show that this huge plant eater roamed North America in large herds. Some skulls show major injuries, suggesting that these animals engaged in fierce contests, probably over mates. *Triceratops* was one of the last of its line, evolving a few million years before the dinosaurs disappeared.

MAXIMUM LENGTH	30 ft. (9m)
TIME	Late Cretaceous
FOSSIL FINDS	Western North America

△ *Like other ceratopsids,* Anchiceratops *was a variable animal, with no two individuals having exactly the same shield and horn shape. Some scientists think that these differences would have allowed these dinosaurs to recognize each other as they mingled in herds.*

ANCHICERATOPS

Considerably smaller than *Triceratops*, this animal had a long and narrow head shield with a serrated edge of backward-pointing spines. Its shield also had a pronounced central dividing ridge. *Anchiceratops* was a swamp dweller and lived on lush vegetation, gathering it up with its parrotlike beak. It could weigh over five tons and probably spent much of its time wading through shallow water and wet mud.

MAXIMUM LENGTH	20 ft. (6m)
TIME	Late Cretaceous
FOSSIL FINDS	North America (Alberta)

CENTROSAURUS

Looking like a gigantic rhinoceros—although from a totally different line of the animal world—*Centrosaurus* was a heavy, powerful, thick-set animal with a large horn on top of its beaklike snout. Unlike many other ceratopsids, it had a relatively short head shield, although it was edged with toothlike horns. The frill was not made of solid bone, but had two openings, reducing its weight. In Canada a find of about 50 specimens close together points to their being herd animals.

MAXIMUM LENGTH	20 ft. (6m)
TIME	Late Cretaceous
FOSSIL FINDS	North America (Alberta, Montana)

ARMORED DINOSAURS

STEGOSAURS

Stegosaurs were slow-moving plant eaters with a double row of bony plates or spines protruding from their backs. These plates were attached to their skin, rather than their skeletons, making it difficult to establish exactly how they were positioned in life. Opinions differ about their purpose; they may have been used for self-defense, but they could also have played a part in heat regulation, helping warm up or cool down the animal's blood. If so, the plates may have been able to blush—something that could have been used as part of a mating ritual or as a warning signal. Stegosaurs were also armed with vicious spikes on their tails, which would have been wielded like a medieval weapon to stab their enemies.

STEGOSAURUS

Stegosaurus weighed about three tons and was the largest member of its family. It had a strangely proportioned body, with its hind legs much larger than its front ones, giving it a massively humped back. Its remarkably small head was held low and housed a tiny brain, which was not much larger than a walnut. Like other stegosaurs, it had a beaklike snout, and chewing teeth at the back of its mouth. *Stegosaurus* probably fed on all fours, although some experts think it could have reared up to reach its food.

MAXIMUM LENGTH 29.5 ft. (9m)

TIME Late Jurassic

FOSSIL FINDS Western North America, Europe (U.K.)

158

▷ *One of the oldest known stegosaurs,* Huayangosaurus *was also one of the smallest, standing only about 6 ft. (1.8m) at the hips— roughly the height of a man—and weighing just over one ton. It may have been the ancestor of later members of the stegosaur family.*

◁ *The five animals shown here give an idea of how stegosaur armor varied.* Tuojiangosaurus *(top left) and* Stegosaurus *(top right) had two rows of broad, flat plates. The plates look impressive, but many paleontologists think they were actually too thin to have been used in self-defense.* Dacentrurus *(bottom left),* Lexovisaurus *(bottom center), and* Kentrosaurus *(bottom right) had narrower plates graded into spikes on their tails. These five animals shared several features typical of their family—elephantlike legs, an arched back, and a relatively tiny head.*

HUAYANGOSAURUS

Like the rest of the family, *Huayangosaurus* was equipped with a paired row of pointed back plates and a further elongated and hornlike pair on its hips. Its tail was armed with two pairs of pointed horns. Unusually for a stegosaur, it had teeth in its beak, rather than just in its cheeks. *Huayangosaurus* is one of several species that have been unearthed in China, making this region the best part of the world for stegosaur remains.

MAXIMUM LENGTH	13 ft. (4m)
TIME	Mid Jurassic
FOSSIL FINDS	China

TUOJIANGOSAURUS

A good picture of this dinosaur comes from the discovery of two sets of fossilized remains found in China. It had pairs of V-shaped plates running along its spine, which were largest in the middle of its back and decreased in size toward its neck and tail. Just like *Stegosaurus*, it had two pairs of long, spiky horns on its tail and a steeply arched back. At its tallest point—over its hips—it was about 6.6 ft. (2m) high.

MAXIMUM LENGTH	23 ft. (7m)
TIME	Late Jurassic
FOSSIL FINDS	China

KENTROSAURUS

First discovered in the early 1900s, during the German fossil-hunting expeditions to Tanzania (page 160), *Kentrosaurus* is one of Africa's best-known stegosaurs, with dozens of additional specimens being unearthed in recent times. Although similar in shape to *Stegosaurus*, *Kentrosaurus* was much smaller. The pairs of plates on its back gave way to spiky horns, about 2 ft. (60cm) long, from midway down its back to the tip of its tail. It was believed to have had a long spike protruding sideways from each of its hips, or perhaps from each of its shoulders. These spikes would have been useful in self-defense. Like other stegosaurs, it had relatively small teeth for a plant eater and may have swallowed stones to help it grind up its food (page 78).

MAXIMUM LENGTH	16.4 ft. (5m)
TIME	Late Jurassic
FOSSIL FINDS	Africa (Tanzania)

LEXOVISAURUS

Named after an ancient tribe from France, where some of the earliest remains were found, *Lexovisaurus* was a typical stegosaur, with pairs of narrow pointed plates down its back, as well as an additional pair of spikes, up to 4 ft. (1.2m) long, thought to have been located on its shoulders. Weighing up to two tons, it was probably faster than some of the larger stegosaurs and may have been able to run at speeds of up to 19 mph (30km/h).

MAXIMUM LENGTH	16.4 ft. (5m)
TIME	Mid Jurassic
FOSSIL FINDS	Europe (England, France)

DACENTRURUS

One of the smaller stegosaurs and also one of the earliest, *Dacentrurus* weighed about one ton and was well armed with sharply pointed back and tail plates up to 18 in. (45cm) long. Its remains have been found in several locations in western Europe, and they include what may have been one of its eggs.

MAXIMUM LENGTH	14.8 ft. (4.5m)
TIME	Mid Jurassic
FOSSIL FINDS	Europe (England, France, Portugal)

FOSSIL HUNTING IN AFRICA

AFTER SOME SPECTACULAR DISCOVERIES DURING THE LAST 100 YEARS, AFRICA IS A KEY DESTINATION FOR PALEONTOLOGISTS. FAMOUS FOR FOSSILS OF HUMAN ANCESTORS, ITS PREHISTORIC INHABITANTS INCLUDED THE LARGEST LAND PREDATORS EVER.

Fossil collecting in Africa began on a truly grand scale with the discovery of an immense "dinosaur graveyard" in Tanzania in 1907. Since the 1920s East and South Africa have produced finds that help us to map out human evolution, and recently major dinosaur finds have been made on the edges of the Sahara Desert and in Madagascar.

FOSSIL EVIDENCE

Paul Sereno, seen here during his 1993 expedition to Niger, has been one of the most successful fossil hunters of recent years. As well as discovering Afrovenator *and rediscovering* Carcharodontosaurus, *he has made some major breakthroughs in the study of early dinosaurs in South America. His finds here include* Eoraptor *and the most complete specimens so far collected of* Herrerasaurus.

△ Afrovenator— *"African hunter"—was an allosaur that lived in the Early Cretaceous. It was up to 29.5 ft. (9m) long and weighed up to two tons.*

THE HUNTER-KILLERS

Ask anyone to name a giant predatory dinosaur, and the chances are that they will think of *Tyrannosaurus rex*. Far less well known, although probably even larger, was an immense allosaur that lived in North Africa in Early Cretaceous times. Called *Carcharodontosaurus*, which literally means "shark-toothed lizard," this awe-inspiring predator was first discovered in the 1920s, when European paleontologists found parts of its skull and a small number of other bones. These remains were eventually taken to

a museum in southern Germany, but during World War II the building was damaged by Allied bombs, and its unique fossils were destroyed.

For the next five decades, it remained on the list of dinosaurs that had been found and then lost. That was the situation in 1996, when a team from the University of Chicago, led by paleontologist Paul Sereno, carried out a prospecting trip in Morocco's Atlas

▽ *Seen next to the extraordinarily large skull of* Carcharodontosaurus, *a human skull looks like little more than a bite-sized snack.*

Mountains. Working on a ridge of eroded sandstone, they extracted a skull measuring 5.2 ft. (1.6m) long: *Carcharodontosaurus* had been rediscovered, and the new specimen was even larger than the one that had vanished during World War II. For Paul Sereno this discovery was both a first and a second, because he had already found another African allosaur—which he named *Afrovenator*—during an expedition to Niger in 1993.

Off the coast of Africa, Madagascar is also a scene of great interest in the dinosaur world. In 1999 remains of primitive plant-eating dinosaurs were found to be over 230 million years old, making them the most ancient species yet discovered.

THE FOSSILS OF TENDAGURU HILL

Paleontologists in Africa often work in remote locations, but they do have the benefit of modern transportation. Things were not so easy in the early 1900s when the German naturalist Eberhard Fraas traveled through Tanzania—then known as Tanganyika—following up information about fossil finds at a site called Tendaguru Hill. On arrival Fraas found that Tendaguru contained a vast array of remains. Between 1909 and 1913 German paleontologists carried out four expeditions to the area and collected over 200 tons of fossils. These were coated in plaster, packed up, and then carried all the way to the coast to be shipped back to Europe.

Among this extraordinary haul were the remains of a large range of plant eaters, including stegosaurs, hypsilophodonts, and diplodocids. But in terms of size the most impressive finds were several partial *Brachiosaurus* skeletons, including—unusually for a sauropod—an almost complete skull. When these eventually arrived in Germany, a complete *Brachiosaurus* skeleton was assembled, creating the largest articulated dinosaur fossil in the world. The skeleton is still housed in Berlin's Humboldt Museum.

HUMAN ORIGINS

One visitor to Tendaguru, after the German excavations were over, was the British anthropologist Louis Leakey. At the time of Leakey's visit most anthropologists believed that human evolution had begun in Asia—an idea that American fossil-hunting

expeditions hoped to prove when they visited the Gobi Desert (page 108). But during his long career, spent largely in Tanzania and Kenya, Louis Leakey and his wife, Mary, helped show that this was not true. Among their fossil finds was *Homo habilis*, a humanlike primate that was a direct ancestor of our own species and lived about two million years ago.

Following Louis Leakey's death in 1972 his son Richard continued the family tradition, making several important finds.

◁ *Standing next to the remains of a* Brachiosaurus, *these Tanzanian laborers were some of the hundreds who excavated and carried fossils during the German expeditions to Tendaguru Hill in the early 1900s.*

◁ *The Tendaguru* Brachiosaurus—*the world's largest dinosaur on exhibit—is at the Humboldt Museum in Berlin. When this skeleton was prepared,* Brachiosaurus *was the tallest dinosaur known, but the number one position has since been taken by* Sauroposeidon.

◁ *Here a group of American and British paleontologists are at work, cleaning sauropod remains in Niger. Once exposed to the surface, fossils like these slowly fracture as they become warm and expand in the desert sunshine, then cool and contract after dark. Some of the resulting fragments can be seen on the ground.*

WEAPONS AND ORNAMENTS

IN THE DINOSAUR WORLD SOME BODY PARTS, SUCH AS HORNS AND SPINES, EVOLVED AS MUCH FOR IMPRESSING RIVALS AS FOR FENDING OFF PREDATORS.

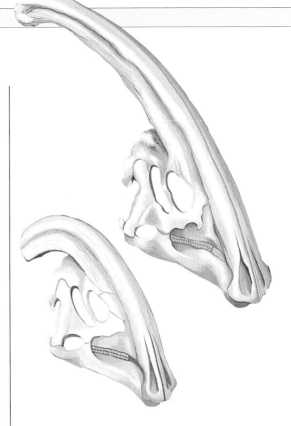

At first glance the huge horns of a *Triceratops* look as though they were designed for one thing only: keeping carnivores at bay. The same is true of their head shields and of the spines, lumps, and bumps that many armored dinosaurs possessed. But studies of living animals show that structures like these are not always what they seem. In modern mammals horns and antlers are often used by males as badges of rank, as well as for self-defense.

SEXUAL SELECTION

In the living world animals evolve because the ones best adapted for survival have the most young, which inherit their characteristics. This is called natural selection. But in many species another kind of selection is at work as well—sexual selection. It occurs when females decide which males to choose as mates. Imagine a species of bird in which males have red tails. If the females find red tails attractive, the males with the biggest and reddest tails will stand the best chance of mating. Those males will father more young, and the proportion of males with large red tails will slowly increase.

◁ *From relatively modest beginnings, shown here by* Protoceratops *(top), the head shields of ceratopsians became increasingly elaborate.* Styracosaurus *(middle) had holes in its spine-edged frill, but in* Triceratops *(left) the frill was solid and extremely heavy.*

△ *The crests of hadrosaurs are typical examples of structures that evolved through sexual selection. This shows two* Parasaurolophus *skulls; the male's crest is longer than the female's.*

Tails will get larger and redder, making males increasingly different from their mates.

What is true of tails is also true of any other feature that females find impressive, whether it is bright plumage, large horns, or the strength and skill to push rivals out of the way. Sexual selection can help exaggerate any of these as time goes by.

Sexual selection is something that paleontologists have to bear in mind when looking at dinosaur armor and weapons. For example, the elaborate head shields of *Triceratops* and its relatives almost certainly started out as a clear-cut form of defense. But over millions of years they became suspiciously large in males and highly elaborate. They also varied enormously from one species to another. To experts in animal evolution this suggests one thing: sexual selection was at work. As these animals evolved it slowly turned their head shields into ornaments as well as armor, helping the males to win mates.

Sometimes these ornaments were simply shown off, making their owner look more striking and desirable. The crests of some

hadrosaurs, for example, probably functioned in this way. But fossil remains show that head shields and horns of ceratopsids were used in ritual combat between rival males.

LOCKING HORNS

At the beginning of the breeding season *Triceratops* and its relatives probably behaved like many grassland animals today, with males sparring with each other for the right

that had this kind of drawback. A *Triceratops* head shield, for example, was an enormous and extremely heavy "attraction" that would have taken a large amount of energy to grow, and even more to carry around. To a lesser extent the thickened brain cases of dome-headed dinosaurs, or pachycephalosaurs, fell into the same category. But one of the best examples of an animal with burdensome body parts is the Irish elk, a prehistoric deer

▽ *In* Triceratops *the head shield and horns were status symbols that were shown off in male-to-male confrontations. However, when turned against predators, they made effective weapons. Here a mature male fights off a* Tyrannosaurus.

to mate. One of the key features of this kind of fighting is that it looks more dangerous than it really is. The two rivals square up to each other in a threatening way, but when they clash, they do so in a fashion that prevents either of them becoming seriously injured. Like today's buffalo and antelopes, ceratopsids had large air spaces in the front of their skulls. This helped cushion the impact of a head-on clash, protecting their brains from damage.

However, injuries did sometimes occur. Many *Triceratops* skulls show shallow nicks in their surface—evidence of painful gouges where an opponent's horns hit home.

GOING TO EXTREMES

An interesting feature of sexual selection is that it can make some body parts so large that they become a handicap. Dinosaurs and other prehistoric animals showed features

from the Pleistocene Epoch (page 211). Males had antlers over 10 ft. (3m) wide, which weighed nearly 110 lb. (50kg). Antlers this large were so cumbersome that they were almost useless as weapons, but amazingly—as in today's deer—they were shed and regrown each year.

▽ *Rhinoceroses use their horns in the same way as dinosaurs. With their horns locked together, these males are unlikely to do each other harm, but one will yield to the other.*

ARMORED DINOSAURS

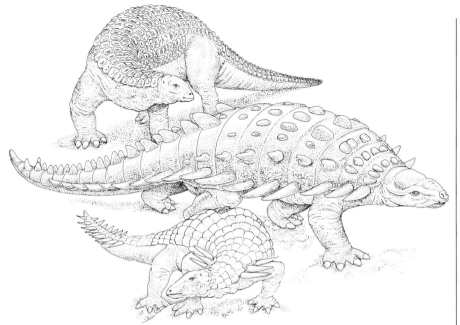

NODOSAURS AND ANKYLOSAURS

Ankylosaurids first appeared in the Late Jurassic, but their heyday was during the Cretaceous. First to evolve were the nodosaurs, which spread across the Northern Hemisphere. They were heavily built, slow-moving plant eaters equipped with body armor of horns and bony plates. Toward the end of the Cretaceous the nodosaurs gave way to the ankylosaurs proper, which had even tougher armor and a bony club at the end of their tail.

△ Nodosaurus (top), Hylaeosaurus (middle), and Silvisaurus (bottom) were all typical nodosaurs and had an extensive protective body armor of horny plates and spikes running over their backs. Only their legs and undersides lacked this protection, but incomplete fossils mean that their exact appearance is still a matter of conjecture.

HYLAEOSAURUS
Hylaeosaurus was first discovered in about 1830 by the famous British paleontologist Gideon Mantell. It was only the third dinosaur to be identified, and only a few isolated fragments of its skeleton have come to light since. As a result its exact appearance is difficult to establish, but it is likely to have shared a range of typical nodosaur features, including armor plating, perhaps backed up by rows of horns projecting sideways from its flanks and along its tail. Like other nodosaurs, its front legs were probably shorter than its hind legs,

giving it a humped profile, and they would have been stoutly built to carry the weight of its armor.

MAXIMUM LENGTH   19.7 ft. (6m)

TIME   Early Cretaceous

FOSSIL FINDS   Europe (England, France)

SILVISAURUS
Like *Hylaeosaurus*, this was an early nodosaur with a range of primitive features, including small, pointed teeth in its upper jaw—in contrast with later species, which typically had toothless beaks. It also had a relatively long neck, which makes it possible that it browsed on tall shrubs as well as eating plants closer to the ground. It was armored with large bony plates and also with spikes, but incomplete fossils make it difficult to tell how these were arranged on the living animal.

MAXIMUM LENGTH   13 ft. (4m)

TIME   Early Cretaceous

FOSSIL FINDS   North America (Kansas)

NODOSAURUS
With an arched back covered in bands of small bony plates, stretching from behind its neck right down its tail, *Nodosaurus*—"lumpy lizard"—looked like a huge prehistoric armadillo. No skulls have yet been found, but its head was likely to have been small, with fairly narrow jaws. Like all ankylosaurids, it fed on low-growing plants and had leaf-shaped teeth. Its heavy build and small brain were typical of an animal that relied on armor to avoid attack, and its lifestyle and diet make it probable that it lived in herds.

MAXIMUM LENGTH   19.7 ft. (6m)

TIME   Late Cretaceous

FOSSIL FINDS   North America (Kansas, Wyoming)

EDMONTONIA
Edmontonia was one of the largest nodosaurs. Several almost-complete fossil skeletons have been found, and they show that it was built even more solidly than a rhinoceros. A band of bony plates extended all the way down its tail, and there were additional plates over its neck and skull. The two vertebrae that joined

its head to its spine were fused together. This means that it would have had difficulty bending its neck. Once it reached adulthood, *Edmontonia* was so well-armored that it was unlikely to be attacked. It had several pairs of giant spikes protruding from its shoulders, which would have been an effective deterrent against predators. It lived in the same time and place as *Euoplocephalus*, but its narrower jaws imply that it had a different diet, reducing direct competition between the two.

MAXIMUM LENGTH 23 ft. (7m)

TIME Late Cretaceous

FOSSIL FINDS North America (Alaska, Alberta, Montana)

EUOPLOCEPHALUS

With body armor extending even in front of its eyelids and a tail ending in a heavy club, *Euoplocephalus* was a typical ankylosaur. It had a large head with protective spikes, and further spikes and nodules arranged in rows down its back and the base of its tail. Over 40 fossil finds have been made so far. These including several skulls, which show that it had a broad, toothless muzzle—one that would have been good at cropping swathes of low-growing plants. *Euoplocephalus* probably weighed about two tons, and although it was solidly built, its tail club suggests that it was quite nimble on its feet in the event of an attack by a predator.

MAXIMUM LENGTH 23 ft. (7m)

TIME Late Cretaceous

FOSSIL FINDS North America (Alberta, Montana)

ANKYLOSAURUS

Largest of the true ankylosaurs and almost the last of its line, *Ankylosaurus* was a massively built plant eater. It weighed up to four tons, but its club weighed over 110 lb. (50kg) and could be swung quickly to smash a predator's teeth or skull. It had armor plating embedded in its skin and the rows of spikes and raised nodules that characterize ankylosaurs. It may have been a herding animal, like many of its relatives, but its size means it would have been safe feeding on its own.

MAXIMUM LENGTH 32.8 ft. (10m)

TIME Late Cretaceous

FOSSIL FINDS North America (Alberta, Montana)

△ Euoplocephalus *(top), with its distinctive club-ended tail, and* Edmontonia *(bottom) coexisted in Late Cretaceous North America. Although they had the same general build, differences in their jaw structures suggest that they fed on different plants.*

◁ *Weighing as much as one of today's elephants, but with its own built-in weaponry and armor,* Ankylosaurus *was one of the best-protected plant eaters during the Age of the Reptiles, but it failed to survive when the Cretaceous Period came to an end.*

ARMORED DINOSAURS

DOME-HEADED DINOSAURS

In the dinosaur world a large head was not necessarily a sign of great intelligence. This is particularly true with the pachycephalosaurs, or bone-headed dinosaurs. These remarkable animals get their name from their reinforced brain case, which in some cases was over 8 in. (20cm) thick. Scientists believe that male bone-headed dinosaurs used their skulls in head-to-head clashes in the same way sheep or goats do today. Alternatively, they may have used them as battering rams to butt rivals in the side.

▽ Homalocephale *(top) and* Stegoceras *(bottom) were both small, bipedal, grazing dinosaurs with thickened tops to their skulls.* Homalocephale *had a flat top to its skull, and* Stegoceras *had a dome. Both lived in herds and used speed and agility to escape predators.*

HOMALOCEPHALE
Homalocephale's head had a thick, flat top of bone with bony protrusions around the edge like a crown. The thick skull bones were flexible and relatively porous. Some experts think that this is evidence against the head-butting theory, because a skull like this would not have been able to withstand a massive impact. Certainly no evidence of skull damage has been discovered. *Homalocephale* had small, leaf-shaped teeth, which indicates that it would have lived on a diet of plants, fruit, and seeds.

MAXIMUM LENGTH 10 ft. (3m)

TIME Late Cretaceous

FOSSIL FINDS Asia (Mongolia)

STEGOCERAS
In size, body shape, and behavior *Stegoceras* was probably very like *Homalocephale*. It too was a small, bipedal plant eater with a steeply sloping snout, and serrated teeth shaped for chewing low-growing plants. The most obvious difference was its head—a raised dome adorned with a prominent crown of bony growths, the largest of which was at the back of the skull. The dome probably got bigger as the animal reached maturity, and it seems to have been more pronounced in males. For males a large head would have been a sign of importance in the same way that large tusks are a badge of rank in bull elephants. *Stegoceras* would have been a fast runner, and like other bone heads, it lived in herds. Although it ran on two legs, it probably dropped onto all fours to feed.

MAXIMUM LENGTH 6.6 ft. (2m)

TIME Late Cretaceous

FOSSIL FINDS North America (Alberta, Montana)

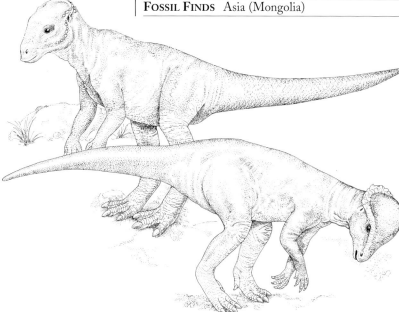

DOME-HEADED DINOSAURS

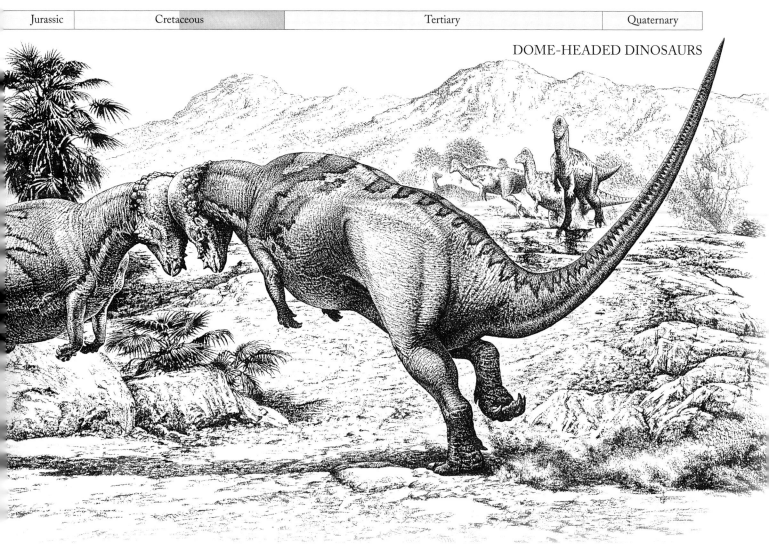

PRENOCEPHALE

In 1974 a superbly preserved skull of *Prenocephale* was found in Mongolia. It had a large, bulbous head with a knobbly ridge running around the edge and looked like a small-scale *Pachycephalosaurus*. *Prenocephale* probably lived by browsing on leaves and fruit and, like its relatives, almost certainly lived in herds. It shared another family feature: a mesh of bonelike tendons in the rear half of its tail, which would have held its tail rigid.

MAXIMUM LENGTH 8.2 ft. (2.5m)

TIME Late Cretaceous

FOSSIL FINDS Asia (Mongolia), western North America

PACHYCEPHALOSAURUS

The biggest of the bone heads, this dinosaur weighed nearly half a ton. It had a very large skull topped with a solid dome up to 10 in. (25cm) thick. Running around the outside of its head, at the base of the dome, was a ring of bony knobs. *Pachycephalosaurus* had tiny teeth for its size. Like other bone heads, it probably had a good sense of smell, which would have been useful for detecting predators. As the only fossil finds have been skull remains, scientists have had to guess what the rest of its body looked like. This dome-headed giant was one of the last of its line, surviving until the mass extinction that wiped out all of the dinosaurs 66 million years ago.

MAXIMUM LENGTH 15 ft. (4.6m)

TIME Late Cretaceous

FOSSIL FINDS western North America

▽△ Pachycephalosaurus *would have used its "bone head" to win in clashes with male rivals.*

167

DINOSAUR DROPPINGS

WITH THEIR OFTEN HUGE APPETITES, DINOSAURS PRODUCED IMMENSE AMOUNTS OF DROPPINGS. SOME HAVE SURVIVED AS FOSSILS, GIVING PALEONTOLOGISTS A DIRECT INSIGHT INTO WHAT DINOSAURS ATE.

Coprolites, or fossilized droppings, are discovered less frequently than fossilized bones. One reason for this is that they have an irregular shape, which means that even expert eyes find them difficult to spot. Another factor is that droppings are considerably softer than bones, which gives them less of a chance of being preserved. Rain washes them away, and scavenging animals, such as insects, often break them apart. Only occasionally does genuine dino dung does come to light, millions of years after it dropped to the ground.

REMAINS OF A KILL
In 1995, a group of scientists working in Saskatchewan, took a stroll from a site where a *Tyrannosaurus* was being excavated. One of the team noticed some pale round objects that were slowly being eroded from a layer of hard mud. These came from a giant dinosaur coprolite, the largest that has ever been found. Roughly cylindrical, it measured about 17.7 in. (45cm) long and up to 6.3 in. (16cm) across, and when fresh, probably weighed about 5.5 lb. (2.5kg).

The fossil was taken back to the lab, where paper-thin slices were shaved off and viewed under a microscope. These revealed pieces of broken bone that had been partially digested. By looking at the pattern of blood vessels inside the bone fragments, researchers were able to tell that the victim was a young dinosaur and probably a plant eater. The animal that produced the coprolite, on the other hand, was undoubtedly a carnivore, the most likely candidate being *Tyrannosaurus* itself.

△ Fossilized droppings are often difficult to identify. The one on the left came from a dinosaur, and the one on the right may have been produced by a marine reptile.

DUNG AND DIET
Plant-eating dinosaurs outnumbered meat eaters and ate more food. Some herbivores had only modest food requirements, but giant sauropods, such as *Argentinosaurus*, probably consumed about three or four tons of food a week. This translates into about one ton of droppings—an enormous potential source of evidence about dinosaur diets.

Unfortunately, compared to carnivores, plant eaters' droppings fossilized less frequently, mainly because they contained no hard fragments of bone. The few sauropod droppings that have been found include specimens from Utah, which look like squashed basketballs up to 15.7 in. (40cm) across. Their shape is explained by the fact that they originally contained water and hit the ground from a height of many feet. Some of these coprolites contain pieces of conifer stems.

At the other end of the scale, geologists in England have discovered large numbers of coin-sized coprolites, thought to have been produced by a plant-eating dinosaur. What the droppings lacked in size, they made up for in numbers. One deposit contained nearly 300 of these pellets, and a close examination showed that they contained the undigested remains of cycad leaves, a common ingredient of dinosaur diets.

DINO DUNG AS RAW MATERIAL
Some coprolites of plant-eating dinosaurs are riddled with fossilized burrows, each up to the thickness of a finger. These burrows were created by dung beetles, which mined the giant droppings as a source of food. Just like dung beetles today, some would have shaped pieces of the dung into balls and rolled them away to make nurseries for their young. By dismantling and scattering piles of dung, these scavenging insects helped to return nutrients to the soil—nutrients that plants in Mesozoic times needed to grow.

REPTILES IN THE AIR

Before birds evolved, reptiles were the only backboned animals that had successfully taken up life in the air. Initially reptiles were gliders rather than true fliers, using specialized scales or skinflaps to cushion their fall as they leaped from tree to tree. But by the end of the Triassic a completely new group of flying reptiles evolved, equipped with muscle-powered wings. These were the pterosaurs, a collection of quick-witted and sometimes gigantic aviators that soared and flapped their way through the skies. They flourished for over 150 million years and left a great treasury of fossils.

WINGS OF SKIN

GLIDING OR FLYING REPTILES EVOLVED ON AT LEAST FOUR SEPARATE OCCASIONS IN THE DISTANT PAST. THE MOST SUCCESSFUL BY FAR WERE THE PTEROSAURS, WHICH TOOK TO THE AIR ON WINGS MADE OF SKIN.

The first flying reptiles appeared toward the end of the Permian Period, over 240 million years ago. These early aviators were all gliders, speeding between trees on winglike flaps that they opened just before takeoff. They included *Coelurosauravus*, which had foldaway wing flaps along its sides, and *Longisquama* (page 62), a Triassic animal with elongated scales down its back. One of the strangest, a tiny animal called *Sharovipteryx* (page 60), had two pairs of flaps. But none of these animals could stay airborne for more than a few seconds, because their wings could not be flapped up and down.

▽ *Coelurosauravus was an early glider from the Late Permian. About 15.7 in. (40cm) long, it had elongated ribs that could hinge outward to form a pair of skin-covered wings. Some of today's lizards glide in exactly the same way.*

FIRST FLAPPERS

With the evolution of the pterosaurs in the Late Triassic, reptiles stopped being simple gliders and developed real mastery of the skies. Pterosaurs are sometimes confused with dinosaurs, and although they were a distinct group, they did share the same direct ancestors. Not only did they appear at the same time as the dinosaurs, they also became extinct at the same time. Until the

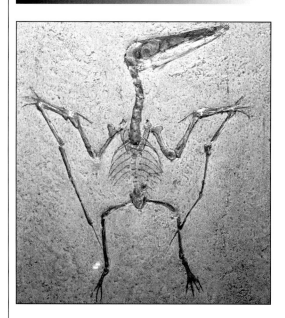

Many pterosaurs fed on fish or squid, catching prey by swimming close to the water's surface. If they crashed, their remains sank to the bottom, where they stood a good chance of becoming fossilized. This Pterodactylus *fossil is a typical example and shows the entire skeleton in superb detail. By contrast, species that lived over land, such as* Quetzalcoatlus, *left a meager amount of fossil evidence.*

global disaster that brought the Age of Reptiles to an end, pterosaurs were by far the largest animals that could fly. Unlike gliding reptiles, they could flap their wings to stay airborne, and they may even have been as maneuverable as today's birds.

DESIGN FOR FLIGHT

Few fossils of the earliest pterosaurs exist, but later forms, particularly from near the end of the Jurassic, have left a wealth of well-preserved remains. They show that pterosaurs had very specialized arms featuring an immensely elongated fourth finger, often as long as the rest of the limb. When the wing was extended, this finger stretched open a double-sided membrane of skin, which ran in a triangle between three points: the shoulder, the wingtip,

and a region near the hind leg. A second and much smaller membrane formed a forward part of the wing. It also started at the shoulder, but ran in front of the main arm bones to a point near the wrist, creating a straight edge in front of the elbow. The remaining fingers were far shorter and clustered together at the wing's leading edge. They were probably used for walking and climbing, and perhaps tearing up food.

Unlike a bird's feathers, which consist of dead cells, a pterosaur's wing membranes were made of living tissue. They were reinforced by tough but elastic fibers, and they contained a network of blood vessels to keep them alive. Compared to feathers, they were simple structures and did not need lots of preening to keep them in good condition. But although minor damage could be repaired, a major tear was likely to be permanent, and therefore potentially fatal.

Apart from their wings pterosaurs showed other physical modifications. Their skeletons were light, with a reduced number of bones, and the rib cage was deep but short. Early species, the rhamphorhynchoids, had long tails. Later ones, the pterodactyls, had tails that were reduced to

a short stub. In these pterosaurs the head was often longer than the rest of the body.

ENERGY FOR FLIGHT

The shape of their beaks, together with the fossilized remains of meals, shows that pterosaurs were carnivorous and fed on a range of animals from

insects to fish or scavenged on remains. Strangely, once flowering plants evolved, pterosaurs do not seem to have branched out into eating fruit and seeds, although these are both packed with energy.

Giant pterosaurs, such as *Arambourgiana* (page 178), were experts at soaring, a highly efficient way of flying that uses very little muscle power. But smaller species would have needed to put a lot of effort into flapping, one of several reasons why paleontologists think that most petrosaurs, or perhaps all of them, were warm-blooded.

◁ *Different tail lengths make it easy to tell rhamphorhynchoids and pterodactyls apart.*

◁ *The largest pterosaurs had a wingspan larger than a hang glider; the smallest were not much larger than a starling when fully grown.*

▽ *Pterosaur wings consisted of a double-sided sheet of skin reinforced by tough fibers. As in birds, most of the bones contained air cavities to minimize weight.*

1 Quetzalcoatlus
2 Pteranodon
3 Dsungaripterus
4 Dimorphodon
5 Pterdactylus
6 Sordes

REPTILES IN THE AIR

LONG-TAILED PTEROSAURS

The long-tailed pterosaurs were the first reptiles capable of true powered flight. They appeared in the Late Triassic Period and were widespread in the Jurassic. Like the pterodactyls, which eventually replaced them, they had leathery wings held open by a lengthened fourth finger, but they also had some more primitive features. These included sharply pointed teeth and slender tails that often ended in a diamond-shaped vane. Many of these pterosaurs fed on fish, but they probably did not spend time in the water. Instead they did all their hunting on the wing.

▽ *Clinging to rocks with wing claws and feet, two* Dimorphodon *bask in the morning sunshine while another flies off to feed. Like other pterosaurs,* Dimorphodon *would have used a lot of energy in flight. It was probably warm blooded and insulated by furlike scales.*

DIMORPHODON
Fossils of this animal were first found in 1828 by the British collector Mary Anning (page 198), and for over a century it remained the most primitive pterosaur known to science. With its bulky, puffinlike beak, *Dimorphodon* was one of the most distinctive long-tailed pterosaurs. Its head was almost as large as the central section of its body, but it was lighter than it looked, because the skull contained large spaces separated by thin struts of bone. Its front teeth were long and protruded from its beak, but the teeth farther back were much smaller. Its wings were equipped with three large, clawed fingers, and its tail was long but probably very stiff, because

it was reinforced by parallel rods of bone. Opinions are divided about how *Dimorphodon* lived and why it had such a large beak. It may have fed on fish or small land animals, but its beak may have acted partly as display, in the same way that toucans' beaks do today.

WINGSPAN 4.6 ft. (1.4m)

TIME Early Jurassic

FOSSIL FINDS Europe (England)

SCAPHOGNATHUS
This long-beaked pterosaur is one of several species that have been found in the Solnhöfen limestone of southern Germany—a geological formation famous as the source of *Archaeopteryx* fossils (page 134). It had the large, protruding teeth typical of long-tailed pterosaurs and short wings. Its tail ended in a diamond-shaped vane—another feature common in early pterosaurs, which would have helped improve its stability when flying. *Scaphognathus'* jaws would have allowed it to catch fish or insects, but there is no evidence whether or not it fed over water or on land.

WINGSPAN 35.4 in. (90cm)

TIME Late Jurassic

FOSSIL FINDS Europe (Germany)

the rest of the body. *Rhamphorhynchus'* jaws were slightly upturned at their tips, and they would have made a very effective fish trap. To feed, the animal probably skimmed close to the surface, with the lower half of its beak slicing through the water. If the beak made contact with a fish, it would have snapped shut instantly—a fishing technique still used by some birds today. Some *Rhamphorhynchus* fossils show the remains of fish in the stomach in various stages of digestion.

WINGSPAN 5.7 ft. (1.75m)

TIME Late Jurassic

FOSSIL FINDS Africa (Tanzania), Europe (England, Germany)

PREONDACTYLUS

Preondactylus is one of the earliest known pterosaurs. It had several primitive features, including long legs and a short skull, but it was a capable flier, skimming over lakes and lagoons to catch fish. One fossil consists of a jumble of bones apparently regurgitated by a large fish; it may have been swallowed after it crash-landed.

WINGSPAN 5 ft. (1.5m)

TIME Late Triassic

FOSSIL FINDS Europe (Italy)

◁ *With a fish clamped in its tooth-filled beak, a* Rhamphorhynchus *flies off to feed. Small fish would have been swallowed whole. Larger ones would be taken to a safe place and then torn apart— as shown by the animal in the background. Unlike today's birds, pterosaurs could hold their catch with their wing claws while they tore it apart with their teeth.*

▽ *Swinging its feet forward and cupping its wings, a* Preondactylus *comes in to land. For pterosaurs—just as for birds—good eyesight and coordination were essential for flight. Studies of pterosaur skulls showed that these animals had well-developed brains, allowing them to carry out precise maneuvers in midair.*

ANUROGNATHUS

Anurognathus literally means "without tail or jaws"—an understandable, if misleading, description of this unusual pterosaur. Known from just one specimen found in Germany in the 1920s, it had a tail that was no more than a stump and a short, blunt head with only a few small teeth. Its legs and feet, however, were well developed. One possible explanation for these features is that the fossil is of a young animal, which would have changed shape as it became an adult. Another possibility is that *Anurognathus* was a lightweight hunter of dragonflies and other insects and may have used dinosaurs as living launchpads to dart after its prey.

WINGSPAN 19.7 in. (50cm)

TIME Late Jurassic

FOSSIL FINDS Europe (Germany)

RHAMPHORHYNCHUS

Rhamphorhynchus is the best-known of the long-tailed pterosaurs, because of some superbly preserved fossils in the Solnhöfen limestone of southern Germany. Several species have been identified, but they all have long, pointed jaws armed with large, crisscrossing teeth. Their wingspan was among the largest of all tailed pterosaurs, but their legs were disproportionately short, suggesting that they were not very agile on the ground. The Solnhöfen fossils show outlines of the wings along with the vane-tipped tail, which was often longer than

REPTILES IN THE AIR

EUDIMORPHODON

Fossils of this animal show a number of interesting details of pterosaur anatomy. Like most other long-tailed species, it had a long beak with large teeth at the front and smaller teeth at the sides. Its large eyes were protected by a circle of thin bony plates called a sclerotic ring, and it had thickened neck vertebrae to support the weight of its head. It also had gastralia, or stomach ribs, so its rib cage enclosed almost the whole of its underside. *Eudimorphodon* was a fish eater and is among the earliest pterosaurs known from the fossil record.

WINGSPAN	3.3 ft. (1m)
TIME	Late Triassic
FOSSIL FINDS	Europe (Italy)

BATRACHOGNATHUS

Like *Rhamphorhynchus*, this pterosaur had a deep, blunt beak. This, together with its small size, makes it likely that it fed on insects. Its skull was about 2 in. (5cm) long and contained large spaces, covered by skin, that helped reduce weight. Fossils show that, like many of its relatives, this species had a uropatagium—a flap of skin stretching between its legs and tail—as well as the flaps that formed its wings. Many of today's bats have a similar skin flap helping them fly.

WINGSPAN	19.7 in. (50cm)
TIME	Late Jurassic
FOSSIL FINDS	Asia (Kazakhstan)

SORDES

When the remains of this animal were first discovered, in the 1960s, it looked very much like a standard pterosaur. But under close examination the fossil showed one astonishing feature—signs of what look like a coat of fur. As with bats, the fur seems to have covered the animal's head and most of its body, but not its wings or tail. Many paleontologists take this as evidence that pterosaurs were warm-blooded—a theory that may explain their highly active way of life. If this is true, it is likely that many pterosaurs had "fur," although it is rarely seen in fossil remains. Apart from its remarkable coat, *Sordes* had large eyes and a long, narrow beak with large, protruding teeth. As with *Batrachognathus*, its small size suggests that it fed on insects rather than fish.

WINGSPAN	2 ft. (60cm)
TIME	Late Jurassic
FOSSIL FINDS	Asia (Kazakhstan)

▽ Sordes *(top and left), had a batlike shape, with a flap of skin connecting its hind legs to the base of its tail. Its furry scales may have been a common feature in pterosaurs, but so far it is the only species that shows this clearly in fossils.*

▽ Batrachognathus *(bottom right) had well-developed wing claws useful for clinging to vegetation when it landed to swallow its catch.*

◁ Circling over a lagoon, a small flock of Dsungaripterus *soar upward on rising air. Although they fed along the seashore, these pterosaurs would have visited freshwater to drink and to bathe.*

DSUNGARIPTERUS

This unusual pterosaur—the first to be discovered in China—had a beak with a vertical crest at its base and an upturned and sharply pointed tip. Its teeth were short, strong, and effective at crushing food rather than grasping it. From these features it seems likely that *Dsungaripterus* fed on mollusks and other hard-bodied seashore animals, prizing them from rocks and then crushing them in its jaws. Its long legs would have been ideal for wading among tide pools as it searched for food.

WINGSPAN	11.5 ft. (3.5m)
TIME	Early Cretaceous
FOSSIL FINDS	Asia (China)

ORNITHODESMUS

Ornithodesmus was one of several pterodactyls that had wide, ducklike beaks. Its beak looks heavy, but the tip was attached to the rest of its skull by remarkably narrow struts of bone, making it far lighter than it appears. It had short but effective teeth at the tip of its beak, making it likely that it fed on fish. The name *Ornithodesmus* is also used for a species of dinosaur; because this was named first, the pterosaur will eventually be renamed.

WINGSPAN	16.4 ft. (5m)
TIME	Early Cretaceous
FOSSIL FINDS	Europe (England)

PTERODACTYLS

The pterodactyls were a group of pterosaurs widespread in the Late Jurassic. By the Cretaceous the long-tailed pterosaurs had died out, leaving the pterodactyls as the only reptiles in the skies. They had very short tails, and some were adorned with bizarre bony crests. Some species were not much larger than pigeons, but others were the largest flying animals that have ever existed on Earth.

▷ A number of pterosaurs had flattened crests at the tip of their beaks. This is Criorhynchus, *which had a wingspan of over 16.5 ft. (5m). In flight, its trailing legs acted as a counterbalance for its head, and they may have helped it to steer.*

▷ Seen from the front, Ornithodesmus' *beak reveals its ducklike shape. This kind of beak may have helped* Ornithodesmus *catch fish in muddy water, where it would have used touch rather than sight to find its prey.*

ORNITHOCHEIRUS

Up to 13 ft. (4m) long and with a wingspan three times the size of the largest flying bird alive today, *Ornithocheirus* (page 182) was a spectacular airborne reptile. Like other pterodactyls, it had a front-heavy build, with a large head and neck, but only the shortest trace of a tail. In many species the beak was highly distinctive, with a vertical crest at its tip. *Ornithocheirus* was not shaped for flapping flight. It traveled by seeking out thermals, or columns of warm, rising air. Having reached the top of one thermal, it could then glide down to the next. This method of flight was highly energy-efficient. *Ornithocheirus* could travel great distances with little effort. It probably fed on squid and fish.

WINGSPAN	39.4 ft. (12m)
TIME	Early Cretaceous
FOSSIL FINDS	Europe (England), South America (Brazil)

▷ *Added together, Pteranodon's beak and crest were nearly 6.6 ft. (2m) long—longer than the rest of its body. Despite its great size, this pterosaur probably weighed no more than 40 lb. (18kg), about the same as the heaviest flying birds alive today. The species shown here is* Pteranodon longiceps.

▽ *Sweeping majestically over a herd of sauropods, a flock of* Quetzalcoatlus *sets off to find food. These huge pterosaurs could have migrated immense distances and would probably have been far more widespread than the few fossil finds suggest.*

PTERANODON

The first remains of *Pteranodon* were found in the 1870s, and for the next 100 years it was the largest pterosaur known. Its wingspan dwarfed that of most other pterosaurs, but its most remarkable feature was its huge and bizarrely-shaped head, which had an extraordinary bony crest. In one species, *Pteranodon sternbergi*, the crest sticks up almost at right angles to the beak, but in *Pteranodon longiceps* it sweeps backward so that the beak and crest are almost in line. This kind of crest would have counterbalanced the beak, but it also acted like an airplane's tail fin, keeping the beak pointing into the oncoming air. The stabilizing effect may have been an advantage, but many other pterosaurs—including the gigantic *Quetzalcoatlus* (below)—managed to fly perfectly well without a crest. *Pteranodon* probably caught fish by skimming close to the waves. Like some of today's fishing seabirds, it is unlikely to have landed on the water because, with its immense wingspan, it would have found it difficult to take off again.

WINGSPAN	29.52 ft. (9m)
TIME	Late Cretaceous
FOSSIL FINDS	Asia (Japan), Europe (England), North America (Kansas, Oregon, South Dakota)

QUETZALCOATLUS

Named after an Aztec god, *Quetzalcoatlus* may have been the largest flying animal ever to have existed. Its claim to the top spot is even stronger if—as some palaeontologists suggest—*Arambourgiana* (pages 178–179) is really a *Quetzalcoatlus* that has been misidentified. The original remains of *Quetzalcoatlus*, which were unearthed in 1971, consist of wing bones built on a gigantic scale. By comparing these with complete skeletons of smaller species, estimates of its wingspan have ranged as high as 50 ft. (15m), although current figures are generally smaller. Unlike most pterosaurs, *Quetzalcoatlus* probably lived inland, and it would have flown largely by soaring, like a living glider. Its toothless beak suggests that it was probably a scavenger, although it may also have caught animals on the ground (page 181).

WINGSPAN	39.4 ft. (12m)
TIME	Late Cretaceous
FOSSIL FINDS	North America (Texas)

TROPEOGNATHUS

This large South American pterosaur had a vertical crest above and below the tip of its beak, like the one seen in *Ornithocheirus* (page 175). Its beak was armed with interlocking teeth, showing that it was a fish eater, and it is possible that the crest may

have helped it catch food. However, an alternative explanation is that the crest was used for display purposes during the animal's breeding season. If so, it probably varied in size between the sexes, although this has not been proven from fossil remains.

WINGSPAN 19.7 ft. (6m)

TIME Early Cretaceous

FOSSIL FINDS South America (Brazil)

ANHANGUERA

Like *Tropeognathus*, *Anhanguera* is known from remains found in northeastern Brazil. It had a typical fish eater's beak, with interlocking teeth, and its complete skull was about 19.7 in. (50cm) long. Like other pterodactyls, its backbone was shaped in an unusual way, with the largest vertebrae in the neck, tapering to the smallest ones in its stumpy tail. By comparison most terrestrial reptiles have their largest vertebrae in the central part of the body, where they carry the most weight. Pterodactyls needed their extra-large neck vertebrae to support their oversized heads.

WINGSPAN 13 ft. (4m)

TIME Early Cretaceous

FOSSIL FINDS South America (Brazil)

CEARADACTYLUS

Another fish eater from modern-day Brazil, *Cearadactylus* had about a dozen unusually long teeth at the tip of its beak, much smaller ones farther back in the jaws, and no teeth at all at the point where its beak hinged. This kind of anatomy, which was common among pterodactyls, meant that *Cearadactylus* could not chew its prey. Instead, it would have swallowed small fish whole or torn larger ones apart after landing with its catch.

WINGSPAN 13 ft. (4m)

TIME Early Cretaceous

FOSSIL FINDS South America (Brazil)

PTERODACTYLUS

The first specimen of this well-known reptile came to light in 1784, making this the earliest pterosaur to be discovered. Its name means "wing finger," and the word "pterodactyl" has often been used mistakenly for pterosaurs as a whole. *Pterodactylus* had a compact body with a small rib cage, long wings with three tiny clawed fingers, and a short tail. Its neck was well-developed to support its large head and beak—but it did not have a crest. *Pterodactylus* was a fish eater with relatively small teeth for grasping its slippery prey. Over a dozen species of *Pterodactylus* have been identified, varying slightly in their anatomy and size.

WINGSPAN 8.2 ft. (2.5m)

TIME Late Jurassic

FOSSIL FINDS Africa (Tanzania), Europe (England, France, Germany)

△ *On the ground most pterodactyls walked on all fours, although some of them could stride on their hind legs alone. Here a* Pterodactylus *shows how the wings folded back when not in use.*

▽ Tropeognathus *(top),* Cearadactylus *(middle), and* Anhanguera *(bottom) were three large pterodactyls found in Brazil. When these animals existed, South America and Africa were just beginning to drift apart as the Atlantic Ocean formed.*

GLIDING GIANTS

Gliding over a Late Cretaceous seascape, two Arambourgiana *watch for fish swimming near the surface. These immense pterosaurs are known from the slenderest fossil remains—a single neck vertebra measuring 2 ft. (60cm) long, which was found in Jordan in 1943. From this one bone paleontologists have deduced that* Arambourgiana *probably had a wingspan of 39.5 ft. (12m), making it perhaps the largest pterosaur of all time.*

HOW PTEROSAURS FED

WITH THEIR WARM-BLOODED BODIES, PTEROSAURS NEEDED A PLENTIFUL SUPPLY OF FOOD. MANY WERE FISHERS OR INSECT EATERS, BUT SOME HAD DISTINCT WAYS OF STAVING OFF HUNGER.

Fossilized pterosaur skulls provided plenty of evidence about their eating habits. Their beaks evolved to fit particular diets. Most seem to have fed over water, but land-based species had a smaller chance of being fossilized if they died.

△ Rhamphorhyncus *probably fed in the same way as skimmers— living seabirds that fish from the water's surface.*

LIVING STRAINERS

Of all the pterosaurs known from fossils, one stands out from all the rest. Called *Pterodaustro*, or "southern wing," it was originally found in Argentina and lived during the Early Cretaceous. Unusually for a pterosaur, *Pterodaustro*'s beak had a strong upward curve, but its strangest feature was a set of about 500 wiry teeth on either side of the lower jaw. These teeth pointed up like the bristles of a toothbrush, and they were so long that they could not fit inside the beak when the upper jaw was closed.

Pterodaustro used its teeth to strain food from shallow water. As water flowed past the bristles tiny animals and plants became trapped in them. The pterosaur would then close its beak so that it could swallow its catch—a feeding system remarkably like the one used by flamingos today.

As a rule fish-eating pterosaurs hunted from the air, skimming the surface, but rarely landing on the water. Some experts think that *Pterodaustro* also fed in this way, but another view is that it waded through the shallows with its wings folded back, sweeping its beak from side to side. If true, it would have been an ungainly sight.

◁ Pterodaustro *uses its bristle-filled beak to feed. The bristles— actually highly modified teeth—were up to 1.6 in. (4cm) long and were made of keratin, the same substance that forms hair and claws.*

△ Starting from the top right and going counterclockwise, this four-stage sequence shows Anhanguera *catching a fish. Its catch is small enough to be swallowed while flying—anything much larger than this would have to be taken back to land and ripped apart.*

▷ Probing into soft mud, a Pterodactylus *catches a worm. Like today's birds, pterodactyls had very good eyesight, moderate hearing, but probably a poor sense of smell. They would have found worms by sight, and perhaps by touch.*

GETTING A GRIP

Apart from *Pterodaustro*, pterosaurs had either widely spaced teeth or no teeth at all. Unusually for reptiles, the toothy species sometimes had several types of teeth, including large, single-pointed ones at the front of the jaws, and smaller ones with a number of points at the sides. This feature must have developed at an early stage in pterosaur evolution because it is visible in some of the oldest species, such as *Eudimorphodon* (page 184).

For pterosaurs that caught fish from the air, spotting prey and snatching it were the first two steps in a complex operation. Once a fish had been grabbed by the front teeth, it either had to be maneuvered into a headfirst position, so that it could be swallowed, or it had to be flicked from the front of the beak toward the back, so that it was secure for the journey back to land. This is where the small lateral teeth came in. Unlike the front teeth, they had a more powerful bite, and because they were short, the pterosaur could carry its victim without its beak gaping.

In some fossils the outlines of what look like throat pouches can be seen. These handy devices would have allowed pterosaurs to carry food back to land without any risk of it wriggling free.

FEEDING ON LAND

Fish eaters were not the only pterosaurs that had teeth. Smaller species based on land probably used their teeth to catch insects, both in the air and on the ground. At one time pterosaurs were thought to be clumsy on land, moving with a scuttling walk, as many bats do today. More recent studies of pterosaur skeletons suggest that they might have been surprisingly agile. In some the rear legs were straight and strong, and with their wings folded back, their wing claws would have given them a tenacious grip.

At a time when giant plant-eating dinosaurs were common, this four-legged stance could have been put to good use. Some pterosaurs might have probed damp ground for insect grubs, but others probably followed dinosaur herds and watched for any insects as they fed. A dinosaur's back would have made a perfect platform for keeping an eye out for food, and with four sets of claws to keep them in position, pterosaurs would have been difficult to dislodge.

SOARING SCAVENGERS

During the Cretaceous the giants of the pterosaur world dispensed with teeth altogether. Instead, species such as *Pteranodon* and *Quetzalcoatlus* had massive, toothless beaks, sometimes over 3 ft. (1m) long. *Pteranodon* was a fish eater, but *Quetzalcoatlus* fossils come from rocks that formed inland.

One theory is that *Quetzalcoatlus* lived like some of today's cranes and storks, striding across the ground or through shallow water, snatching any small animals it found. But it is more likely that it was not a hunter at all, but a scavenger. Its huge wings, combined with excellent eyesight, would have made it the supervulture of the Late Cretaceous, soaring high over open landscapes in search of dinosaur remains.

For a scavenging *Quetzalcoatlus* breaking through over an inch of dead dinosaur skin to reach the meat was a problem. Pterosaur teeth would not have been much help, but a daggerlike beak was perfect. With a few well-aimed blows, *Quetzalcoatlus* could have punctured the toughest of hides.

HOW PTEROSAURS BRED

FOR PTEROSAURS, RAISING YOUNG WAS A DEMANDING BUSINESS. INSTEAD OF LAYING EGGS AND THEN ABANDONING THEM—LIKE SOME DINOSAURS—THEY PROBABLY SPENT TIME CARING FOR THEIR YOUNG.

Fossils reveal little about the family life of pterosaurs, but there are a few clues about how they bred. One is that female pterosaurs generally had a narrow pelvis; this makes it unlikely that they gave birth to live young, unless the young were small and poorly developed. They are more likely to have laid eggs. They would have laid them in inaccessible places, such as cliffs and trees, away from predators.

▷ *Back from a fishing trip, an adult* Ornithocheirus *regurgitates food for one of its offspring.*

DELIVERING FOOD

If pterosaurs were warm-blooded, they would probably have incubated their eggs. The young hatchlings would have looked like miniature versions of their parents, but with shorter beaks and wings. They would not have been able to fly, which means that they would have depended on their parents for food. Some adult pterosaurs may have brought back pieces of food in their beaks, but for fishing species—which often wandered far out to sea—this would have been an inefficient method of delivery. Instead, they probably fed their nestlings on regurgitated and partly digested food, a system that allowed them to catch several fish before having to head back to shore.

For most pterosaurs the work of feeding and guarding the young is likely to have kept both parents fully occupied. Because they had to operate as a team, the two adults would have stayed together for the whole of the breeding season, or perhaps even for life.

FLYING LESSONS

Today's flying vertebrates—birds and bats—have to wait until they reach adult size, or very close to it, before they fly. A remarkable feature of pterosaurs is that the young seem to have begun flying when they were still a lot smaller than their parents. Evidence for this comes from fossils of *Pterodactylus*, which include some specimens less than 4 in. (10cm) long. These have well-developed wings; but some of their other features, such as the shape of their beak, show that they were juvenile animals.

This discovery has some intriguing implications for pterosaur family life. Young pterosaurs had to learn to fly, and most likely they were instructed by their parents. But even when they were fully at home in the air, they may still have been partly dependent on their parents for food. While the parents hunted for prey their youngsters may have flapped around them in a family flock until the time came when they could catch all their own food.

REPTILES IN THE SEA

Although reptiles evolved on land, many slowly abandoned terrestrial life and moved into the sea. During the Mesozoic Era these included dolphinlike ichthyosaurs, long-necked plesiosaurs, and a number of other predators, some almost as large as today's baleen whales and far more dangerous. Together they were the dominant marine animals, but their supremacy was not to last. The ichthyosaurs died out during the Cretaceous, and of the other animals featured in this chapter, only turtles survived into modern times.

ADAPTING TO LIFE IN WATER

FOR AIR-BREATHING, FOUR-LEGGED REPTILES, MOVING FROM LAND TO WATER MEANT SOME MAJOR CHANGES IN SHAPE AND ALSO IN BEHAVIOR. DIFFERENT GROUPS OF REPTILES MADE THE CHANGE IN DIFFERENT WAYS.

Because reptiles were so successful on land, it seems even more remarkable that so many kinds took up life in the sea. But evolution does not work in a set direction, and if a change brings advantages, that change is likely to be made. For marine reptiles the advantage was reduced competition for food—a factor that made life increasingly difficult on land. The ancestors of today's turtles were among the first to make the transition, followed by a variety of other groups. Interestingly, dinosaurs were not among them, although it is likely that most could swim.

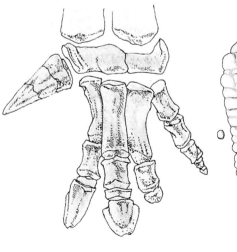

▽ *The hand bones of an iguanodon (left) compared with those in the flipper of an ichthyosaur (right). Ichthyosaurs evolved large numbers of additional bones, which made their flippers more rigid.*

SHAPES FOR SWIMMING

For land animals gravity is a tiring fact of life, but air resistance is rarely a problem. In the sea things are the other way around. Here animals are buoyed up by the water around them, so they weigh little or nothing. But the moment they start to move, water resistance slows them down. The faster they swim, the more energy this resistance wastes.

The best way to minimize resistance is to have a streamlined body—something that all marine reptiles evolved at an early stage. Turtles developed flatter, smoother shells; pliosaurs had bodies with long heads and short necks. The true specialists, however, were the fastest-moving of all prehistoric marine reptiles—the ichthyosaurs. With their beaklike snouts and barrel-shaped bodies, they could swim as fast as dolphins.

As well as different body shapes, marine reptiles also had different swimming styles (pages 194–195). But while some wriggled their way through the water and others sped along with their flippers or tails, almost all had one thing in common—a large number of phalanges, the bones that make up fingers and toes. Typical land-dwelling reptiles, such as lizards, have four phalanges in each finger or toe, the same number as humans. Marine reptiles could have as many as 17, and some had extra fingers and toes. All these bones were bound together by strong ligaments, turning their feet into reptilian fins.

This proliferation of finger and toe bones is known as hyperphalangy. Millions of years after most marine reptiles died out, exactly the same adaptation evolved in the cetaceans, the group of mammals that includes today's dolphins and whales.

COMING UP FOR AIR

Despite some far-reaching changes in shape, marine reptiles still needed to breathe air. In fact, this is one area in which evolution has never quite managed to turn back the clock in reptiles or in sea mammals. Instead of losing lungs, marine reptiles developed ways of breathing more easily at sea.

One of the first and simplest adaptations was nostrils high up on the head, equipped with flaps that allowed them to be closed. Another was a secondary palate—a flap at the back of the mouth that could shut off the windpipe, or trachea. This would have been vital because marine reptiles did not have lips, so they could not keep water out of their mouths while they were submerged. The palate prevented water from flowing down the windpipe and into their lungs.

With the help of these two modifications they could take a breath at the surface and then dive down to search for prey. No one knows how long they could stay underwater, but today's crocodiles may provide a guide. When they are active, large species surface

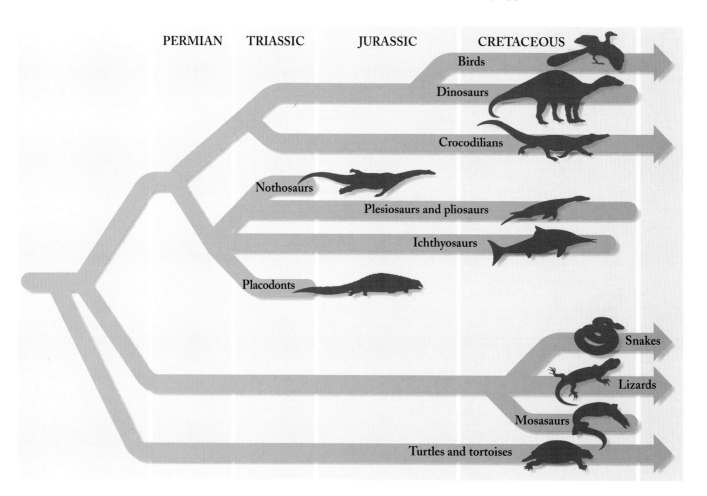

Young ichthyosaur emerging tailfirst

roughly every five to ten minutes, but they can rest underwater for several hours. In prehistoric times the deepest divers were the ichthyosaurs, and some, such as *Ophthalmosaurus*, may have been able to stay underwater for an hour or more, but not nearly as long if swimming at high speed.

EGGS OR LIVE BIRTH?

Apart from their need to breathe air, ichthyosaurs were fully equipped for life at sea. Fossils show that they gave birth to live young, which meant that they never had to return to land. But for other marine reptiles in these distant times evidence about reproduction is extremely thin on the ground. No remains have ever been found of young animals developing inside their mothers or of embryos inside eggs. As a result paleontologists can only guess how these animals might have bred.

It is possible that smaller species might have dragged themselves onto land to lay eggs, as turtles do today. But with giant species, such as the whale-sized *Liopleurodon* (page 191), this is likely to have been physically impossible. For this reason most experts believe that animals like this gave birth, instead of laying eggs.

◁ *This fossil shows a female ichthyosaur in the act of giving birth. The young animal is emerging tailfirst, and its head is partly hidden by its mother's hind flippers.*

▽ *This family tree shows how marine reptiles were related to other reptiles of the Mesozoic. Several marine groups died out well before the Age of Reptiles ended.*

PERMIAN	TRIASSIC	JURASSIC	CRETACEOUS

Birds

Dinosaurs

Crocodilians

Nothosaurs

Plesiosaurs and pliosaurs

Ichthyosaurs

Placodonts

Snakes

Lizards

Mosasaurs

Turtles and tortoises

REPTILES IN THE SEA

NOTHOSAURS

The nothosaurs, with the unrelated placodonts, were early marine reptiles that showed different degrees of adaptation to life in water. Some of them lived in lagoons and along shallow shores and spent much of their time on land, but others were sea creatures that may have wandered far into open water. A fossilized embryo found in Switzerland shows that some or perhaps all of these animals reproduced by laying eggs, a primitive characteristic that made them partly dependent on land.

△ Pistosaurus *had well-developed flipperlike limbs, although the outlines of toes were probably evident beneath the surface of its skin. Its tail was cylindrical and did not have a fin.*

▽ Ceresiosaurus *had a characteristic nothosaur body, with a long neck, finned tail, and well-developed flippers with distinct toes. It probably hunted for fish in rocky crevices on the seabed, instead of in open water.*

CERESIOSAURUS

Ceresiosaurus was a typical nothosaur, with a slender, streamlined shape. It had a long, highly flexible tail and extra bones in its toes—a feature that evolved on many separate occasions in marine reptiles and mammals. Its head was relatively small, but its jaws were armed with small, sharp teeth—the hallmark of a fish eater. Opinions differ about how *Ceresiosaurus* swam. Instead of using only its tail, like the placodonts (see opposite), or its flippers, like the plesiosaurs (page 188), it may have used both, perhaps switching from one form of movement to the other as it adjusted its speed. Along with many other marine reptiles from the Triassic, its remains have been found in ancient marine sediments in the European Alps, an area which once formed part of the Tethys Sea.

MAXIMUM LENGTH	13 ft. (4m)
TIME	Mid Triassic
FOSSIL FINDS	Europe (Italy, Switzerland)

PISTOSAURUS

Unlike *Ceresiosaurus*, *Pistosaurus* had some advanced features that made it even better equipped for life in open water.

Its flipperlike legs were smooth and elliptical—without any visible toes—and its backbone was relatively stiff, allowing it to move by paddling instead of by waving its tail. Its head was small and almost cylindrical, another adaptation that would have helped to reduce energy-wasting turbulence as it slipped through the water. *Pistosaurus* is classified in the same order as the nothosaurs, but in a family of its own. It could clearly have ranged far out to sea, but if it laid eggs, as other nothosaurs seem to have done, it would have had to return to land to breed.

MAXIMUM LENGTH	10 ft. (3m)
TIME	Mid Triassic
FOSSIL FINDS	Europe (France, Germany)

LARIOSAURUS

Only about half the size of an otter, *Lariosaurus* was much smaller than some of its nothosaur relatives, although at the other extreme some nothosaurs were not much larger than a human hand. It had a lizardlike shape, with a short neck and toes. Its hind limbs still retained distinct toes and claws, although its feet would have been webbed.

It would probably have been amphibious, feeding in shallow water but spending much of its time resting on the shore. Because they had small bodies, animals like *Lariosaurus* would have been quickly chilled by cool seawater. As a result most of them were restricted to the tropics. Between swims they would have basked on rocks to warm themselves—like marine iguanas do today.

MAXIMUM LENGTH	2 ft. (60cm)
TIME	Mid Triassic
FOSSIL FINDS	Europe (Spain)

NOTHOSAURUS

Nothosaurus was a highly successful and widespread animal, appearing at the beginning of the Triassic Period and surviving, with relatively few changes, for over 30 million years. Several particularly well-preserved specimens have been found, clearly showing its webbed feet with five long toes.

Its front legs were shorter than its hind ones—a characteristic that is more useful for moving on land than it is for swimming at sea. This reptile had a sinuous, streamlined body, and spines on its vertebrae make it likely that its tail had a vertical fin. *Nothosaurus* was a fish eater, but its leg anatomy suggests that it spent a substantial amount of time on the shore, like modern seals do today.

MAXIMUM LENGTH	10 ft. (3m)
TIME	Triassic
FOSSIL FINDS	Asia (China, Russia), Europe (Germany, Italy, Switzerland), northern Africa

PACHYPLEUROSAURUS

At one time this animal and its relatives were thought by scientists to be nothosaurs, but they were probably close cousins, rather than members of the same family. *Pachypleurosaurus* itself was slim and lizardlike, with paddles that worked like a seal's flippers, allowing it to drag itself out onto land. Compared to the rest of its body, its head was small, perhaps allowing it to probe underwater crevices in search of fish to eat. There were several species of *Pachypleurosaurus*, and they varied a great deal in size. The smallest species were only about 2 ft. (60cm) long.

MAXIMUM LENGTH	8.2 ft. (2.5m)
TIME	Mid Triassic
FOSSIL FINDS	Europe (Italy, Switzerland)

PLACODUS

Looking like a large, humpbacked lizard, *Placodus* was one of the earliest marine reptiles. It had webbed feet and a flattened tail, but apart from this, it showed few modifications for life in the water. Its head was short, and it had three different types of teeth: protruding incisors at the front of its jaws, rounded molars along the sides, and a set of six flattened molars on the roof of its mouth. This suggests that it fed on mollusks in shallow water, prizing them from rocks and crushing them in its jaws. *Placodus* belonged to a group of reptiles called placodonts, which were protected by reinforced skeletons or sometimes bony shells (page 202). The placodonts became extinct before the Triassic came to an end.

MAXIMUM LENGTH	6.6 ft. (2m)
TIME	Early Triassic
FOSSIL FINDS	Europe (France)

△ Nothosaurus *was one of the larger members of its family, with a seallike lifestyle. Because it was cold-blooded—like its relatives—its oxygen consumption would have been relatively low, allowing it to stay submerged for several minutes at a time. Its nostrils were positioned halfway down its muzzle and would have been closed by flaps of skin when it dived.*

REPTILES IN THE SEA

PLESIOSAURS

Plesiosaurs first appeared in the Late Triassic, but had their heyday in the Jurassic. There were two basic forms: species with long necks and small heads, the true plesiosaurs; and species with short necks and large heads, the pliosaurs (page 190). Both types had four flipperlike fins, and they swam by beating these up and down like wings, instead of by waving their tails. All of them were oceangoing carnivores that returned to land only when they laid their eggs. Compared to early marine reptiles, some of them were enormous, even rivaling modern whales in size.

△ Plesiosaurus *would have fed by powering through the water with its paddles while using its flexible neck to lunge after fish and squid. Its head was triangular with a pointed snout— an efficient shape for slicing through the water.*

▷ Rhomaleosaurus *was the Early Jurassic equivalent of a killer whale, hunting fish and perhaps other reptiles with its well-armed jaws. Unlike small-headed plesiosaurs, it could have torn large animals to pieces by tossing them in the air.*

PLESIOSAURUS

Some of the earliest *Plesiosaurus* fossils were discovered by the English fossil collector Mary Anning in the 1820s (page 197). The specimens she found were well-preserved and remarkably complete— a result of rapid burial by a soft blanket of marine sediment, which prevented the remains from being disturbed. Her finds and many others show that there were several species of *Plesiosaurus*, all of them variations on the same successful design. They had narrow heads, slender necks and tails, and two pairs of paddles roughly equal in size. Their teeth were numerous, pointed, and slightly curved—a shape that evolved for catching fish, which would then be swallowed whole. *Plesiosaurus'* large paddles and sturdy build make it likely that it pursued its prey, instead of waiting for fish to come within range.

MAXIMUM LENGTH	9.8 ft. (3m)
TIME	Early Jurassic
FOSSIL FINDS	Europe (England, France, Germany)

RHOMALEOSAURUS

With its relatively long neck and large head, *Rhomaleosaurus* looked like a halfway stage between true plesiosaurs and the pliosaurs. Its classification is still a matter of debate, and at times it has been allotted to both these groups. Its lifestyle is more certain, because fossils clearly show a powerful body, two pairs of roughly equal paddles, and crocodile-like jaws, sometimes nearly 3.3 ft. (1m) long, armed with large, protruding teeth. Some recent research suggests that *Rhomaleosaurus* and its relatives may have swum with their jaws slightly ajar, allowing water to go in through the mouth and out through the nostrils. This unusual arrangement—a reversal of the normal water flow—would have allowed them to track prey by smell rather than by sight.

MAXIMUM LENGTH	23 ft. (7m)
TIME	Early Jurassic
FOSSIL FINDS	Europe (England, Germany)

CRYPTOCLIDUS

A large plesiosaur with a 6.6 ft (2m) long neck, *Cryptoclidus* had a number of evolutionary refinements for life at sea. Its flippers were much larger than those of earlier plesiosaurs, giving it more power underwater. Its teeth were long, pointed, and interlocking so that they formed a cagelike trap for fish, shrimp, and squid. Fossils of this animal are often very well preserved, and some of the best came from clay quarries in England at a time when clay was dug out by hand. This kind of quarrying is now carried out by machine, so complete fossil skeletons are much more rarely found today.

MAXIMUM LENGTH	26.2 ft. (8m)
TIME	Late Jurassic
FOSSIL FINDS	Asia (Russia), Europe (England, France)

MURAENOSAURUS

Muraenosaurus—"moray eel lizard"—belonged to a group of reptiles called elasmosaurs, renowned for

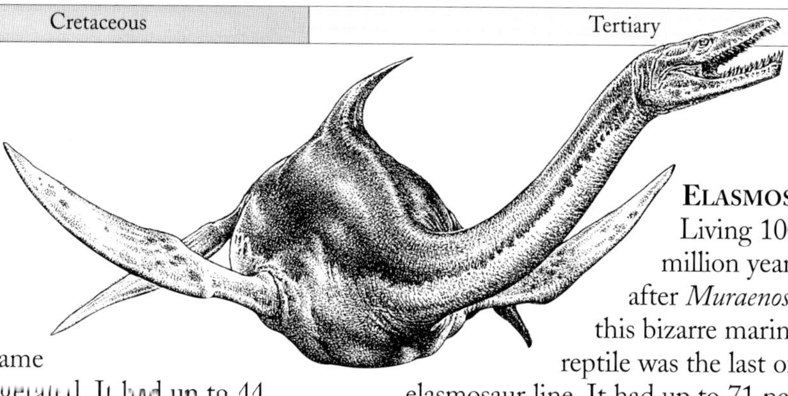

PLESIOSAURS

their very long neck. It was one of the early examples of the neck-stretching trend, which became increasingly exaggerated. It had up to 44 neck vertebrae, and altogether they accounted for over half its entire body length. Its head was relatively tiny—just 15.7 in. (40cm) long. It also had relatively small flippers for its size and a stubby tail. This combination of features suggests that *Muraenosaurus* was not an active hunter. Instead, it probably rested on the seabed in shallow water, where it could attack fish either from beneath the surface or from above it. To feed, it would have drawn its neck back into a curve and then suddenly straightened it to grab its prey. Its small head would also have allowed it to extract fish from crevices among rocks.

MAXIMUM LENGTH 19.7 ft. (6m)

TIME Late Jurassic

FOSSIL FINDS Europe (England, France)

ELASMOSAURUS
Living 100 million years after *Muraenosaurus*, this bizarre marine reptile was the last of the elasmosaur line. It had up to 71 neck vertebrae, contributing to a snakelike neck—19.7 ft. (6m) long. The central part of its body was also much larger than in *Muraenosaurus*. *Elasmosaurus'* feeding technique was probably similar to its earlier relatives, although its increased neck length would have given it a greater reach. The theory that it was a sit-and-wait predator has been bolstered by the discovery of gastroliths, or stomach stones, which it may have used as ballast.

MAXIMUM LENGTH 46 ft. (14m)

TIME Late Cretaceous

FOSSIL FINDS Asia (Japan), North America (Kansas, Wyoming)

◁ *Powered by its well-developed paddles,* Cryptoclidus *would have "flown" through the water.*

▽ Elasmosaurus *homes in on a school of fish. This plesiosaur is often portrayed as a sea monster, but its narrow head meant it could tackle only very small prey.*

189

PLIOSAURS

Descended from plesiosaurs, pliosaurs became the top marine predators from the Early Jurassic into the Cretaceous. With short necks, massive heads, and viciously armed jaws, they could attack animals almost their own size, ripping off chunks of flesh like today's sharks or killer whales. They probably hunted alone, and they may have relied partly on their sense of smell to track down food. In pliosaur evolution natural selection favored increasing size. After more than 60 million years the outcome of this process was *Liopleurodon*, perhaps the largest predator ever to have existed on the planet.

△ Kronosaurus' *head accounted for about a third of its entire body length, and its jaws ran almost the entire length of the skull, giving them a depth of nearly 10 ft. (3m). It had two other distinguishing features that set it apart from other pliosaurs: the top of the head was unusually flattened and the ribs were thicker.*

MACROPLATA
A relatively primitive pliosaur from the Early Jurassic, *Macroplata* still had features in common with its plesiosaur ancestors: a long neck with 29 vertebrae and a fairly small head. Two specimens from England, dated about 15 million years apart, highlight the trends in pliosaur evolution—the more recent species had a longer head, as well as a slightly larger body. In pliosaurs as a whole the limbs also became larger and stronger than those of plesiosaurs, allowing them to power through the water after their prey.

MAXIMUM LENGTH	16.4 ft. (5m)
TIME	Early Jurassic
FOSSIL FINDS	Europe (England)

SIMOLESTES
Simolestes was slightly larger than *Macroplata* and had a more typical pliosaur shape, with a short neck, massively built head, and large, paddlelike legs. Its neck contained only 20 vertebrae, far fewer than many plesiosaurs, but still more than pliosaurs of later times.

Its jaws had blunt ends, giving it a snub-nosed appearance, and the lower one was equipped with half a dozen extra-large teeth, which stabbed upward into prey. It would have killed small prey outright, but with larger animals it probably attacked and then circled at a distance, waiting for the moment when its victim was too weak to fight back. Sharks use the same technique.

MAXIMUM LENGTH	19.7 ft. (6m)
TIME	Mid Jurassic
FOSSIL FINDS	Asia (India), Europe (France)

PLIOSAURUS
First identified in the 1840s, the original pliosaur has proven difficult to classify. Many paleontologists believe that it is actually a form of *Liopleurodon* because their remains look so similar. Among the few differences are the teeth. *Liopleurodon's* were round viewed in cross section, while *Pliosaurus'* were triangular. *Pliosaurus* had about 20 neck vertebrae, and its skull was up to 6.6 ft. (2m) long.

MAXIMUM LENGTH	39.4 ft. (12m)
TIME	Mid Jurassic
FOSSIL FINDS	Europe (England), South America (Argentina)

PELONEUSTES

A compact Late Jurassic pliosaur, *Peloneustes* shows the developing trend in the family for a larger head and shorter neck, as well as a more streamlined shape. Its hind paddles were slightly larger than its front ones—the reverse of the situation in many plesiosaurs. However, as in plesiosaurs, both pairs of flippers were used in swimming, although the rear pair are likely to have done more of the work. Each

flipper would have twisted as it beat up and down through the water, creating a backward thrust that drove the animal forward (page 194). The remains of suckers, preserved as fossils in *Peloneustes'* stomach, show that squid formed an important part of its diet. Its teeth were relatively small, making it unlikely that it attacked large prey.

MAXIMUM LENGTH	10 ft. (3m)
TIME	Late Jurassic
FOSSIL FINDS	Europe (Russia, U.K.)

LIOPLEURODON

Once it reached maturity, this colossal pliosaur was so large that it had no enemies apart from its own kind. Estimates of its length range from about 39.4 ft. (12m) to as much as 82 ft. (25m)—a figure that suggests it might have weighed over 100 tons. This is much larger than the sperm whale, which is the largest living predator that tracks down and attacks individual prey. *Liopleurodon* would have fed on any marine animal large enough to attract its attention. Although it was fully equipped for life in the open sea, it may also have swum into shallow water, where it could pick off

dinosaurs foraging near the shore. It relied mainly on vision and smell, lunging forward to make a kill with an array of widely spaced, daggerlike teeth. These were conical in shape and up to 1 ft. (30cm) long—twice the length of those of *Tyrannosaurus*. They projected from the front of its jaws, which hinged at a point close to the back of the skull—a distance of up to 13 ft. (4m). Given its size, *Liopleurodon* would have been able to travel immense distances, but little is known of its breeding behavior. On land it would have been as helpless as a beached whale, which suggests that it gave birth to live young instead of laying eggs.

MAXIMUM LENGTH	82 ft. (25m)
TIME	Late Jurassic
FOSSIL FINDS	Europe (France, Germany, U.K.)

KRONOSAURUS

The first pliosaur fossil finds in Australia were made in Queensland and date back to the 1880s. In 1990 cattle ranchers in the same area stumbled across another set of fossilized bones protruding from the ground like tree stumps. They turned out to belong to *Kronosaurus* or a similar animal and are among the most complete pliosaur remains currently known. Although *Kronosaurus* was only generally a little over half the size of *Liopleurodon*, it was still larger and heavier than most land-based predators of the Cretaceous, with a head measuring 8.2 ft. (2.5m).

MAXIMUM LENGTH	33 ft. (10m)
TIME	Early Cretaceous
FOSSIL FINDS	Australia (Queensland), South America (Colombia)

◁ Liopleurodon *was a terrifying marine predator of enormous size and power. Armed with murderous, projecting teeth and protected by platelike bones on its underside, it would have reigned supreme in the Jurassic seas.*

▽ *Although a midget compared to some of its relatives,* Peloneustes *was still a substantial predator, the size of a large modern dolphin. It would have been a fast and agile swimmer, powered by its four paddles. It caught fish and squid in its narrow, toothed mouth.*

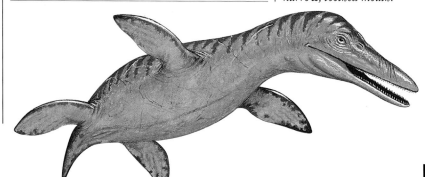

191

REPTILES IN THE SEA

ICHTHYOSAURS

Ichthyosaurs, or "fish lizards," were the first reptiles that were fully adapted to life in the sea. Ichthyosaurs had streamlined bodies and flippers instead of legs, and most had crescent-shaped tails. Like all reptiles, they breathed air, using nostrils at the base of their snouts. Some fossilized ichthyosaurs died with embryos inside their bodies, or even while they were giving birth—dramatic proof that they did not lay eggs.

▷ *Like other ichthyosaurs,* Mixosaurus *had four pairs of flippers, and a single upright fin on its back. The fin would have helped to keep it on a straight course while its tail moved from side to side.*

MIXOSAURUS

Mixosaurus (meaning "mixed lizard") lived about 220 million years ago, when ichthyosaurs were already well-established. Although it was fully adapted to life at sea, it still had several primitive features. The most obvious one was its tail, which ended in a point, instead of having two vertical lobes. *Mixosaurus* fed on fish, and its distribution—in warm, shallow seas worldwide—shows that it was very successful.

LENGTH 3.3 ft. (1m)

TIME Mid Triassic

FOSSIL FINDS Asia (China), Europe (France, Germany, Norway), North America (Alaska, Nevada), New Zealand

ICHTHYOSAURUS

Looking like a small dolphin, *Ichthyosaurus* is one of the best-known marine prehistoric reptiles, with hundreds of fossils having been found. A powerful swimmer, it could probably have reached speeds of 25 mph (40km/h), powered by its vertical two-lobed tail. Its snout was long and narrow and was armed with small but sharp teeth—ideal for gripping squid and other slippery animals.

LENGTH 6.6 ft. (2m)

TIME Early Jurassic to early Cretaceous

FOSSIL FINDS Europe (England, Germany), Greenland, North America (Alberta)

▷ *Compared to most ichthyosaurs,* Shonisaurus *was a vast and bulky animal. At one fossil site in Nevada the remains of more than 30* Shonisaurus *have been found close together. This suggests that these giant reptiles lived in schools, like many of today's whales.*

▽ *With its streamlined body and long jaws,* Temnodontosaurus *was shaped for catching fast-moving prey. Fish made up most of its diet, but it also ate squid and other cephalopod molluscs. Their hard remains have been found inside* Temnodontosaurus *skeletons.*

TEMNODONTOSAURUS

Also known as *Leptopterygius*, this large ichthyosaur had a long snout, a barrel-shaped body, and a powerful two-lobed tail. Most ichthyosaurs had good eyesight, but this one's eyes were the biggest of any known animal, alive or extinct. They measured up to 10 in. (26cm) across, and as in most ichthyosaurs, were surrounded by a ring of thin, overlapping bony plates, which helped to protect them during dives. *Leptopterygius'* large eyes may have been an adaptation for hunting at night.

LENGTH	29.5 ft. (9m)
TIME	Late Jurassic
FOSSIL FINDS	Europe (England, Germany)

SHONISAURUS

With a body as long as a bus, *Shonisaurus* is the largest ichthyosaur that has yet been discovered. It appeared relatively early in ichthyosaur evolution and had some unusual features that set it apart from its relatives. Among these were a deep, bulky body; long, equal-sized flippers; and teeth only in the front of its jaws. Its diet is uncertain, but its size alone means that it would have been a formidable predator, capable of tackling many other sea animals.

LENGTH	49 ft. (15m)
TIME	Late Triassic
FOSSIL FINDS	North America (Nevada)

193

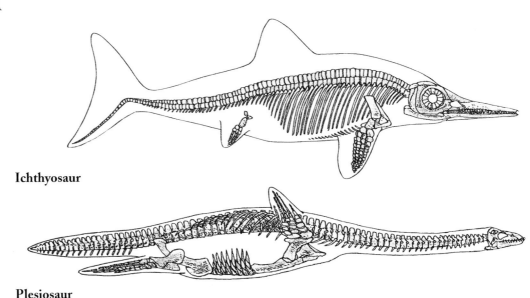

▷ *Ichthyosaurs, plesiosaurs, and turtles all had different swimming styles. Ichthyosaurs, the most fishlike of the three, swam with side-to-side undulations. Plesiosaurs used a complex swimming technique with two pairs of paddles moving in alternate directions. Turtles swim with their front legs, with very little push coming from the pair at the rear.*

Ichthyosaur

Plesiosaur

SWIMMING STYLES

WHEN REPTILES TOOK UP LIFE IN WATER, THEY EVOLVED DIFFERENT METHODS OF SWIMMING. SOME SWAM LIKE FISH, BUT OTHERS MOVED IN WAYS THAT HAVE NO DIRECT EQUIVALENT IN LIVING ANIMALS.

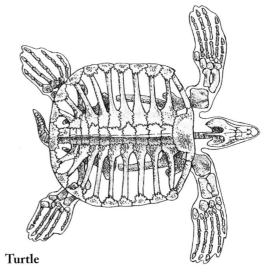

Turtle

To swim, an animal has to push against the water around it. This backward push drives the animal forward in the same way that the push from a propeller moves a boat. Reptiles evolved swimming styles with modified versions of two different body parts: tails and limbs. Tail propulsion is the common swimming style in fish and was the method evolved by ichthyosaurs. Limb propulsion is used by seals and penguins, but reptiles evolved some versions of it that were uniquely their own.

POWER AT THE REAR
To swim efficiently, an animal has to push against the water with minimum turbulence. This creates a smooth water flow as the animal moves—the exact opposite of what happens when somebody splashes around as they learn to swim.

Tail propulsion is ideal for this, and it is no accident that most fish use their tails to swim instead of rowing with their other fins.

The earliest marine reptiles, such as *Placodus* (page 187), had long, webbed tails that they rippled from side to side in conjunction with the rest of their bodies. For animals that originated on land, this way of swimming needed relatively few physical changes, but it had the disadvantage of being fairly slow. Ichthyosaurs, on the other hand, evolved shorter, bladelike tails, much more like those of fish. Most of their body movement took place at the tail end, and their paddlelike limbs acted as rudders and stabilizers, keeping them on course. This swimming style is almost exactly the same as that used by the fastest fish today.

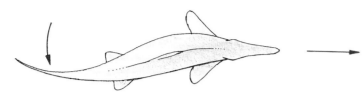

△ *In fish and ichthyosaurs the body and tail push against the water as they bend from side to side.*

∧ *The side-to-side movements generate a force that drives the animal forward through the water.*

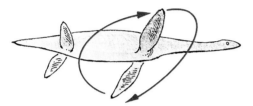

△ *In plesiosaurs the tip of each flipper follows a roughly elliptical path (assuming the animal is still).*

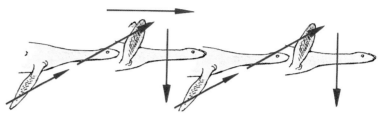

△ *The backward push comes during the downstroke. The flipper then twists to move upward edge-on.*

△ *Turtles move both sets of flippers together, but the front pair does the work.*

△ *The flippers work like oars, although they can also glide like wings.*

△ *To push the turtle forward, flippers move downward and backward.*

PADDLES AND FLIPPERS

In most other marine reptiles evolution followed a different course. These animals also developed paddlelike limbs, but instead of being fairly immobile, their limbs kept some of the movement they had on land. For some of these reptiles the tail helped in propulsion. In others, particularly turtles, it became so small that it played no part in swimming at all.

Evolution often exaggerates differences between front and back legs, and this is exactly what happened with turtles. Their forelimbs became longer and more powerful, beating up and down like a pair of wings to push the animal through the water. The back legs were much smaller and used mainly for steering and stability. But in plesiosaurs, the four paddles stayed roughly similar in size. Plesiosaurs probably swam with all four limbs working simultaneously, a highly unusual swimming style that has not been seen either before or since.

THE PLESIOSAUR PUZZLE

For stability plesiosaurs' two pairs of legs would most likely have beaten in opposite directions, but the exact path of each paddle is not easy to work out. They may have pushed horizontally (like oars), diagonally, or vertically up and down. From studies of plesiosaur skeletons the second theory is generally accepted as the most likely of the three. Each flipper generated a backward push as it came down and then twisted so that it could slide back into the up position with minimal resistance against the water. The upstroke was aided by the animal's spine, which bent rhythmically as it swam.

▽ *Plesiosaurs used their flippers for steering and braking as well as for building up speed. Here an* Elasmosaurus *carries out a sharp turn to pursue a school of fish.*

FAMILY GROUP

Guarded by their mother, two young Temnodontosaurus *swim past a rocky reef in search of food. Because female ichthyosaurs gave birth to live young, they had small families. The females probably looked after their offspring and showed them how to hunt.*

FOSSIL HUNTING IN EUROPE

EUROPE WAS THE BIRTHPLACE OF PALEONTOLOGY. EUROPEAN FOSSIL FINDS HAVE INCLUDED A NUMBER OF SIGNIFICANT FINDS, BEGINNING WITH THE DISCOVERY OF FOSSIL REPTILES OVER 250 YEARS AGO.

Fossils are common objects in some parts of Europe. During the medieval period they were thought to be the remains of animals that had perished in the biblical Great Flood—something that some people still believe today. But by the 1700s fossils of truly gigantic animals started to come to light, making scientists increasingly doubtful about the traditional version of the earth's history. They gradually realized that the earth was far older than previously thought, and that a wide range of animals had lived in the distant past, only to become extinct.

▷ *Carefully splitting open thin sheets of limestone, quarry workers in Germany reveal well-preserved fossils of Jurassic fish that have been entombed in limestone for over 150 million years.*

▷ *This is a fossil shrimp from the famous Solnhöfen limestone quarries in southern Germany. Because the rock particles are so fine, all the details of its body have been preserved. Solnhöfen has also yielded fossils of soft-bodied animals, such as jellyfish.*

BROUGHT TO THE SURFACE
In the early days of paleontology most fossils were discovered by accident, often by workers in Europe's quarries. One of the most spectacular of these early finds was the Beast of Maastricht—a giant crocodile-like skull that was found in a chalk quarry in the Netherlands in 1776. The Beast was actually a mosasaur (page 200), but scientists of the time imagined that it must belong

FOSSIL EVIDENCE

Born in 1799, Mary Anning was the world's first professional collector of fossils. Her home town, Lyme Regis, England, is flanked by seacliffs of Jurassic shale and mudstone, and it was here, in 1811, that she found the first known remains of an ichthyosaur, which had fallen out of the cliffs onto the shore. Thirteen years later she discovered another first: the almost complete fossil skeleton of a plesiosaur.

to an animal that still existed, probably either a crocodile or a whale.

The confusion over this animal was understandable, because the tooth-filled jaws of a mosasaur do look distinctly crocodilian.

But in 1784 an Italian naturalist published an account of an even more remarkable fossil that he had found in the Solnhöfen

limestone quarries in southern Germany. Unlike the Maastricht mosasaur, this animal was small, but it looked unlike anything that scientists had ever seen or heard of before. Resembling a cross between a bat and a bird, it was actually a pterosaur—the first one to be studied in a systematic way. This fossil was the scientific equivalent of front-page news, and as interest in paleontology mushroomed quarry workers kept a sharp lookout for interesting specimens, which by now were fetching record prices.

During the early 1800s quarries like Solnhöfen generated a steady stream of fossil remains. At this time a young woman named Mary Anning became the first person to collect fossils for a living. Mary Anning lived on the coast of Dorset, England, in an area where fossil-filled cliffs are being steadily eroded by the sea. Her finds included an almost complete ichthyosaur, which was identified as an extinct marine reptile. The idea of extinction was becoming widely accepted, and this helped prepare the way for more momentous discoveries in the years that followed.

THE FIRST DINOSAURS

The first dinosaur fossil to be formally described was found in 1676 by the English museum curator Robert Plot. At the time Plot's discovery—the knee end of a giant thighbone—was thought to be from a large mammal, perhaps even a giant human being. Over 140 years passed before more remains of the animal were found in an English quarry. These fossils were examined by pioneering geologist William Buckland, who recognized that they belonged to a carnivorous reptile, which he named *Megalosaurus*. The following year another English geologist, Gideon Mantell, identified the remains of *Iguanodon*, again correctly deducing that they were from a reptile, rather than a mammal.

The name *Megalosaurus* means "giant lizard" and shows that even in the 1800s geologists were still trying to squeeze their newly discovered animals into known branches of the reptile world. But this situation was not to last for long. In 1841

the leading English anatomist Richard Owen showed that *Megalosaurus* and *Iguanodon* were different from living reptiles in many ways, even apart from their size. He proposed a new name for this extinct group of reptiles— "the dinosaurs."

MAMMALS AND PEOPLE

After this breakthrough European paleontology began to move quickly. The first fossil of *Archaeopteryx* was found at the Solnhöfen quarries in 1861, and as the 1800s drew to a close European fossil hunters began to send back fossils from other parts of the world. These formed the basis of magnificent museum collections in cities such as London, Paris, and Berlin. Paleontologists continued to unearth a wide range of reptiles in Europe, particularly marine forms such as ichthyosaurs and plesiosaurs, but their finds also included extinct mammals— mammoths, bears, and rhinoceroses—that flourished in Europe during ice age times.

In the last 150 years Europe has also been an important source of fossils and artifacts belonging to early humans, who spread northward through the continent after the move from Africa. The finds include the remains not only of our direct ancestors, but also those of Neanderthal man (page 216).

◁ *The crumbling cliffs of Lyme Regis, on the south coast of England, are a fossil hunter's paradise. Their layered rock, formed from seabed sediment in Jurassic times, contains the remains of a wide variety of animals— from ammonites to ichthyosaurs.*

△ *The Solnhöfen quarries in southern Germany produce limestone with an extremely fine grain. The rock was built up by tiny specks of sediment that settled in coral reef lagoons during the Late Jurassic. The quarries are famous for being the source of* Archaeopteryx *and half a dozen kinds of pterosaur, but they have also yielded many fish and over 100 kinds of fossils insect.*

REPTILES IN THE SEA

MOSASAURS

Mosasaurs were latecomers to the ranks of Mesozoic marine reptiles, appearing late in the Cretaceous Period and disappearing when it came to a close. Unlike other reptiles in the sea, they belonged to the same line of animals as today's monitor lizards. They had scaly, lizardlike skin, and they swam by rippling their long bodies, which ended in a flattened, fin-bearing tail. Some of them grew to a great size, and they had unusual jaws that could bend sideways to engulf and crush their prey.

▽ Tylosaurus (below) had the sinuous shape, small limbs, and narrow head characteristic of the mosasaur family.

▷ Platecarpus (right) had a large number of finger and toe bones, a typical feature of marine reptiles.

MOSASAURUS

Mosasaurus has a unique place in the study of prehistoric life. When the first skull was found in a Dutch quarry in 1776, it was assumed to belong to an unknown animal—perhaps a crocodile or whale—that was still alive somewhere on Earth. But as the decades went by without a living Mosasaurus being found, scientists began to grasp a crucial fact: animal life in the past included species that have become extinct. The creature that triggered this breakthrough was one of the deadliest marine predators of the Late Cretaceous. Its limbs had evolved into

△ Mosasaurus *and its relatives were alive when the ichthyosaurs had died out, making them among the largest marine reptiles in the Late Cretaceous.*

two pairs of widely saced, finlike paddles, containing many more toe bones than in its land-dwelling ancestors. Its tail was vertically flattened, and this—together with its wedge-shaped skull—made it look like a fish crossed with a crocodile. Like all mosasaurs, its jaws had a joint about halfway along their length, allowing them to extend sideways, and they were equipped with a battery of sharply pointed teeth. It probably fed on fish, squid, and turtles, but it also ate ammonites. This is known because fossilized ammonites have been discovered with bite marks that match *Mosasaurus'* teeth.

MAXIMUM LENGTH 33 ft. (10m)

TIME Late Cretaceous

FOSSIL FINDS Europe (Belgium, Holland), North America (South Dakota, Texas)

TYLOSAURUS

Similar in form to *Mosasaurus*, although slightly smaller, *Tylosaurus* would have been an equally formidable predator of the Late Cretaceous seas. Like *Mosasaurus*, it drove itself through the water with its tail, using its paddle-shaped flippers for steering and perhaps for stabilizing itself when it rested inshore. Its teeth were up to 2 in. (5cm) long and 1.2 in. (3cm)

wide at the base and would have constantly been replaced throughout its lifetime. Its eyes were surrounded by a sclerotic ring—a circle of small, flattened bones that acted as a protective shield in front of the eyeball. Like other mosasaurs, *Tylosaurus* lived in shallow seas. But although hundreds of mosasaur fossils have been found, unlike ichthyosaurs, none shows signs of carrying embryos. This makes it probable that most mosasaurs laid eggs, dragging themselves onto sandy beaches like turtles. Their flippers would have been ineffective on land, so they may have writhed their way up the shore.

MAXIMUM LENGTH	26.2 ft. (8m)
TIME	Late Cretaceous
FOSSIL FINDS	North America (Kansas, Texas), New Zealand

PLATECARPUS

Remains found on both sides of the Atlantic show that *Platecarpus* was a fairly common marine reptile in the Late Cretaceous. Although very small compared to other mosasaurs, it was about the same size as many of today's open-water sharks, and its long jaws would have made it an effective predator. It probably fed on fish and squid, but exactly how it hunted is unclear. It may have fed in the same way as modern seals, cruising through the shallows close to the shore and catching animals frightened by its approach.

MAXIMUM LENGTH	19.7 ft. (6m)
TIME	Late Cretaceous
FOSSIL FINDS	North America (Alabama, Colorado, Kansas, Mississippi; Manitoba, Northwest Territories), Europe (Belgium)

GLOBIDENS

When *Globidens* first came to light in Alabama in 1912, it was given its name because of its remarkable teeth. They had rounded crowns and looked like a row of golf balls set in the animal's jaws. Teeth like these were clearly useless for grasping fish or squid, and instead *Globidens* probably fed on mollusks and crustaceans, cracking open their shells and body cases with its jaws. Only a handful of *Globidens* skulls have been found—all in North America—but isolated teeth have been found in other parts of the world.

MAXIMUM LENGTH	19.7 ft. (6m)
TIME	Late Cretaceous
FOSSIL FINDS	North America (Alabama, Kansas, South Dakota)

PLOTOSAURUS

One of the largest of about 20 mosasaurs so far discovered, *Plotosaurus* had a long body and a snakelike tail with a flattened vertical fin. Its small flippers were widely spaced, making them ineffective for propulsion but good for steering and stability. Skin impressions found near some *Plotosaurus* fossils show that it was covered in small scales, like today's monitor lizards. With its sleek shape and sharp teeth, it would have been a major threat to fish and squid in shallow seas as the Cretaceous neared its end.

MAXIMUM LENGTH	33 ft. (10m)
TIME	Late Cretaceous
FOSSIL FINDS	North America (Kansas)

△ *With its jaws gaping open,* Globidens *(top) reveals a mouth full of bulbous and extremely hard teeth. The main teeth were up to 1.2 in. (3cm) across; the ones at the front of the jaw were smaller and peglike.*

△ Plotosaurus *(above) was so well adapted to marine life that it would have had difficulty moving on land. This suggests that it gave birth to live young, unlike some of its relatives.*

REPTILES IN THE SEA

SHELLED REPTILES

During the Mesozoic Era two different groups of marine reptiles evolved shells as a protection against predators. One group, the placodonts, were relatives of some of the earliest reptiles in the seas (page 197). They emerged in the Triassic but were extinct before it came to an end. The other group were the chelonians—animals that also appeared in the Triassic and were the ancestors of today's tortoises and turtles. Although they lived at different times, these two groups evolved similar adaptations to suit similar ways of life.

△ With its streamlined shell and huge "wingspan," Archelon (top right) roamed vast distances throughout the seas of the Late Cretaceous.

▷ Placochelys (right) is a combination name that means "placodont-turtle"—a fitting description of this remarkably turtlelike animal.

▽ Henodus (below) had a rectangular shell. Its legs were relatively short and stumpy, suggesting that it spent most of its time crawling across the seabed.

ARCHELON
Chelonians first appeared on land, and although tortoises remained there, turtles took up life in freshwater or the sea. By the late Cretaceous, one marine species—Archelon—became the largest sea turtle that has ever lived. It weighed about three tons and swam by beating its winglike front flippers, which were 14.8 ft. (4.5m) from tip to tip. Its shell was formed by an open lattice of struts, instead of a complete shield of bone, and it probably had a rubbery surface, like the shells of modern leatherback turtles. Like other chelonians, Archelon's jaws formed a toothless beak, and it fed on jellyfish and other soft-bodied animals. Despite its great weight, it reproduced by hauling itself onto beaches and laying eggs.

MAXIMUM LENGTH	13 ft. (4m)
TIME	Late Cretaceous
FOSSIL FINDS	North America (Kansas, Dakota)

HENODUS
Long before *Archelon* appeared in the seas, *Henodus*, a placodont, had evolved a shell for self-defense. Unlike a turtle's shell, this one was made up of several hundred bony plates, which fit together like a mosaic. The edges of the shell were drawn out into a pair of rigid flaps, giving a flattened shape. *Henodus* had a blunt mouth without any teeth, and it ate mollusks and other slow-moving animals in shallow water.

MAXIMUM LENGTH	3.3 ft. (1m)
TIME	Late Triassic
FOSSIL FINDS	Europe (Germany)

PLACOCHELYS
The shell of this placodont was shallow and almost rectangular and was covered with a scattering of bony plates that made it harder to attack. It had flat-toothed jaws, ending in a narrow beak that was ideal for prying mollusks from rocks. It had flattened legs that worked like flippers, and their size meant that it was probably a good swimmer. However, like all marine turtles, it could not pull its legs within its shell if it was attacked. *Placochelys* most likely reproduced by laying eggs, and it would have had no difficultly crawling out onto land.

MAXIMUM LENGTH	3 ft. (90cm)
TIME	Late Triassic
FOSSIL FINDS	Europe (Germany)

THE AGE OF THE MAMMALS

During Earth's long history most of the changes involving animal life have been extremely slow. But 66 million years ago something happened that had an abrupt and disastrous effect on the world's dominant animals. The 150-million-year reign of dinosaurs came to an end, and many other reptiles, including pterosaurs and plesiosaurs, also disappeared. The surviving reptiles never completely recovered from this setback, but for mammals it brought new opportunities. The Mesozoic Era had ended, ushering in the Cenozoic—the era in which we live today.

THE END OF THE DINOSAURS

BEFORE THE AGE OF MAMMALS BEGAN SOME DINOSAUR FAMILIES HAD ALREADY BECOME EXTINCT. BUT WITHOUT THE CATASTROPHE THAT OCCURRED 66 MILLION YEARS AGO, DINOSAURS MIGHT STILL BE DOMINANT TODAY.

In the earth's crust only the thinnest of lines separates the last rocks of the Age of Reptiles from the first ones formed during the Age of Mammals. But this geological turning point—known as the K-T boundary—has been studied by scientists in minute detail in places all over the world. The reason is that it holds the secret to what happened at the end of the Cretaceous Period, when as many as fifty percent of all the world's plant and animal species became extinct. Those studies point to one likely culprit: an object from outer space.

▷ *Terrified by the light released by a giant meteorite, a tyrannosaur reacts by running for its life. It has only seconds to live because the impact has already set off an atmospheric shock wave that will burst over the horizon, sweeping away almost anything that can be moved, from animals and plants to boulders weighing many tons.*

THE EVIDENCE

Dozens of theories have been put forward for the extinction of the dinosaurs, often without any evidence. But in the 1980s two American scientists, Luis Alvarez and his son Walter, published research showing that a massive meteorite up to 9 mi. (15km) across might have smashed into the earth, causing devastation on an unimaginable scale. Their evidence was the unusually high level of iridium that they found in the K-T boundary. Iridium is a chemical element and is normally ten times rarer than gold. The most likely explanation for the raised level, according to the Alvarez team, was that it had come from a giant meteorite that had vaporized on impact about 66.4 million years ago.

When they first proposed this idea, the site of the impact was unknown. But in the 1990s geologists investigated the remnants of a huge crater off Mexico's Yucatán Peninsula and found that its age almost exactly matched the time of this event. The crater is about 186 mi. (300km) across, indicating that the meteorite that made it would have sent shock waves right around the world.

THE IMPACT

Some scientists are not convinced by the meteorite theory and think that, as with the Permian extinction (page 66), the true causes might have been volcanic eruptions and other natural events. If a giant meteorite did crash into the earth, the results would have been incredibly destructive immediately after, as well as in the weeks and months that followed. In the second or so that it took to fall through the atmosphere, its outer surface would have melted, creating a burst of light brighter than thousands of suns. Once it struck the earth and vaporized, shock waves would have reverberated throughout the planet, triggering off landslides and earthquakes. Millions of tons of dust would have been blasted into the air, replacing the intense light of the impact itself with day after day of deep gloom. Choked by dust and deprived of light, plant plankton soon would have died in the sea, followed by plants on land. And without plants, animals would have had no food.

VICTIMS AND SURVIVORS

The few remaining species of sauropods would have soon died out, followed by other plant-eating dinosaurs. Predatory theropods might have been able to hold out for longer by scavenging, but the disintegration of food chains would have made life increasingly difficult. Eventually, after perhaps centuries or millennia, the last dinosaurs would have disappeared. Small animals fared better, perhaps because they were less exposed, but the checklist of survivors raises some puzzling questions. Why did pterosaurs vanish, while birds managed to pull through? What physical features allowed crocodiles to survive, while most other aquatic reptiles perished? More than 60 million years after the K-T event answers to these questions are still not known.

THE AGE OF MAMMALS

EARLY TERTIARY

The Tertiary Period (meaning "third") was given its name in the 1700s, when it was thought to be the third major interval in Earth's distant past. The Tertiary began after the Cretaceous mass extinction, and it continued until 1.6 million years ago, which means that it includes almost all of the Age of Mammals. During the Early Tertiary—often known as the Paleogene—some of the continents were close to the positions they occupy today, but Australia was still in the process of becoming an island, and North and South America were separated by the sea.

▷ Pakicetus *(top right) is the earliest known cetacean—the group of mammals that includes today's whales and dolphins. About 6.6 ft. (2m) long, it had long jaws with flesh-tearing teeth.*

▽ Pristichampus, *a land-dwelling crocodile, attacks a* Hyracotherium, *one of the earliest known members of the horse family.* Hyracotherium *stood just 8 in. (20cm) high at the shoulders.*

CHANGING DIETS

When the Tertiary Period began mammals had already existed for at least 150 million years, and two major lines—the placental mammals and the marsupials—were well established. However, during this long phase in their history neither of these lines played a major role in Earth's animal life. They were about the size of today's mice and voles, and they emerged under the cover of darkness to feed. Most of them ate insects, earthworms, and other small animals, cutting up their prey with tiny but sharp teeth.

With the disappearance of the dinosaurs and many other groups of animals, mammals were confronted with new opportunities on an extraordinary scale. Practically all of the large plant eaters had disappeared, leaving a huge and largely untapped source of food. There were no large meat eaters at all. From modest beginnings mammals went through an astounding surge of evolution. They eventually filled both these gaps, becoming the most important plant eaters and hunters on land and even spreading into the air and sea.

Some of the first large carnivorous mammals were the creodonts, a group of placental mammals that included species that looked like weasels, cats, and hyenas. Creodonts flourished for several million years, but became extinct before the Early Tertiary came to an end. Marsupial meat eaters were important predators in Australia and South America. But a group of placental, meat-eating mammals, the carnivores, became the leading predators in all other parts of the world.

Early Tertiary carnivores included the ancestors of all the main families of mammalian hunters, including cats, dogs, and mustelids (animals that include today's badgers, otters, and skunks). One feature that all these animals

shared was a set of teeth shaped for gripping and slicing flesh. Their gripping teeth, or canines, were near the front of their jaws, ideally placed for stabbing into prey. As carnivores evolved, some species developed very long canines, a feature that reached its high point in the saber-toothed cats. These were equipped with two stabbing teeth up to 6 in. (15cm) long, which were flattened from side to side. True saber-toothed cats were all placentals, but some marsupials—for example, *Thylacosmilus* (page 208)—developed in a similar way, an example of convergent evolution.

THE RISE OF THE PLANT EATERS

For mammals that fed on insects the switch to eating plants was more complicated than the switch to hunting larger prey. They gradually evolved front incisors to harvest their food and grinding teeth or molars to reduce it to a pulp. More importantly, they developed complex digestive systems filled with microorganisms that helped them break down food. Many of these animals developed long legs and hooves, which meant they could run for safety if attacked.

During the Early Tertiary several lines of hooved placental mammals developed in different parts of the world. They included the early ancestors of today's elephants, as well as tapirs and rhinoceroses. Horses evolved in the Northern Hemisphere, but they were mirrored by convincing horse look-alikes, litopterns, which developed in isolation in South America. The most impressive of these plant eaters would have been the brontotheres, animals that looked like giant rhinoceroses with head shields and horns. One of the largest, *Brontotherium*, lived in North America, had a forked horn, and weighed up to two tons.

REPTILES AND BIRDS

Apart from the mammals, other survivors from the Cretaceous extinction made the most of new opportunities in a dinosaur-free world. Among them were the reptiles that emerged from the extinction unscathed: lizards and snakes, turtles and tortoises, and —largest of all—the crocodilians. Most crocodilians kept to their original watery habitats, but some, such as *Pristichampus*, abandoned this kind of life and took up hunting on land, running on powerful legs that ended in hooflike claws.

For birds the disappearance of pterosaurs meant less competition for fish. But on land the extinction of their immediate relatives—the predatory theropods—opened up some new and different ways of living. Giant, flightless hunters evolved, capable of running down other animals and tearing them apart with their beaks. One of the best-known examples of these feathered predators was *Diatryma*, which lived in North America and Europe about 50 million years ago. Standing about 6.6 ft. (2m) tall, it probably fed on mammals, but declined when predatory mammals became larger and more widespread. Similar birds survived for much longer in South America, perhaps because large predatory mammals were rare on this island continent, which was cut off from the rest of the world.

◁ *Crouched in shallow water,* Moeritherium *feeds on water plants. This portly, pig-sized animal was an early proboscidean—a relative of today's elephants and of extinct mammoths and mastodons. Its ears, eyes, and nostrils were in a line along the top of its head, allowing it to float with most of its body submerged.*

▽ *With its long legs and powerful beak,* Diatryma *was well equipped for making sudden raids among herds of small grazing mammals. Small animals were swallowed whole, but larger ones were torn up by the hook at the beak's tip.*

THE AGE OF MAMMALS

LATE TERTIARY

The Late Tertiary, or Neogene, began about 23 million years ago. Life had fully recovered after the great Cretaceous extinction. Mammals continued to flourish and reached a peak of diversity as the global climate became cooler and drier. The continents were less scattered than they were in Early Tertiary times and, toward the end of this period a significant event occurred in the Western Hemisphere: North and South America became joined by a narrow isthmus of dry land.

▷ *Hapalops was a ground sloth that lived in South America about 20 million years ago. It was about 4 ft. (1.2m) long—a modest size compared to some of its later relatives, such as* Megatherium *(page 213).*

▽ *The South American marsupial, saber-toothed cat* Thylacosmilus *attacked its prey with a pair of enormous canine teeth. True placental cats evolved similar weapons independently— one well-known example is* Smilodon *(page 212).*

SEPARATION AND CONNECTION

Marsupial mammals first appeared during the Late Cretaceous Period, when many of the continents were still connected. Fossils show that they spread across Europe, North America, and South America and reached Australia in the Tertiary. Marsupials and placental mammals lived side by side, with marsupials proving just as successful as their relatives in the struggle to survive. But during the Tertiary Period, continental drift caused great changes in these two mammal lines. Some of the continents began to separate, carrying their mammals with them. Marsupials died out in Europe and North America, but in South America and Australia—now both isolated—they thrived.

Today Australia is well known for its marsupials, but South America had almost as many kinds in Tertiary times, including opossums—rodentlike insect eaters that spent their life in trees—and ground-based predators that looked like hyenas and bears. The largest of the South American predators were the saber-toothed, marsupial cats. One of these, *Thylacosmilus*, had the longest canine teeth of any hunting mammal.

In Australia marsupials remained in isolation until humans arrived, perhaps 60,000 years ago. There were no placental mammals to compete with, so they evolved into an extraordinary array of forms. In South America things were different partly because placental mammals also existed on the continent. But as the Tertiary neared its end the Central American land bridge allowed mammals from North and South America to mix. For some of South America's marsupials, particularly the opossums, this brought a chance to spread north, but for plant-eating species and placentals, it meant extra competition as hooved mammals, such as horses and deer, spread south.

UNLIKELY PARTNERS

During the Late Tertiary, as the world's climate grew drier, grassy plains became a major animal habitat for the first time. Plant-eating mammals gradually adapted to this, switching from a diet based on the leaves of trees and shrubs to one based on grass.

Grasses grow from the bottom up, rather than at their tips. As a result they can grow back if they are eaten down to the ground, whereas other plants, such as tree saplings, become stunted and die. By killing the plants with which grasses compete, mammalian grazers help grass spread.

This improbable partnership proved to be one of the great success stories in mammalian evolution, particularly in the interior of northern continents. In North America larger and faster horses evolved, as well as the antelope-like pronghorns. In Europe and Asia the main grazers were bovids, animals that include today's cattle and sheep.

OUT OF THE TREES

The Late Tertiary was an important time for primates, a group of mammals that adapted to life in trees. The earliest remains—just five teeth—date back to the Late Cretaceous. By the Early Tertiary ancestors of monkeys and apes make their first appearance in the fossil record. Primates had hands that could grip, forward-facing eyes, and large brains—features that helped them judge distances and jump from branch to branch.

Throughout the Tertiary primates in the Americas remained forest-dwellers, just as they are today. But in Europe, Africa, and Asia an increasing number of species took up life on the ground, probably because forests were giving way to grassland. These ground dwellers included the ancestors of today's baboons, as well as hominids—animals related to today's chimpanzees and gorillas, and also to us. Unlike monkeys, hominids did not have tails, and most could stand on their back feet to get a better view of their surroundings. This upright posture freed their hands for other tasks, such as carrying food or even making tools. It was a major development, and one that would have momentous consequences for the whole of the living world.

◁ Merychippus *was a Late Tertiary member of the horse family. About 3.3 ft. (1m) high at the shoulder, it was larger than* Hyracotherium *(page 206). And its weight was supported by just one toe on each foot, rather than three or four. As horses evolved all traces of their other toes disappeared.*

▽ *Keeping a careful watch for danger, a troop of* Ankarapithecus *forages on the ground.* Ankarapithecus *lived in the Near East about 10 million years ago— well before the split between the line that led to the great apes and the one that led to human beings.*

THE AGE OF MAMMALS

QUATERNARY

Upheavals caused by climate change have been a common feature in the history of life, but few periods have seen such abrupt swings as the last 1.6 million years. The Quaternary Period is divided into two geological epochs: the Pleistocene, which spanned the whole of the last Ice Age, and the Holocene, which began about 10,000 years ago, when the ice staged its most recent retreat. For land animals the Quaternary has been a challenging time.

▷ *The woolly mammoth evolved in Europe and Asia but spread to North America via the land bridge that formed across the Bering Sea (page 23). The hump on its head stored fat that acted as a food reserve.*

▽ *The European cave bear is one of several Ice Age species that are known from the fossilized remains of animals hibernating in caves underground.*

EBB AND FLOW
Ice ages are much more than periods of intense and long-lasting cold. During a typical ice age average temperatures swing up and down; with each steep drop, or glaciation, the world's polar ice caps advance, and glaciers creep farther down mountains in other parts of the world. During the warm intervals, or interglacials, the reverse happens, and the ice goes into retreat. We are currently experiencing an interglacial—one that started when the Holocene Epoch began.

Ice ages are impossible to predict, although they are almost certainly linked to variations in the earth's orbit around the sun. As well as changing average temperatures and ice cover, they have other effects on plant and animal habitats. One of these is a drop in sea level, caused by more water being locked up as ice. Another is a change in rainfall patterns, which can make some areas drier than they are in warmer times.

For plant life during the Pleistocene, climate changes were often problematic, particularly in the far north and south, where the ground was bulldozed by slowly moving ice. But for land animals falling sea levels sometimes proved useful, because they allowed species to cross land bridges to areas that they had not been able to reach before.

MAMMOTHS AND MASTODONTS
At their maximum spread the ice caps of the Pleistocene stretched as far south as present-day New York and London. To the south of these giant ice sheets was tundra—a bleak and vast expanse of boggy grassland, crisscrossed by icy rivers carrying meltwater to the sea. It was a hostile landscape, but despite the cold, summer brought a rich supply of plant food. For warm-blooded mammals it was a good place to be.

The most celebrated of the Ice Age mammals were the mammoths and the mastodonts, two

210

groups of animals belonging to the
elephant line. The steppe mammoth,
Mammuthus trogontheri, which lived in
Europe about 500,000 years ago, was one
of the first species to become adapted to
severe cold by developing a coat of long,
thick fur. Unlike today's elephants, it had
a high-crowned head and sloping back, and
in males the tusks were sometimes more than
16.4 ft. (5m) long. The more familiar woolly
mammoth, *Mammuthus primigenius*, was a
more compact animal, measuring less than
10 ft. (3m) high. Its tusks were also smaller,
and it probably used them to scrape away
snow as it searched for food. The American
mastodont, *Mammut americanum*, looked
similar and roamed the coniferous forests
on the tundra's southern edge.

The steppe mammoth died out long
ago, but the woolly mammoth and American
mastodont survived into the relatively recent
past. The mastodont is thought to have died
out about 8,000 years ago, and the woolly
mammoth clung on for another two
millennia. Human hunters were probably
responsible for making both species extinct.

ICE AGE RHINOS

The northern tundra was also home to
the woolly rhinoceros, *Coelodonta antiquitatis*,
another animal whose modern relatives live
in much warmer parts of the world. Standing
about 6.6 ft. (2m) high, it had a pair of solid
horns made of matted hair—a family feature
that distinguishes rhinos from other hooved
mammals. Its thickset shape and long coat

were characteristic
of Ice Age mammals,
because large bodies
can generate plenty
of heat from their
food, and thick fur helps
retain it. Woolly rhinos
lived in Europe and in Siberia and survived
until the ice retreated at the end of the
Pleistocene. Specimens have been found
frozen in permafrost, but some have also
been recovered from naturally occurring
oil seeps in parts of central Europe.

Another Ice Age species, *Elasmotherium*,
had what was probably the largest horn of
any member of the rhino family. It was about
the same size as a white rhino—the largest
species alive today—but its horn was up to
6.6 ft. (2m) long, with a spreading base that
covered almost all of its forehead and muzzle.

SURVIVING THE WINTER

For plant eaters on the tundra, summer
may have been a season of plenty, but winter
was a testing time. Many grazing mammals
migrated south, heading for forested regions
where there was some shelter and food in
the form of bark and buds. These included
reindeer and the so-called Irish elk, whose
remains have been found in many parts of
northern Europe and Asia. Reindeer follow
their traditional migration routes today, but
the Irish elk is now extinct.
In some remote parts
of Europe the
species may
have lasted
until 500 B.C.

Unlike grazing
animals, ice age
bears spent the
winter in a dormant
state, which meant that
they did not have to search for food.
In some caves in Europe, mud still carries
scratch marks made by bears traveling to
and from their hibernation dens.

◁ *Unlike the woolly
mammoth, the woolly
rhinoceros did not
manage to spread from
Asia to North America,
but it did have a wide
distribution from the
northern tundra to the
grasslands farther south.
As with modern rhinos,
its horns evolved
partly for impressing
rivals and partly
for self-defense.*

▽ *With its enormous
antlers the male Irish
elk would have been one
of the most spectacular
animals in Europe and
northern Asia during
Ice Age times. There
were several species of
these remarkable deer,
all with extravagant
antlers that were shed
and regrown each year.*

THE AGE OF MAMMALS

DEATH AT RANCHO LA BREA

Some of the most vivid evidence of life in Pleistocene times comes not from the far north, but from the heart of modern Los Angeles. This is the unlikely setting for one of the world's most remarkable fossil sites—the famous tar pits of Rancho La Brea. Here pools of sticky asphalt, or tar, existed in Ice Age times, creating traps for animals on a massive scale.

For much of the Late Pleistocene the climate of this part of California was cooler and wetter than it is today, and the well-watered landscape was home to a wide variety of animals, including mammoths, giant ground sloths, and saber-toothed tigers. The tar pits were often covered with the remains of dead plants, and in the winter animals could walk across the surface in complete safety, because the asphalt was cold and firm. But during the summer the asphalt absorbed the sun's heat and started to liquefy, like hot tar on the surface of a road. At this time of the year animals walking across what looked like solid ground could suddenly find themselves falling into sticky black pools,

with no hope of getting out. As they struggled to save themselves these trapped animals attracted predators and scavengers, which also became stuck.

After each summer's deadly toll winter rains covered the victims with sand and sediment, and the process of fossilization began. Unlike most fossils, the ones at Rancho La Brea consist of original bones, rather than ones that have been mineralized, or turned to stone. Impregnated with oily tar and cut off from oxygen in the air, they have escaped the normal processes of decay for over 10,000 years.

TREASURE IN THE TAR

Many of the tar pits have now been excavated, yielding fossils on a truly staggering scale. These Late Pleistocene treasure chests have disgorged the remains of nearly 60 mammal species, with over 2,000 skeletons of saber-toothed tigers alone. The largest victims were mammoths, and the smallest included flying insects that had made the mistake of settling on the surface of the tar, instead of flying on. Birds feature

▽ In Ice Age California 20,000 years ago, an imperial mammoth lies in a tar pit while a saber-toothed tiger fights off scavengers that have already gathered in hopes of feeding on the mammoth's remains. The scavengers include storks, vultures, and the dire wolf—the largest known member of the dog family. Most of the animals in this scene became extinct about 10,000 years ago.

▷ *The giant moa*
Diornis maximus *was the largest of about two dozen species whose remains have been found in New Zealand. Until Polynesian settlers arrived about 1,000 years ago, it lived in a world entirely free of land mammals apart from bats. An adult giant moa could hold up to 5.5 lb. (2.5kg) of stones in its gizzard, helping it grind its food. Moas laid just a single egg.*

in the catch. Their fragile skeletons break easily, but in the tar pits they were well preserved. The only animals that managed to avoid this deadly trap were nocturnal species. This was because the surface of the tar hardened after sunset.

RULED BY BIRDS

Although mammals were the largest plant eaters of Ice Age times, some remote islands, such as Madagascar and New Zealand, had no large land mammals of their own. Their largest animals were flightless birds, which grew to colossal sizes. In Madagascar the biggest species were the elephant birds, some of which weighed almost half a ton. One species, *Aepyornis maximus*, laid the world's largest known bird egg (page 16). New Zealand's counterparts, known collectively as moas, included one species, *Dinornis maximus*, that measured up to 12 ft. (3.7m) high, making it the tallest bird ever.

Birds like these were able to evolve on remote islands because there were no predatory mammals to attack either them or their chicks. Most fed on seeds, berries, and shoots, and they ground up their food with gizzard stones, which were very like the gastroliths of dinosaurs (page 78). They survived the changes at the end of the last Ice Age, but sadly they were not able to survive the arrival of human beings, and their spears, bows and arrows, and dogs. Madagascar's last elephant bird probably died about 1,000 years ago, and the last of the moas is thought to have died out much more recently— perhaps as late as 1800.

▷ *The giant ground sloth* Megatherium *lived in South America during Ice Age times. Almost as large as a modern elephant, it could stand on its back legs to reach up into trees and hook down leafy branches with its long claws. Today's sloths belong to the same group of mammals, but rarely set foot on the ground.*

THE PLEISTOCENE EXTINCTION

One of the tantalizing features about Ice Age animals is that—in geological terms—they existed not that long ago. Few of them lasted as long as the moas, but a whole host of large mammals were still alive and well about 10,000 years ago. However, as the last glaciation came to an end hundreds of species abruptly died out. North America was one of the worst-affected regions, losing three fourths of all its large mammals, including many whose remains have been dug up at Rancho La Brea.

Why did this massive round of extinctions take place? Some paleontologists believe that it was triggered mainly by the sudden change in climate as the ice retreated and the world warmed up. According to this theory, rapid changes in plant life—such as the switch from tundra to forest—left many mammals without a source of food. But similar changes had happened in previous times, without the same widespread species loss. Many paleontologists point the finger at a very different cause: the rapid spread of human hunters. According to this theory, migrating humans targeted large animals, killing so many that natural food chains began to collapse, and animals were unable to recover.

213

THE AGE OF MAMMALS

HUMAN EVOLUTION

The origin of our own species is one of the most closely studied areas of prehistory. Although humans are unique in many ways, paleontologists have no doubt that we developed through evolution, just like all other inhabitants of the living world. Our closest living relatives are the great apes, but our own ancestors were humanlike animals called hominids, which split from the line leading to apes about 5 million years ago. Following that split, evolution produced a succession of hominid species, but today only one is left—ourselves.

△ *Australopithecus afarensis lived in Eastern Africa between about 3 and 4 million years ago. Adults stood about 4 ft. (1.2m) high, and had brains about one third the size of ours. Because they stood upright, their hands were free to use sticks and stones as tools, but unlike later hominids, there is no evidence that they shaped them for particular tasks.*

THE FIRST HOMINIDS
At one time experts believed that the ape and hominid lines parted up to 20 million years ago, meaning that this was the time when our last shared ancestor was alive. Since then human genes have been compared with those of other living primates. They show that our genes are remarkably similar to those of the great apes— particularly gorillas and chimpanzees. This connection has prompted some rethinking, and today most experts date the split between the apes and hominids at 4 to 5 million years ago.

At the beginning of the last century many paleontologists thought humans evolved in Asia, but today there is no doubt that Africa was the birthplace of the human line. The first known hominids belonged to the genus *Australopithecus*, which literally means "southern ape." With their long arms, short legs, and protruding jaws, australopithecines had many apelike characteristics, but even the earliest of them walked upright on their back legs more than 4 million years ago.

THE SOUTHERN APES
The first southern ape discovery was also one of the strangest. It was a child's skull found in a South African quarry in 1924. Raymond Dart, the anatomist who examined it, concluded that it belonged to an extinct species that linked humans and apes, which he named *Australopithecus africanus*. At the time many other scientists strongly disagreed, preferring the idea that humans evolved in Asia. But with further discoveries it became clear that Dart was correct and that the southern apes were very likely to have been among our ancestors.

Since the 1920s experts have identified at least six separate species of australopithecines from remains found at more than 20 sites in eastern and southern Africa. Most of these sites have been in Africa's Great Rift Valley, where periodic eruptions have engulfed hominids in volcanic ash. The remains often consist of no more than teeth or fragments of jaws. But in 1974 two American anthropologists stumbled across an amazing find—almost half a female skeleton belonging to a species called *Australopithecus afarensis*. Nicknamed Lucy, its owner lived nearly 3 million years ago. Trace fossils (page 19) have also been found. One of the most evocative, a trail consisting of three sets of footprints, was discovered in 1978. Left by two adults and a child, this family outing predated Lucy by about 500,000 years.

THE TOOLMAKERS
The last australopithecines died out between 1.6 and one million years ago. But long before they disappeared, they gave rise to a new group of hominids that lived alongside them for several hundred thousand years. These newcomers were our immediate ancestors and had much more humanlike

▷ *After a successful hunt a group of* Homo heidelbergensis *cut up a dead rhinoceros— a kill that will provide them with food for many days. This hominid was first found in Europe but originally evolved in Africa perhaps 250,000 years ago. Thought by some experts to be a form of* Homo erectus, *it probably gave rise to our own species.*

HUMAN EVOLUTION

features. They are classified in the genus *Homo*, the small group of primates to which modern humans belong.

Unlike australopithecines, these anatomical humans were adept at making stone tools. One of the earliest species, *Homo habilis*, or "handy man," made simple tools by smashing stones to give them a sharp edge. *Homo erectus*, or "upright man," was a later species that evolved at about the time the australopithecines disappeared. It had a more skillful technique, using flakes chipped from stones, rather than the original stones themselves. These flakes were carefully shaped, creating spearheads and a wide range of other

implements. *Homo erectus* was not particularly good at inventing new designs, but as a stone toolmaker he (or she) would have been far more expert than almost anybody alive today.

No australopithecine remains have been found outside Africa, which makes it likely that the southern apes became extinct without spreading to other parts of the world. But *Homo erectus* was much more adventurous and spread throughout Europe and Asia, taking with it the art of toolmaking and also perhaps the knowledge of how to use fire. Shorter than modern humans and with a brain slightly smaller than ours, it was the most successful hominid so far, and our direct ancestor.

◁ *Peking man was a form of* Homo erectus *that lived in the Far East. Excavations at caves at Zhoukoudian, in northeast China, have revealed layers of ash near its remains, showing that this hominid knew how to use fire. Peking man probably lit fires from natural blazes and kept them going for weeks or months at a time.*

215

THE AGE OF MAMMALS

△ *A simple pebble tool (left) made by* Homo habilis *over two million years ago contrasts with a superbly crafted spearhead (right) made by prehistoric people called Cro-Magnons. The Cro-Magnons date back to about 35,000 years ago and lived in Europe and Asia.*

▽ *In this imaginary meeting somewhere in Ice Age Europe a group of Neanderthals (left) confront a hunting party of modern humans. Both sides are well armed, and events threaten to turn violent, because the Neanderthals sense that their home and livelihood are at stake. Whether scenes like this took place is not certain, but one fact is known— the Neanderthal species did not survive.*

MODERN HUMANS

Humans almost certainly evolved from *Homo erectus*, perhaps through the intermediate species *Homo heidelbergensis*, but there was no precise moment when modern humans suddenly stepped onto the prehistoric stage. Instead, our ancestors' features slowly changed, first going through an archaic form and then reaching a modern form indistinguishable from ourselves. The first modern humans probably appeared between 120,000 and 100,000 years ago. In geological terms this is remarkably recent, and it means that the family tree of modern humans stretches back no more than about 7,500 generations.

Modern humans are also thought to have evolved in Africa. Fossils show that they reached the Middle East by about 90,000 y.a. and the Far East by about 60,000 y.a. As a species, we have been spreading ever since.

EARLY MODERN HUMANS

In 1856, long before anything was known about hominids in Africa, workers in a German lime quarry found a collection of bones in the mud of a cave. The bones were heavily built and clearly very old, and among them was part of a skull with large brow ridges over the eyes. When these remains were examined by anatomical experts, many concluded that they belonged either to a subnormal human or an apelike animal.

Neanderthal man, as it came to be called, turned out to be one of the most extraordinary discoveries in the search for our ancestors. Known only in Europe and the Middle East, this hominid lived between about 120,000 and 35,000 years ago, at a time when modern humans had already made the move out of their African birthplace. At the end of this period the Neanderthals disappeared without trace.

Anthropologists are still not certain who the Neanderthals were and what happened to them. One theory is that they belonged to our own species and merged with modern human beings. A more likely possibility is that they were a separate species—one that lost out in the struggle for food and space and eventually became extinct.

SUCCESS STORY

If sheer numbers are a guide, humans are the most successful large animals that have ever lived. At present the human population totals about 6 billion, and it is expected to level off at about 11 billion at some point. Many factors have been responsible for our

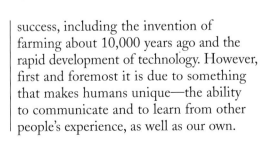

success, including the invention of farming about 10,000 years ago and the rapid development of technology. However, first and foremost it is due to something that makes humans unique—the ability to communicate and to learn from other people's experience, as well as our own.

GLOSSARY

Adaptation A feature of an animal that helps it survive. Adaptations develop through evolution and may include physical features and different kinds of behavior.

Algae Simple plantlike organisms that grow by collecting energy from sunlight. Most algae live in water. Many are microscopic, but the largest, the seaweeds, can be many feet long.

Ammonoids Extinct mollusks with tentacles and spiral shells containing a row of separate chambers. Ammonoids lived in the sea and were distant relatives of today's octopuses and squid.

Anapsids Reptiles without any skull openings behind their eye sockets. Today's anapsids include tortoises and turtles.

Archosaurs The group of reptiles that includes pterosaurs and dinosaurs, as well as the crocodilians and the birds. Archosaurs are often known as the "ruling reptiles."

Arthropods A huge and highly successful group of invertebrate animals that have a flexible body case, or exoskeleton, and legs that bend at joints. Living arthropods include insects, arachnids, and crustaceans; extinct ones include trilobites and sea scorpions.

Bacteria The smallest, simplest, and most ancient living things on Earth. Bacteria live in a variety of habitats, including on and in living animals. Most are harmless, but some, called germs, can cause disease.

Bipedal Standing and moving on two legs instead of four.

Camouflage Protective coloration that allows an animal to blend in with its background. Plant eaters use camouflage to avoid predators; some predators are camouflaged to launch surprise attacks on prey.

Canine tooth A tooth with a single point, shaped for stabbing into prey. Enlarged canine teeth are a common feature in hunters such as saber-toothed tigers.

Carnivore Any animal that lives by eating other animals. The word "carnivore" is also used for a particular group of mammals that includes today's cats, dogs, and bears, together with their extinct ancestors.

Carnosaurs A group of giant, flesh-eating dinosaurs or theropods. Unlike smaller hunters, carnosaurs used teeth, not claws, to bring down prey.

Carrion The remains of dead animals.

Cenozoic Era The part of Earth's geological history that started after the extinction of the dinosaurs 66 million years ago and continues today.

Cetaceans Whales, dolphins, and their relatives. Cetaceans live in water, but they are air-breathing mammals, evolving from animals that lived on land.

Chelonians Tortoises, turtles, and their relatives. Chelonians are an ancient group of reptiles that have hardly changed in 250 million years.

Chordates Animals that have a reinforcing rod, or notochord, running the length of their bodies. Some are soft-bodied, but in most, the vertebrates, the notochord is enclosed inside a hard backbone, making up part of a complete internal skeleton.

Clade An ancestral species, together with all the other species that have evolved from it. Because the members of a clade share the same ancestor, they make up a complete and self-contained group in evolution. Dinosaurs and birds are examples of clades; fish are not, because they evolved from several different ancestors.

Cladogram A diagram that shows clades.

Cold-blooded See **Ectothermic.**

Continental drift The gradual movement of continents across the earth's surface. Continental drift is driven by heat from deep inside the earth, which keeps the solid crust on the move.

Convergent evolution The evolution of similar features in animals that share similar ways of life. Convergent evolution can make unrelated animals difficult to tell apart.

Coprolites Fossilized animal droppings.

Cyanobacteria Also known as Blue-green algae, it is bacteria that live in the same way as plants—by collecting the energy in sunlight.

Cycads Cone-bearing plants, resembling small palm trees, that were a common food of dinosaurs. Cycads still exist.

Diapsids Reptiles with two skull openings on either side of the head, behind the eye sockets. The diapsids include the dinosaurs, as well as the crocodilians, snakes, and lizards.

Ectothermic Having a body temperature that rises and falls with the temperature outside. Ectothermic animals include invertebrates, fish, amphibians, and living reptiles.

Endothermic Having a body temperature that stays warm and steady whatever the conditions outside. Living endothermic animals include mammals and birds; extinct ones included pterosaurs and some dinosaurs.

Estivating Spending hot or dry times of the year dormant, or asleep. When cooler times return, an estivating animal wakes up.

Evolution A gradual change in living things as each generation follows the one before it. Evolution allows animals to adapt to changes around them.

Exoskeleton A hard case that protects an animal's body from outside, instead of supporting it from within. Exoskeletons are a common feature in invertebrates; arthropods have exoskeletons made of separate plates, which meet at flexible joints.

Extinct No longer alive anywhere on Earth.

Fossil The preserved relics of living things. Some fossils are formed by animal remains, but others are traces, such as footprints, that animals leave behind.

Gastralia Extra ribs that protect the part of the body containing the stomach and the intestines.

Gastroliths Stones, swallowed by dinosaurs and other animals, used to help grind up food.

Gastropods Mollusks that have a coiled shell and a single suckerlike foot.

Gondwana A giant continent that formed part of Pangaea. Gondwana eventually broke up to form South America, Africa, India, Antarctica, and Australia.

Herbivore Any animal that lives by eating plants.

Hyperphalangy An evolutionary trend that increases the number of bones in an animal's feet. Hyperphalangy was a common feature of marine reptiles in prehistoric times.

Ichnologists Scientists who study fossilized footprints, tracks, and other trace fossils.

Ichthyosaurs A group of extinct marine reptiles that evolved fishlike bodies and narrow, tooth-filled "beaks."

Incisor tooth A tooth at the front of the jaw, used for cutting into food. Incisors usually have a single, straight cutting edge.

Invertebrates Animals that do not have a backbone or a bony skeleton. Invertebrates were the first animals to evolve, and they make up over 95 percent of all the animal species on Earth.

Laurasia A giant continent that once formed part of Pangaea. Laurasia broke up to form North America, Europe, and northern Asia.

Mesozoic Era The part of Earth's geological history that began 245 million years ago and ended when the dinosaurs became extinct.

Microorganisms Living things that can be seen only with the help of a microscope. They include bacteria, as well as other forms of life. For several billion years microorganisms were the only living things on Earth.

Molar tooth A tooth at the rear of the jaw, used for crushing and grinding food. Molars often have a flat surface with bumps or ridges that grind against each other.

Mollusks Invertebrates that have a soft body, which is often protected by a hard shell. Fossil mollusks are common, because their shells often fossilized when they settled on the seabed.

Nautiloids Extinct mollusks with tentacles and straight or spiral shells containing a row of separate chambers. Like ammonoids, nautiloids lived in the sea and were distant relatives of today's octopuses and squid.

Notochord A reinforcing rod that runs down an animal's body, allowing the animal to move by bending from side to side. Notochords are found only in chordates.

Ornithischians One of the two overall groups of dinosaurs, ornithischians had birdlike hip bones and were all plant eaters.

Ornithopods A group of ornithischian dinosaurs that included a range of small or medium-sized plant eaters, such as iguanodonts and hadrosaurs.

Osteoderms Bony plates that form on the surface of the skin.

Paleontology The study of fossil remains.

Paleozoic Era The part of Earth's geological history that saw the development of the first hard-bodied animals, about 540 m.y.a. During this era living things made the transition from water to land.

Pangaea The supercontinent that existed during much of the Mesozoic Era, when reptiles ruled the land.

Placentals Mammals that give birth to well-developed young. The young develop inside their mother's womb, or uterus, and are fed through a spongy pad called a placenta, which is connected to their mother's blood supply.

Plankton Small or microscopic animals and plants that drift near the surface of the sea. Plankton is an important food for many marine animals.

Predators Animals that catch and eat other living animals— their prey. Unless they hunt in packs, predators are usually larger than their prey. They are always less common.

Pterodactyls A group of short-tailed pterosaurs, or flying reptiles. The pterodactyls included the largest flying animals that have ever existed.

Pterosaurs Flying reptiles that lived at the same time as the dinosaurs. Pterosaurs had leathery wings and bony beaks with or without teeth. Early forms had long tails.

Saurischians One of the two overall groups of dinosaurs. Saurischians had lizardlike hip bones, and they included predators as well as plant eaters. The largest and heaviest dinosaurs belonged to this group.

Sauropods Plant-eating dinosaurs with giant bodies, long necks and tails, and relatively tiny heads. The sauropods included the largest land animals to have existed.

Scavenger An animal that feeds on dead remains.

Species A group of living things that share the same features and that can breed with each other in the wild. Each species has its own two-part scientific name— for example, *Tyrannosaurus rex*. The first part of the name indicates a genus, or collection of species, while the second part indicates one particular species in the genus.

Stromatolite A rocklike mound produced by microorganisms growing in shallow water. Fossilized stromatolites are among the oldest signs of life on Earth.

Synapsids Reptiles and other animals that have a single skull opening on either side of the head, behind the eye sockets. The synapsids include today's mammals and their ancestors, the therapsids.

Tetrapods Animals with backbones and four limbs. Most tetrapods use all their limbs for moving although some (humans and many dinosaurs) stand on their back legs alone.

Therapsids A group of extinct animals that had features somewhere inbetween reptiles and mammals. Also known as "mammal-like reptiles."

Theropods Predatory or omnivorous dinosaurs that usually walked on their back legs.

Trilobites A group of prehistoric arthropods named after the three lengthways lobes of their bodies. Trilobites lived in the sea and survived for over 250 million years.

Vertebrates Animals that have backbones. Vertebrates include fish, amphibians, reptiles, birds, and mammals.

Warm-blooded See **Endothermic.**

INDEX

Page numbers in **bold** refer to main sections.
Page numbers in *italic* refer to illustrations.

Websites

www.dinodata.net
A giant compendium of facts and figures about dinosaurs

www.dinosauricon.com
One of the most comprehensive dinosaur sites on the web, with information on hundreds of genera

www.enchantedlearning.com/subjects/dinosaurs
A site that covers dinosaurs and other prehistoric animals, with up-to-the-minute news about excavations and discoveries

www.nhm.org
Website of the Natural History Museum of Los Angeles County. Contains extensive information about prehistoric animals from the tar pits at Rancho La Brea

www.ucmp.berkeley.edu
Website of the Museum of Paleontology at the University of California, Berkeley. Features a comprehensive guide to life at all stages in the earth's past

www.ucmp.berkeley.edu/pin/pinentrance.html
An English-language website that provides access to the Russian Paleontological Institute (PIN)—the world's largest fossil collection.

www.fieldmuseum.org
Website of the Field Museum, Chicago, which features details of Sue—the world's most complete specimen of *Tyrannosaurus rex*

www.tyrrellmuseum.com
Website of the Royal Tyrrell Museum of Palaeontology, Alberta, Canada. Contains a virtual tour of fossil exhibits, including the Burgess Shale

www.pterosaurs.net
The most comprehensive guide to pterosaurs on the web

Acknowledgments

The publisher would like to thank the following for their contribution to this book:

Editorial assistance Sheila Clewley, Julie Ferris, Elizabeth Longley
Design assistance Mark Bristow
Picture reseach assistance Audrey Reynolds
Artbank assistance Wendy Allison, Steve Robinson

Photographs
Every effort has been made to trace the copyright holders of the photographs. The publishers apologize for any inconvenience caused.

(*t* = top; *c* = center; *b* = bottom; *l* = left; *r* = right)
Front cover: *tc* (back cover) Ardea London/Francois Gohier; *tr* (back cover) Ardea London; *cl* (back cover) Ardea London; *b* (cover—spine) Ardea London; (cover—front flap) Ardea London; 3*c* Ardea London/Francois Gohier; 10*tr* Ardea London/Francois Gohier; 11*cl* Science Photo Library/Michael Abbey; *c* Science Photo Library/Sinclair Stammers; 12*tr* Ardea London; *cl* Geoscience Features Picture Library; 14*tl* NHPA/Daniel Heuclin; *clt* Ardea London/P. Morris; *clb* Geoscience Features Picture Library; *bl* Geoscience Features Picture Library; 15 *br* The Natural History Museum, London/M Long; 16*tr* Ardea London/Masahiro Lijima; *cl* The Natural History Museum, London; *cl* Ardea London; 17*tr* Science Photo Library/Paul Zahl; *b* Novosti; 18*tr* Ardea London/Francois Gohier; *cl* Science Photo Library/Sinclair Stammers; 19*c* The Natural History Museum, London; 20*cl* Ardea London/Francois Gohier; *b* Geoscience Features Picture Library/Dinosaur Nat. Mon.; 21*tl* Geoscience Features Picture Library/Dinosaur Nat. Mon.; *tc* Geoscience Features Picture Library/Dinosaur Nat. Mon.; *tr* Geoscience Features Picture Library/Dinosaurs Nat. Mon.; *c* Geoscience Features Picture Library/Dinosaur Nat. Mon.; *cr* Science Photo Library/Peter Menzel; 25*tc* /www.osf.uk.com/Phil Devries; *tr* Still Pictures/Bryan & Cherry Alexander; 30*tr* Science Photo Library/Louise K. Broman; *bc* Frank Lane Picture Agency; *br* Ardea London; *br* Science Photo Library/Jim Amos; 56*c* Science Photo Library/Sinclair Stammers; 64*tr* NHPA/Dan Griggs; 78*tr* Corbis; 84*tr* Ardea London/Francois Gohier; *bl* Ardea London/Francois Grohier; 86*tr* The Field Museum/#GEO85673_2c; *bl* Science Photo Library/Carlos Goldin; 87*tc* Derek Hall; CR Science Photo Library; 103*tr* Ardea London; 108*tr* The Natural History Museum, London; *cl* Ardea London; *bc* Ardea London; 109*tr* Humboldt University, Berlin; *c* Frank Spooner Pictures; 110*tr* National Geographic Society/O. Louis Mazzatenta; *cl* Frank Spooner Pictures; *bc* Frank Spooner Pictures; 111*tr* National Geographic Society/O. Louis Mazzatenta; *b* The Natural History Museum, London; *c* Ardea London; 146*tr* Science Photo Library/Simon Fraser; *cl* The Natural History Museum, London; *bc* Science Photo Library; 147*tr* Geoscience Features Picture Library; *cr* Ardea London/Francois Gohier; *bc* Frank Spooner Pictures/J. M.Giboux; 148*c* Ardea London/Peter Steyn; *bc* BBC Natural History Unit Picture Library; 149*tl* Quarto/Dr. Reed; 150*bl* Bruce Coleman Collection; 152*tr* Ardea London/Francois Gohier; 153*c* Ardea London/Francois Gohier; 160*tr* University of Chicago; *cl* University of Chicago; *br* University of Chicago; 161*tl* Humboldt University, Berlin; *tc* Humboldt University, Berlin; *c* The Natural History Museum, London; 162*l* Quarto; *br* NHPA; 168*cl* Ardea London/P. J. Green; 170*tr* Ardea London; 171*tr* Quarto; *b* Quarto; 184*bl* Quarto; 194*tr* Quarto; 195*t* Quarto; 198*tr* The Natural History Museum, London; *bc* Geoscience Features Picture Library; 210*c* The Natural History Museum, London; *bl* The Natural History Museum, London/M. Long; 211*tl* The Natural History Museum, London/M. Long; 213*tl* The Natural History Museum, London; 216*tl* Michael Holford; *tc* Michael Holford

RIDDELL

HONORING THE PAST